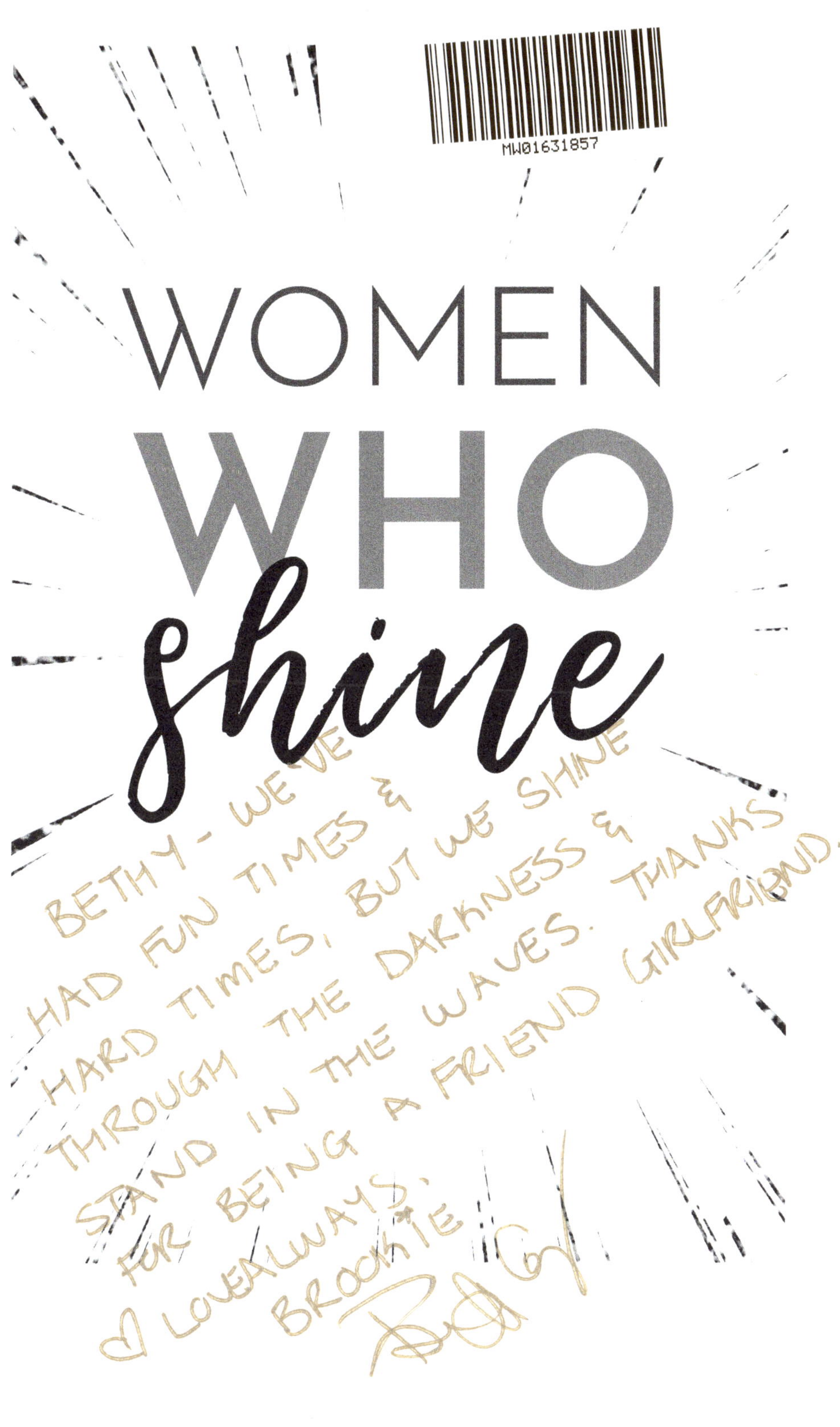
MW01631857
WOMEN
WHO
shine
BETHY - WE'VE
HAD FUN TIMES &
HARD TIMES, BUT WE SHINE
THROUGH THE DARKNESS &
STAND IN THE WAVES. THANKS
FOR BEING A FRIEND GIRLFRIEND.
♡ LOVEALWAYS,
BROOKIE

WOMEN WHO *shine*

30 INSPIRING STORIES OF SHINING LIGHT INTO THE WORLD

First Edition

www.katebutlerbooks.com

Design by Melissa Williams Design
mwbookdesign.com

This book is dedicated to you. We see you, we feel you, we relate to you, and we connect with you, because . . . we are you. At the core we are more alike than we are different. We are beings of light and love who deeply desire to make a positive influence on the world with our unique type of brilliance. The pages of this book promise to fill you with the wisdom, insights, and inspiration that will align you further with your soul's path. Our hope is that the vulnerability and authenticity of these stories will remind you deeply of who you are and inspire you to rise up and shine your light in the world.

It is your time. It is our time. It is time.

Enjoy the unfolding . . .

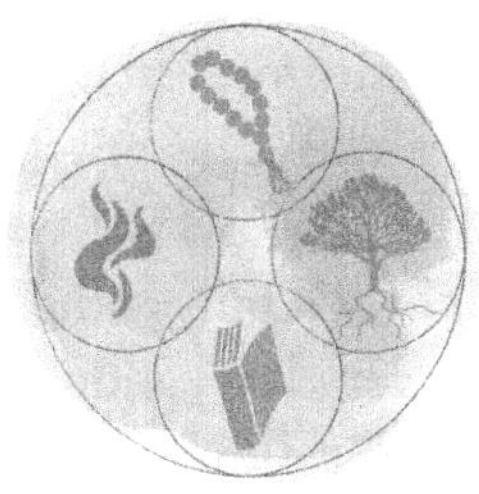

FOREWORD: THE FACADE OF I'M OKAY

Taja V. Simpson

Dear Women Who Shine,

I grew up in Louisiana during the era of the brown paper bag test. This test was a colorist discriminatory practice where a person's skin tone is compared to the color of a brown paper bag to determine which privileges they could have. Lighter-skinned people were afforded more social and economic advantages than darker-skinned people. As a child, and obviously darker than a brown paper bag, I wasn't allowed in certain homes, I couldn't play with some of the kids down my street, and I was bullied daily, all because of my skin tone. It was the culture of my everyday surroundings and the mindset of that time. It was normal. Everywhere I went, I would get teased and bullied for being dark-skinned. I was the butt of all jokes, "You dark this, or You black that." Being a dark-skinned young child during that time was tough to navigate. I always felt less than because of the amount of melanin in my skin.

I was 4 or 5 years old when I first began to understand the

differences and it started with my sister. She was beautiful, super smart, athletic and to me could do anything. And yes, she was light-skinned. I became acutely aware I wasn't on her same level when I would see my aunt for family gatherings a few times a year. She was a big personality, very loud and the center of attention in every room she walked in. She didn't seem to like me and gave me the nickname that would ultimately tarnish my self-esteem. She called me "Ugly Thang." I can recall her voice when she'd yell for me, "come here ugly thaaaaang." As if being called Ugly wasn't enough, the way she would allow the vibrato in her voice to linger in the air when she said THAAAAAANG, would break me, every time. I remember spending summers at my Grandmother's house and there was a really long drive-way. My aunt would pull in and blow her horn and everyone would go out to greet her and help her unload the car. All I ever wanted to receive was her love so I would try to be first hoping that maybe she'd give me a hug this time. I'd grab her around her waist and without her touching me back she would look at me, laugh and say, "Move ugly thang, get over there." She'd then extend her arms to my sister and say with a smile, "Come here my Albino baby!" I would stand there looking at them, and then looking back at myself and wondering why God made me like this. Why did he make me in such a way that would automatically make people dislike me? Why would my appearance make my aunt dislike me? I would cry and cry. My parents would try to make her stop, but that never worked, if anything, it made it worse. My aunt gave everyone nicknames, but the one she gave me was so demeaning it made me feel less of a person. She would proudly call my sister her "Albino Baby" and it was clear she was her favorite. She showered her with gifts and it was very apparent she loved her more than me. Her care and affection toward my sister really showed me there was love in her to give, but she chose not to give any to me. I would try to be strong, but the more I saw her the more she made me devalue myself. As a result, I never felt like I was enough.

This idea of not being enough was reinforced because I was as dark as I was. Certain people couldn't be friends with me because I was darker than the brown paper bag. I didn't pass the test. If you're darker than this, you can't come in. If you're darker than this, you can't play. If you're darker than this, you have to go home. Ultimately what you're hearing as a child is, If you're darker than this, you are no good. If you're darker than this, you have no value. This is what the test was saying to me. I was surrounded by it, but it was the norm, the culture, the time.

Every night I would sit in the tub and pray to God. I would say, "God, could you just make me a little lighter? Maybe the shade in between my knuckles, because when you look at the skin tone in between your knuckles they are lighter. So I'm not asking for a lot, just a little bit lighter Lord, that way it won't be as drastic and no one would notice. Then maybe my aunt would love me and people would like me." As a young child that was my exact prayer, I would say it all the time, really thinking and believing it would solve things. But, it never happened. My tub became my only safe zone. There I didn't have to hear insults from my sister, my aunt, my neighborhood, my school, my city. This was my secure haven. Outside of that bathroom, I lived in a façade, but in reality, those words were killing me on the inside.

My parents were also born and raised in Louisiana and were products of their environment. They experienced racism, segregation, colorism and worked really hard to give my siblings and I a great upbringing. We grew up as part of the middle class with a built-in pool in the backyard and a basketball court in the front driveway. We were the house all the kids wanted to come to. We allowed everyone over our house, you didn't have to pass a color test to get in. The one thing my parents didn't play about was school and they only allowed friends over if those friends were doing their best and making good grades. We were all honor roll and banner roll students because of it. My parents were the most supportive in everything we did. If we played a sport, they were either the coach, manager or attendee as they cheered us on the entire game. They were definitely our biggest cheerleaders. They gave me all the love and support I needed. They poured verbal affection into me, using phrases like "You're beautiful," "of course you're good enough," and "You can do anything." It was really hard to believe their words when the world around me was saying something vastly different. It was like the people vs. my parents. Whenever they would tell me I was beautiful, I would say, "you have to say that, you're my parents." It was hard for me to believe that about myself when only two people in the world were telling me I was good enough and beautiful, but the environment and everyone else around me would say the total opposite. I was an offspring of our environment and this is how the dichotomy of my paradigm started to develop. The world around me was conditioning me to believe one thing, but my parents conditioned me to believe something else.

In junior high school my self-esteem was so low that it was under my shoe. Even as I began to develop friendships and have more relationships, I still had to deal with bullying all the time. One day, I decided to share with my mom what was happening at school and she started to teach me come backs, which are things to say back to a bully to get them to leave you alone. I learned you can't just sit there and take it, you have to verbally come back at them and as the bully sees that their taunts aren't affecting you they will eventually leave you alone. When someone would call me a black this or a black that, she told me to say, "I may be black, but I'm beautiful" or "Yep, and I'm beautiful!" When my mom first taught me to say these things I said, "No one is going to believe that." She would say, "if you believe it, they will. If you say it with confidence, I promise you, they will leave you alone. Just try it. You're mama's chocolate star, you're destined for greatness!"

I went to school the next day and I felt armored and ready. I even practiced how I would say it. Sure enough when we were at recess, the bullying started and I just kept saying, with confidence, "I may be black, but I'm beautiful." Then I'd say, "Yep, and I'm beautiful." Those were the only two bullets I had in my verbal gun so I simply used it over and over and over again. And you know what? Eventually it stopped! I learned that bullies are attracted to fear so the less fearful I was, the more they would leave me alone. It started to seem like I was developing confidence when really I was learning to cope with the skin I was in. While learning those comebacks, I also learned to hide anything that drew attention to me. I learned how to wear certain clothes and how to pose in photos that would hide my butt, because I would get teased so much about it. I stopped wearing bright colors, I stopped wearing bright lip gloss, and I learned to stay under the radar so nothing about me stood out. I couldn't show up in my true value or true worthiness because the world had shown me that wasn't safe. At the time, I thought I was properly dealing with things, but I was actually pushing down all my insecurities and covering them up with "I'm Okay, Everything's cool." I noticed the popular kids weren't bullied so I shifted my focus. I played every sport my schedule would allow, basketball, softball, volleyball, cheerleading and track. The more of a success I was, the more popular I became and the bullying eventually stopped. I masked all my feelings in sports and lived in the facade of I'm Okay. The facade was so good I actually started to believe it myself.

On the outside I was good. I was a leader in my school and an honor student. I was learning to stand up for myself. I thought I'd gotten over those 'not enough' insecurities until one day when I was with one of my friends who lived down the street from me. A lady came up and said, "Ya'll look so much alike, ya'll could be twins." People always thought we were related because we resembled one another and this was a statement we got all the time, but on this day my friend said, "yeah, but she's darker than me. I'm not THAT dark." This shook me. I can remember this moment so vividly.

I realized two things that day. First, I learned just how my friend felt about me. I also learned that it was a big deal to her that she was a couple of shades lighter than me. She wasn't "THAT dark." This shifted my awareness and I would stay out of the sun as much as possible. If I was outside too long I would hear a little voice in my head telling me to reapply sunscreen so I wouldn't get darker. I would wear long sleeve shirts so my arms wouldn't tan, I would dismiss going to the beach because it was just an open space of sunlight and there was nowhere to hide. I would always say, "The sun is the one thing in the world that doesn't discriminate." This became yet another coping mechanism of what I would do to make sure I wasn't getting darker.

I stayed the course and I excelled in all of the sports I participated in. I even added dancer to the long list of extracurricular activities. I excelled so much in school that I was able to finish a year early. I skipped my junior year and graduated high school at 16. There was something bubbling up inside of me with these big dreams I had for myself, but they didn't match my beliefs, my passions, or my deepest wants. I thought I had it all figured out, but there were little situational reminders that would sneak up on me to let me know that I still wasn't enough. I can recall being at my best friend's house, laughing and joking with everyone having a great time. I left the room to go to the bathroom and when I walked out one of her sister's friends came up to me and asked earnestly, "how do you feel, are you okay?" That was a peculiar question to me at the time, but I was in great spirits and I replied, "Yes, I'm great, why?" She said, "Well, you're the only dark-skinned person here and I didn't know if you were uncomfortable." It was like a ton of books slapped me in the face. I was shocked. I was in a safe place, my best friend's house, where I was never made to feel less than, but here I am defending my skin tone again. After a long pause I looked at her and said, "I actually hadn't noticed that until right now, but I'm good." She walked away and I just stood there in my feelings trying to mask how that made me feel, but there I was, yet again reminded of being too dark. dark-skinned women have always been last in the demographic poll. There's white women at the top, all other races in between and when you get to black women, that is usually broken down from light to dark. So if I'm at the bottom how could I ever expect to gain any type of success?

I had no idea this was something others even thought about. I walked away from that moment while adding it to the long list of things I have to carry around about myself. It brought me back to being a young girl and self-identifying in this hierarchy of the world. After that experience I couldn't walk into a room and not notice how I stood out. You can't unknow something like that. Now every time I went anywhere I became more and more aware of it. I'm the only dark-skinned person in the room and I wonder how that makes everyone else feel?

Then came the normal compliments like "You're pretty for a dark-skinned girl." It seemed awkward to say and I would often respond with a "thank you?" It seemed like every guy I ever spoke to on the phone said, "You're the first dark-skinned girl I've EVER been on the phone with" or "I've always said if you ever see me with a darkie, know that she has to be the baddest chick walking." So I guess I should be happy right? I'm your first, I'm the girl you thought never existed. I was the exception to the rule. I was always told the criteria for a dark-skinned girl is a lot higher than a light-skinned girl. If a guy decided to date me I had to be damn near perfect. Where I'm from, if you're light-skinned with what's considered good hair or light colored eyes you were idolized. Dating men from the south, men of that mentality, of that culture, and of that speech, always made me feel not quite good enough. As I was working on myself to get over the mindset that was ingrained in me through the environment I grew up in, men who still thought like that would stand out so much that

I would quickly remove myself from that situation. However, when I moved out of Louisiana and started to meet men and women from the east coast or midwest, I would notice how proud they were to be black and proud to be a dark-skinned man or woman. I'd never seen that before in my life. The first time I was complimented on my nose and lips I thought, "you love my what?" The nose and lips I've been teased about my entire life? I couldn't believe it. I had been discriminated against so much that I decided to take on the mantra "love sees no color" and would date inside and outside of my race. I always focused on the heart and soul of a person, the intelligence of a person because that's what really matters and that's what was attractive to me. Plus I never wanted to make anyone feel how I once felt.

I was tired of feeling less than and I no longer wanted to allow fear to dictate my life. The exterior of me was never going to change so I had to shift what was within myself. I needed to learn to love me, but I actually never worked on self-love. I said these comebacks, but my belief in them didn't support what I was repeating. That was the opportunity for me to really take a step back and analyze all the damage that had been done. I had to go back to the beginning. Where was that beginning? It was dealing with the paper bag test as a child, and my aunt having a good laugh about a nickname. What I realized was these situations created a belief system inside myself where I actually self-elected into believing that I was not valuable, I was not worthy, and I was not good enough. Intellectually, I also held onto the dichotomy of what my parents had taught me. I am enough, I am worthy, I am capable, I have this dream and it is possible. I knew I needed to dig into the foundation of the problem and yank up the root belief of what I intellectually knew was real. It took me 25 years before I looked in the mirror and accepted what I look like and another 5 to look in the mirror and love what I saw. It was time to retrain my beliefs.

Once I started to work on self-love and a belief in myself, I realized, oh boy, I have some work to do. It was very difficult to retrain my beliefs at first. Primarily due to my profession. Here I was this young woman with very low self-esteem and lots of insecurities and I selected businesses that were all about appearance, modeling & acting. I have dealt with more rejection than one would ever dream of. This definitely affected me in my career. I would go to auditions, get a call back, and go to producer's sessions, but I would notice a pattern. The girl who always got the part was the lighter skinned woman. I would see the commercial or film/tv role I was up for and it was never another dark-skinned woman in the role. I began to look at breakdowns and say to myself, "they won't cast ME for that, they will cast a light-skinned girl. Are they really going to give the LEAD role to a dark-skinned girl?" I would go on so many auditions, but every time the booking would go to the ethnically ambiguous looking girl with the big hair. Don't get me wrong, these aren't just my feelings. In 2012 when Kerry Washington booked the lead role in Scandal, that was the first time a black woman had the lead role on a primetime network drama since Diahann Carroll debuted in "Julia" in 1968. That's 44 years before a black woman of any shade would obtain that type of role. Women of my type were typically the friend or the maid, but you're certainly not the beautiful lead that every guy wants in a romantic comedy. So here I am, trying to get work in this industry, all the while living in the skin I'm in and realizing I need to work on myself to overcome what the world is again showing me within my environment, television, movies, magazines, etc. Representation matters. Seeing is believing. Seeing gives hope, it starts the belief and helps to plant the seeds of possibility. It still amazes me that a girl with such low self-esteem ended up as an actor. Yet, if I really sit and think, it makes total sense. Acting is living in a make believe world, which is somewhat like the facade I began to live in as a kid when I told myself I was okay, although I really wasn't.

The first time I looked in the mirror and said, "I am beautiful,

I am worthy, I am enough," I burst out crying. I'd never said that to myself in the mirror like that before. This time was different. My intention was different and I was changing my belief. My confidence grew tremendously. I started to really believe what I was saying and that hit me differently. I walked more upright, my head up high, and things really started to shift for me. I'm healing and I feel empowered and happy. I was making strides in my career and I fell head over heels in love with the man of my dreams. When we met it was unlike anything I'd ever imagined. If I had a checklist he would've checked all the boxes. He was absolutely wonderful to me. He decided to take me to Hawaii for my birthday and little did I know that wasn't all he had in store. I can still remember that moment. We were on a cruise. Fireworks were literally going off in the background when he got on his knee and asked me to marry him. I sat there in shock and the first thing I said was, "Is this real life?" He said, "yes, baby, can I have your answer?" I said. "YES!" Everyone around us applauded and it was a beautiful moment. It was a complete fairytale; it was real to me. I could touch it, feel it, it was exactly in my reach.

We started planning our lives together. We moved into a beautiful condo while we planned the wedding. On a whim he bought me a convertible BMW and this life was now unlike anything I'd ever dreamed for myself. I was happy, in love, and feeling better than ever about myself. The first few months of this engagement were great and slowly things started to shift. Sometimes he would be really happy and other times really sad. I didn't think anything abnormal about it as I too would have felt the same way if my business gained or lost thousands of dollars. Then things started to get worse and in the matter of a week, during the Christmas holiday, I looked up and didn't recognize the man I was living with. It was literally like a Dr. Jekyll and Mr. Hyde experience. He went on Facebook and started exposing family secrets and he is from a well-known and well to do family. His father tried to get him to take down the posts because the information would definitely ruin the brand and image his father worked so hard to build. I don't know if what he posted was true or not. All I knew is that he was acting extremely different. I spoke to his father and he kept asking me, "What triggered him? What did YOU do to trigger him?" I didn't know what he meant and he began to tell me his son was bi-polar and he was acting that way because he was having an episode. I was in total shock. I literally stood there and held the phone for what felt like forever. So many thoughts ran through my mind. What did this mean for him? How do I help him? What should I do or say? His father wanted me to get his phone and take the posts down, but I was afraid for my life and wouldn't dare cross him. Whoever he was at the moment, I didn't want to make him mad so I refused. I spoke to his mother about it and she said to me, "He told me, he told you he was bi-polar." I said to her, "so the bi-polar man told you he mentioned this to me and you didn't follow up with me about it? That's something you talk about in great detail. I need to know how to handle this situation. What should I do?" She said, "Well, we thought you had given him the balance he needed in this life and we were just so excited to see our son again. I see now that you were just an episode." During this episode, my fiancé decided he no longer wanted a life with me and he moved all of his things out and left.

I'd finally gotten myself to a point where I knew I was worthy of love, but when his father asked if I was the trigger I started asking myself, "was this me, did I bring this on myself?" Someone who was made to feel less than, called ugly thang, I felt I wasn't worthy of this love, this condo, this car, this marriage, this relationship and all of the goodness that I thought it was. Was this all a facade too? Who did I think I was that I could have it all?

I was devastated. I got depressed. I stayed on my sofa for months. I couldn't sleep in the bed we once slept in. I would stay on that sofa and simply watch the days go by. Somehow I had to tell everyone, my family, my bridesmaids, friends that the wedding was off. But I couldn't talk. Friends were calling to ask about the bridal shower details, but I literally couldn't utter any words. It took me two weeks to muster up the courage to do that. Instead of having individual conversations with everyone I decided to tell them the same way I asked each of them to be in the wedding. I made a video. I set up my camera and looked into the lens, only this time, instead of a happy moment asking them to be my bridesmaids, I told them how my fiancé had left me. For 18 minutes and 17 seconds I cried my way through, telling them the most disappointing news of my life.

I didn't know what to do. I called my dad and told him how broken I was and expressed that I didn't know how to bounce back from this. He said, "Taja, we need you. I believe in you and you can do this. I know it seems hard now, but let's just take it one step at a time and I will be with you every step of the way." Every time I would get low I thought about that moment with my dad and it would get me through. I could hear this very faint voice inside of me saying to get up, you can do it. You can get past this. I was knocked off my new foundation and this was the biggest pain I'd ever experienced. After months of living on my sofa I decided I couldn't keep doing the same thing and expecting different results, that's the exact definition of insanity. I started to exclusively focus on me and my personal development. I was on the phone with one of my friends and she told me about a book called, *The Wisdom Of Florence Scovel Shinn.* I immediately ordered it and started to read it. This book changed my life. It started me on a journey of the self-discovery of gratitude, law of attraction, the power of the spoken word, and intention. I learned about the Game of life and how to use your words as your wands. I stayed consistent and my beliefs started to match my desires and that's when things would really happen for me. I realized how to really stand in my faith and I now know that belief starts with an in depth feeling. The vibration of what you desire proceeds the manifestation of it. The energy shifted in my life.

I started to refrain from those old beliefs. I stopped telling myself I wouldn't book certain jobs because of what I looked like. Instead I only spoke on what I desired and I never spoke or gave energy to what I didn't. I really understood this when I booked a lead role in a movie ranked number one in the world! I started to gain more credibility and I booked so many acting jobs. I achieved more exposure on television, red carpets, various media outlets and I started to have the opportunity to speak at an expert level on TV. I was opening up, standing in my power and getting my voice back.

One day I was being interviewed on FOX and I shared a piece of my story because, at this point, I understood the power of sharing the story and being a representation to someone else out there. The interviewer asked me, "What was it like meeting Beyoncé?" I don't know if she was expecting a fluff answer, but I told the interviewer that when I was introduced to her, I honestly didn't know what I was going to say. I spoke my truth. I said, "Thank you for your song 'brown skinned girl.' I'm from Louisiana and growing up there didn't give me a lot of pride in being dark-skinned, but your song, even now, helps me stand in my greatness and I wanted to say thank you." She was sitting at the time. She got up and gave me a hug and said, "You are beautiful and thank you for telling me that. That's why I wrote it. I want my kids to be proud of who they are and what they look like. And you are so beautiful." She had no idea how much that meant to me. The little brown girl in the tub that would pray to be lighter would really appreciate that moment.

The next day my dad called me. He'd watched the interview and he called to apologize to me. He said, "I never knew the depth of how you were affected as a kid and for that I'm sorry. I should have done a better job of protecting you, especially where your aunt came into play. When she was calling you 'Ugly Thang' and all those names I didn't do enough to protect you and I feel like I failed you in that way as your father and I'm so sorry. I allowed the fact that we didn't get along and tried to keep the peace, get in the way of what it was doing to you and I sincerely apologize to you for that." He broke down with tears during that and so did I. I received an apology I never knew I needed. I believe the universe rewarded me with this immense healing because I was authentic to my story, to my voice and ultimately my power.

When I look back now, the worst thing in my life birthed the best version of me and daily affirmations are what helped my beliefs. I had to affirm myself. I had to learn that it was okay even if I didn't fully believe it right away. When affirming yourself it takes constant repetition until that affirmation starts to resonate with you. That made it palatable for me. My big goal was to love myself but I had to take baby steps to get to my goal.

I had to find gratitude in who I was, exactly as I am. That was my first step and this time I did it with intention. Once I shifted my intention so that it supported the affirmations I started to feel good. I felt better about myself. I felt better about my own skin and I grew confident from within, not just externally. Those were the practical steps I had to take to get me to this place.

Now, I can bless everyone, including my aunt, for all the discouragement along the way because it's made me who I am and I love me. As much as I thought I would never be here, something in me always knew I would. I affirm myself daily. I'm a successful working actor and living my dream. Words have power and my mom always said I would be her stardom baby, her Chocolate Star. Now that I understood the power of the spoken word, I was able to finally live up to it. I had to believe it before I could ever see the power of those words manifest in my life. I'm so grateful that I've always had the best relationship with my parents and it's because of their support that I was able to get through the toughest times in my life.

Today I live by these 4 pillars, gratitude, belief, intention and manifestation. My daily practice is what allows me to continue to excel in my life and be the best version of myself. I no longer run from the sun. Instead I live near the beach and I go there all the time because it's become my happy place. I love to wear bright colors. I even wear lipstick and created my own lipstick collection. It took me a long time to get here, but I can proudly say that I am grateful for what I look like and I love being in the skin I'm in.

ABOUT TAJA V. SIMPSON

Taja V. Simpson is an actor, director, writer, and entrepreneur. As an award winning actor she has over 20 years' experience in acting with more than 50 credits in TV and film. As a businesswoman, Taja is the founder and CEO of the Dream is Real, Inc. and The Working Actors Academy. Through her companies Taja has directed, written and produced over 40 productions from theater and music videos to television and film. She has coached and mentored hundreds of actors helping them navigate the various aspects of Hollywood and evolve into becoming working actors.

Versatility is Taja's greatest accomplishment, which is what led her to guest star in multiple roles on some of the most popular television shows of our time. She received her first breakout role in The Bold & The Beautiful as Adele, where she recurred on the show for over two years. Since then some of the shows she has appeared in are; Grey's Anatomy, NCIS, Insecure, A House Divided, Raven's Home, NCIS:LA, KC Undercover, Lethal Weapon & All-American.

Taja can now be seen weekly as Priscilla Owen in BET's #1 Scripted Cable drama, Tyler Perry's "THE OVAL." She is also in Christopher Nolan's "My Online Valentine" on Amazon, BET, BETHer & BET + where she leads this film down the dating woes in this hilarious Romantic Comedy, and "LOLA", a boxing film where she plays the lead role of a female boxer on Amazon and Tubi. Taja can also be seen in other films on Netflix, Amazon and Hulu.

As a Louisiana native Taja attended McNeese State University and graduated with a Bachelor of Science in Mass Communications. She initially was on the path to a career in broadcast journalism as a reporter and anchor, but couldn't shake the calling of being an actor that she discovered as a 7 year old child playing pretend with her cousins. Eventually, she would answer the call and the journey to becoming a working actor would begin. Nothing fills Taja with joy more than being able to take a character and bring it to life in a way that touches, inspires and evokes an emotional connection with her audience.

Taja has always had a passion for acting and a desire to serve and uplift others so she decided to combine the two by creating The Working Actors Academy which allows her to mentor and coach aspiring actors everywhere. The Working Actors Academy is an online acting course that not only teaches actors practical tactics to help them evolve as professional actors, but also instills in each student the importance of learning about yourself and engaging in personal development to become the best version of you. She believes by truly knowing yourself and doing the work to become a better person you will become a better actor.

Taja's personal and professional journey has led her on a mission to help others embrace the power of believing in yourself, consistently doing the necessary work to evolve as a person, and ultimately become the person that you always dreamed you could be and live an authentic, full and purposeful life. In the essence of every role and every business venture Taja engages in this mission, which is always ever present. Believe. Evolve. Become.

To Learn more about Taja, visit her website at www.tajavsimpson.com

You can also follow her on social media, she'd love to connect with you!

www.instagram.com/tajavsimpson/
www.facebook.com/tajavsimpson
www.twitter.com/tajavsimpson

table of contents

Foreword:The Facade of I'm Okay **vii**
Taja V. Simpson

Introduction: Be Her Now **1**
Maya Comerota

A Note from the Creator of the Inspired Impact Book Series, **11**
Kate Butler

Abandon Fear and Engage **17**
Diana Buckwalter

Ignite Your Inner Spark **26**
Stacy Kuhen

Stars Can't Shine Without Darkness **37**
Christine Lavulo

Becoming Your Best **44**
Laurie Maddalena

Planting Seeds in the Mind to Shine **55**
Denise McCormick

Via Combusta: A Sacred Journey **68**
Tatjana Obradovic

You Light Up My Life **79**
Kristi Ann Pawlowski

Ascend With Me **87**
Candice Shepard

The Art of Transcending Abundance **94**
Tara Truax

Luminary Insights **103**
Ivanna Mann Thrower Anderson

Unstoppable Me **110**
Heather Beebe

Light That Shines Bright **119**
Tracey Watts Cirino

Stand In the Waves **129**
Brooke A. Conaway

Choosing Grace **139**
Sarah Grafton

The Other Side **149**
Susan E. Grubb, LPC

Becoming My Own Hero **156**
Gaby Juergens

Clearing the Path to Stand Up and Shine **164**
Ann Klossing

Transport to Joy **173**
Shari Lillico

I Was Never Alone **180**
Christina Macro

Trust is a Must! **194**
Lori Parks

Belly of the Whale **203**
Dr. Lisa Patierne

Finding My Inner Shine **214**
Maria Ramos

We Are Medicine **223**
Emma Alexandra Williams

Worthy **232**
Kristina Williams

Light Through the Cloud **240**
Peggy Wright

Say Yes to Your Deepest Calling **247**
Dianne A. Allen

Honoring Self As You Steer Your Career **255**
Dr. Agatha Ampaire

Triumphantly Risen **263**
Anita Lucia La Pierre

Love Yourself First **268**
Melissa A. Malland

A Hoarder's Heart **276**
Melanie Renee

Give Back and Impact: Be a Force for Good **285**
Ellie D. Shefi

Reprinted with Permissions **302**

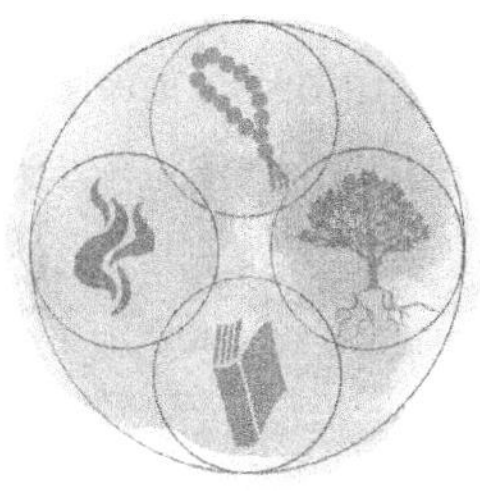

INTRODUCTION: BE HER NOW

Maya Comerota

When I was a little girl growing up in Elkins Park, Pennsylvania, I'd pretend to be Madonna and sing "Cherish" into my hairdryer while getting ready for school. In the afternoons, I was Eponine from *Les Miserables* belting out "On My Own" for anyone who would listen. And when my parents had friends and family over, no one could leave until they had congregated into the living room for one of my "performances."

I was going to be the first Broadway star that was also a doctor. I was going to live a legendary, exciting, fun life of musical adventures while also healing people, changing their lives and saving the world.

Twenty-five years later, after working hard to get good grades and working even longer and harder as an employee, I wasn't a doctor but I did have a new dream job: Global Head of Innovation for a fortune 100 biotech company, supervising a team of over 100 nurses who were supporting hundreds of thousands of patients with lifelong autoimmune illness.

I was making a difference *plus* I had a lake house, a boat, a shiny company car, a gorgeous husband and a beautiful son.

Anyone peeking in the window of my perfectly decorated house would think, "Maya has it all."

What no one could see, though, was how much time I spent wondering, "Is this it?"

Why did it always seem like something was still missing?

I knew I was making an impact but I was still desperate for "more" even when I wasn't sure what "more" was.

Then on a beautiful sunny afternoon in August of 2015, I found out.

My three-year-old son, Hunter, was playing downstairs with the nanny, Julia.

I longed to go downstairs and play with him. Just one more email I promised myself, then you can play. But that was over an hour ago.

Bing!

I get a text from Matthew, the VP of Strategy.

For months he's been sending me texts.

Come on Maya. Come to dinner with me.

Maya, we need to spend more time together.

Maya it's important I get to know you on a more personal level.

He knows the terms of my contract say that I can't quit or get fired without owing the company $250k so he keeps pushing, I keep saying "no," and he keeps getting more annoyed and upset.

Today's text reads:

Maya I'm with Tara. She's asking me what kind of job you're doing. Do you want me to tell her you're doing a good job? Or should I tell her you're not delivering?

Tara is VP of HR!

I can feel blood rushing through my body. I know I want him to stop but I don't know how to get him to stop. And I'm tired. Tired of him emailing. Tired of him texting me at all times of the day and night. I've barely been eating and sleeping because of this.

I keep saying, "I just want to do my job."

I've been at this company for 15 years. I've worked hard to get here, I have a team I love, I have a great pension, I'm making a difference and I want to retire here.

Why won't he listen?

Finally, my husband, James, and I go to see an attorney to find out what my options are. I don't want to cause trouble or sue the company. I just want Matthew to stop.

The attorney tells us, "Your case is open and shut. You've done nothing wrong but if and when you report this, your career is over."

I remember looking at James and thinking, "Maybe he'll stop."

That was three weeks ago.

I desperately wanted to be playing downstairs with Hunter, but instead I'm in my office afraid to move.

I have to get away, to escape, to get some perspective and think for a minute.

I grab the keys to my husband's truck and call out, "Hunter, mommy will be back in an hour."

"Mommy, mommy, take me with you," he says, with outstretched arms.

"No, little man. Mommy will be back soon. You stay here and play with Julia."

Twenty minutes later, I somehow passed my exit and I'm stopped at a red light wondering, "How did I get here?" I can't remember the last 20 minutes I've been on the road and I realize I am in the wrong lane.

As I turn the wheel to cross the lane and take the entry ramp back onto the freeway, a big, black SUV crashes into the side of my truck—right where Hunter would have been sitting!

The car starts to spin. Everything becomes slow motion.

> The SUV crashes through the railing . .
> crashes through the green highway sign . .
> slides down the embankment . .
> comes to a stop . .
> seconds before hitting oncoming traffic.

I think, "Please God, don't let the driver die. Don't let there be a child in that car."

Then I see a vision.

It's Hunter, standing in front of James. They're both dressed in black, crying. My parents and brothers stand next to them. Everyone looks sad.

I hear a voice, or, more accurately, I feel a voice, in every cell of my body.

> *You did not do what you came here to do.*

At the same time, I'm overwhelmed by the deepest sense of sadness I've ever felt.

Then another vision arises.

It's the day Hunter was born. I'm holding him in my arms, placing a gentle kiss on his head, promising to love him with all my heart.

I feel that love again. True unconditional love.

Then another scene.

This time it's my wedding. James and I are at the altar. He's looking at me with such love in his gaze before kissing me.

It's been so long since he looked at me and touched me like that.

A wave of regret washes over me. Regret that I haven't fully lived my life.

Yes, I've had fleeting moments of joy and love, but I knew I hadn't yet *really* lived.

That's when I make a promise, "If I live through this I will be the woman I was born to be. I will live the life I was meant to live. I will be her."

It was my first conversation with God and I was praying for another chance. The chance to do what I was put here to do.

When the police arrived, the other woman and I were embracing. The police looked at us and asked, "How did you get out of there?"

Both of our cars were totaled yet neither one of us had a scratch on us.

While I'm not sure how the other driver's life was impacted that day, I knew there was only *one reason* we had both survived.

That day changed everything. Not all at once. But little by little.

I knew I had to stop *doing* so much and *decide* to be the woman I was destined to be.

I didn't know exactly who or what that was yet, but I was determined to figure it out and I committed to myself that I would *Be. Her. Now.*

A couple months later, I was flying to Budapest to be part of a big global innovation meeting. I had routed my flight through London specifically so I wouldn't have to travel with Matthew, even though he hadn't been bothering me much since my accident.

Bing!

As we're landing, I get a text message from him.

> *I had them change your travel plans. You're staying two extra days with me so we can be together.*

Adrenaline coursed through me.

"Be Her Now," I whispered.

I didn't want to be her. I wanted to run and hide.

"Be Her Now," I whispered again, then dialed my boss.

"Jack, there's something I need to tell you."

"Everything OK? Aren't you in Budapest?"

"Yes, but I'm getting on the first flight home," I said. "Matthew's been harassing me for the past six months. He keeps threatening to fire me if I don't do what he wants. I won't be at the meeting tomorrow and Jack, I think he may be doing this with others, too."

After a formal investigation, Matthew was fired. And, just like the lawyer predicted, my career as I knew it was over.

That January, after 15 years with the company, I handed in my resignation, my computer, and my phone and walked out of my office for the last time with my shoulders back and my head held high. I noticed the crisp, fresh air on my cheeks and the little gust of wind through my hair.

As I drove away, for the first time in years, I felt free. Free to be the me I was created to be.

I was no longer Maya, the Head of Global Innovation. I was just Maya. I wasn't even sure who that was anymore, but I knew it was up to me to discover who God put me on this earth to be.

> *"If there was no tomorrow, Maya, what would you do? Who would you want to be? What would you want to make sure the people you loved knew?"*

The answer filled my chest and lungs and I wanted to scream from the rooftops.

> *"There is something you are uniquely here to do. Go, live your life, have fun, laugh, play, dance in the rain, sing! Be the person you are meant to be."*

I didn't want anyone to feel the sadness and regret I felt in the car on the day of my accident, the regret of coming to the end of life and feeling like you hadn't really lived.

So my journey began. I listened to the voice that I heard and felt in the car and I let it lead the way.

It was peace, joy, compassion, love and faith speaking as a whisper in my body. As a swelling in my heart. Or a tingle in my nose. It was a feeling. A knowing.

> *When it gets hard, it will be okay.*
> *You are never alone.*
> *Your heart always knows.*
> *Your dreams are your destiny*
> *Lean in to the longing*
> *You don't need to know the whole plan, just take the next step.*
> *You are Born For This*

When it rained, the whisper said, *Dance.* When a song I loved came on the radio, the whisper said, *Sing.* It told me what books to read, what lectures to go to, what courses to take.

At first it was hard to hear and sometimes even harder to follow. You want me to do what? You want me to go where?

But I learned to listen to its message. And the more I listened and the deeper I listened, the louder it became and the whisper drowned out any other noise.

I began to study and keep company with some of the greatest transformational teachers in the world. I put pictures of them on my wall and had conversations with them in my head. I dreamed that one day I'd do what they do and impact people's lives at a grand scale. That simply by being who I am, and sharing what I came here to share, lives could be transformed.

It didn't come without challenges. My marriage was in turmoil, our bank account dwindled. We sold our lake house and my car. I even sold the suits I wore as a corporate executive, all the while whispering, through tears sometimes, "*Be Her Now. We're going to be okay.*"

Today, over a million people have been impacted by my programs and messages and I speak on some of the world's largest and most prestigious stages. But I never forget that every invitation that comes in to share my story and support others to change their lives is only because I dared to dream and first transform my own.

Hunter is now 10 years old and we have a morning ritual.

Every morning, Hunter calls, "Family cuddle!" and we all pile on the couch. Me. James. Hunter. And our wheaten terrier puppy who Hunter named Coco Comerota Stewart Bean McGee, or Coco for short.

Before he leaves for camp, I sing Hunter "Cherish" and he giggles.

"Mom, you're acting like you're 11 years old!" Then he busts out to take center stage, singing and dancing along with me.

"I love you, Mom." Then adds, with a big kiss, "You're the best mom in the world!"

James walks in and tries to wrap his arms around me while I continue to belt out notes and try to get him to dance with me.

Bing!

We're interrupted by a text from one of my students.

> *I was at a shop and it started to rain. Everyone took shelter but I ran into the parking lot and danced and twirled in the rain! It was so much fun! Thank you!"*

Even after all this, I still want more. But now it's a loving longing instead of a desperation. I realize that we will always want more, because we *are* more.

In fact, I have fallen in love with the desire for *more* as an expanded expression of self.

I still want more.
I want more of me.
And I want more of you.
Be. Her. Now.

ABOUT MAYA COMEROTA

Maya is a luminary, visionary entrepreneur and top transformational teacher and coach on a mission to unlock human potential.

She has built multibillion dollar initiatives, 7 figure companies and supported over 1.5 million people worldwide to live a life they love living and make seemingly impossible dreams a reality.

Maya is an expert at personal innovation, with certifications from the world's leaders in high performance, neuroscience and life mastery.

As a highly sought after speaker, Maya has been invited to speak on stages with Tony Robbins, Mary Morrisey, Dean Graziosi, Bo Eason and Kyle Cease among others. She has also been a featured expert on television shows and publications such as NBC, Entrepreneur Magazine, Entrepreneur Mindset and Yahoo News.

Maya is the CEO of 528HzInc and the creator of Born For This, Living Legendary Mastermind and Living Luminary Mastermind.

As a high performance consultant and coach, Maya has worked with NFL athletes, entrepreneurs, executives, and fortune 100 companies such as AbbVie, Abbott, Shire, Baxter, Quintiles, and The Magic Johnson Foundation.

She was recently a featured speaker on Richard Branson's island and featured in Project Next, Tony Robbins' and Dean Graziosi's latest Digital Product.

Her greatest accomplishment, however, is being a devoted wife to her husband James and a proud Mom to her son, Hunter.

To connect with Maya, visit mayacomerota.com

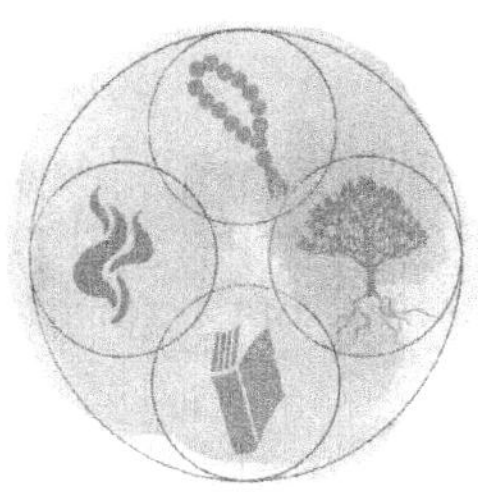

A NOTE FROM THE CREATOR OF THE INSPIRED IMPACT BOOK SERIES, KATE BUTLER

I was putting away the kid's clothes and my phone rang. I glanced at the number and it looked familiar. When I answered, it was Sarah, a woman I had spoken to about six months prior who was interested in writing a book. She had this fascinating story to share, but what made her project even more interesting was her desire to put her journey into a book so she could share it with her children, and eventually her grandchildren. Sarah had the entire vision mapped out. She would use this book to begin tough family conversation and heal certain family dynamics. I had never spoken to a potential author before that was so clear about the outcome she desired. Yet, there was something holding her back.

Money was a little tight, so we had figured out a way for us to work together that felt good for both of us. She had the outline of the book completed. She even had about seventy percent of the book written. We had discussed the parts that would bring the book full circle and she was excited at how it would all come together. Yet, something was still holding her back.

It would be another 6 months before I would speak to her again and it was the same conversation. This time, I pushed back a bit. I said, "Sarah, this is the third time now that we are having the same conversation. You know you want to do this. Your book is practically done. Money is no longer a roadblock. So, what is still keeping you from moving forward?" Sarah said, "I'm paralyzed with the fear that I am just not good enough to do this."

I was stunned. And then my heart broke. Sarah had been suffering for a year-and-half with this fear. She had been allowing her thoughts to torture her and keep her stuck. And it was all a lie. Sarah was a complete Rockstar. Her story was engaging, liberating and unique. This story not only had the potential to heal her family, but millions of families out there.

I said, "Sarah, I am just going to be straight with you. If you allow this fear to continue, not only will you not publish your book, but you are also setting yourself up for many more dreams to not come true. You've got to do this now."

She agreed. She knew she had a story to tell, a dream to live and people that were waiting for it.

Sarah was incredible to work with. She brought a really neat energy and perspective to the table and the closer we came to finishing her book, the more I began to see how far this book could go.

A few months later Sarah stopped returning my emails. It was so unlike anything I had experienced with her but I did not give it too much thought. A few weeks later I tried calling her instead. I did not get a return call back. Then I received an email from my team that Sarah's payment did not go through. I thought, "Oh, ok, this must be it." Even though we had worked out a plan, maybe things had changed on her end. So, I reached out again to talk this through with her and come up with a new plan. Crickets.

Three weeks later I received a communication stating that Sarah had passed away.

She died with the last part of her story still in her. She passed before she could see her dream come to life. She left before she could see the impact her story had on so many people. She was gone.

This forever changed me.

We are not given a dream that we do not have the fullest capacity to achieve. Period. Our time is now. It is right now. Sarah taught me this and so much more.

Sarah taught me, deeply, the importance of living a life worth living.

Life is short.
Make it count.
Make it all count. All the moments.

Do the right thing, even when it's hard. Scratch that, especially when it's hard.

Take the risks, big and small.

Love so deeply you feel your heart expand.

Be grateful when that person shatters your heart, because it means you loved and created meaningful moments.

Stop blaming others. If it's a part of your life, YOU played a part in it too. Own your part and say you're sorry, without conditions. And move on.

Don't wait. Do it now.

Smile.
Giggle.
Belly laugh.

Remember its rarely about what you say and almost always about how you make someone feel.

Have grace knowing only hurt people, hurt people.

Forgive. Give people a break. Be gentle with relationships. Give them the benefit of the doubt.

No matter how many times you've messed up, try again. You're worth it.

One more time, YOU ARE WORTH IT.

Everyone always thinks they are the ones reaching out first, making all the effort and putting in more . . . do it anyway. Keep calling, keep reaching out, keep making the effort. Do it anyway.

Take a long walk, the downloads that happen are extraordinary.

Push yourself beyond a current limit.
Do something tough because you can.
Stretch beyond the norm.

Learn a lesson each day from your kids, they have SO much to teach you.

Remember you can only be appreciated if you don't expect it.

No one owes you anything. No matter how much you do for them. That was your decision, not theirs. And by the way, keep giving. In fact, give more. When you're being honest with yourself, you'll always be thankful you gave more than you had to.

Make people feel so ridiculously special. Because . . . THEY ARE.

Every moment in your life is meant for you. Period. Some moments are lessons, while others are openings. Figure out which one and get on with it.

Get fairy hair.
Hike the red rocks in Sedona.
Kiss under the sparkling lights of the Eiffel Tower.
Fly first class (Even if it's just once.)
Hug your partner when they walk in the door.
Tell your kids you are proud of them.

Say I love you freely.

If people can hate for no reason, I can love for no reason . . . and so can you.

Dig deep. Shine your light. Shine it bright.

Don't be afraid to dream, if you're breathing it's possible. And no, you're not too old to go for it.

Live a life worth living.

I love you with all of my heart, Kate

ABOUT KATE BUTLER, CPSC

Kate Butler is a #1 International best-selling and Award-winning author and speaker. As a CPSC, Certified Professional Success Coach, she offers clients dynamic programs to help them reach their ultimate potential and live out their dreams. She does this through Mindset, Success and Book Publishing programs. Kate is also the creator of the Inspired Impact Book Series, which has published the titles: *Women Who Ignite*, *Women Who Inspire*, *Women Who Influence*, *Women Who Impact*, *Women Who Illuminate*, *Women Who Rise*, and *Women Who Empower*.

Kate received her degree in Mass Communications and Interpersonal Communication Studies from Towson University in Maryland. After 10 years in the corporate world, Kate decided it was time to fulfill her true passion; she studied business at Wharton School of Business at The University of Pennsylvania, and received her certificate in Entrepreneur Acceleration.

Kate now brings her expertise to mainstream media where she has been featured as the Mindset and Publishing expert on Fox 29, Good Day Philadelphia, HBO, in the Huffington Post, and various other television, news, and radio platforms. Kate was named "Top 10 Inspiring Women To Look Out For In 2021" by The NYC Journal and also "Top 20 Female Entrepreneurs Disputing Their Industries in 2021" by Disruptors Magazine.

To learn more about becoming an author in the Inspired Impact Book Series, or to learn how to work with Kate directly on achieving your goals, or publishing your book (including children's books), visit her website at www.katebutlerbooks.com.

Kate would love to connect with you!

FB: @katebutlerbooks
IG: @katebutlerbooks

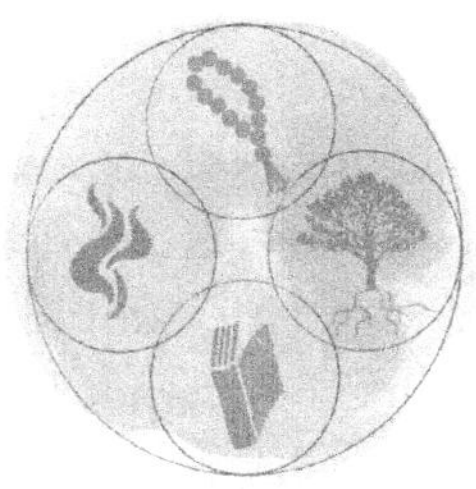

ABANDON FEAR AND ENGAGE

Diana Buckwalter

Once again, I was crying myself to sleep, the kind of crying where you can barely catch your breath, gasping for air between sobs, gasping for air even after falling asleep. I was bad again. My daddy told me so. I am 5 years old and I made too much noise playing in my bed after the lights were out. Daddy came in and grabbed me out of my bed, ripped my clothes off and hit me over and over with his belt. This happened frequently. I don't know how I am bad all the time, I try so hard not to be. Mama told me to try harder to be a good girl. Maybe one day I can be good all day long. Growing up in Texas in the 1960s, where men rule supreme, they own their families. No one can tell a man how to parent or how to be a husband.

Mama had just come home from the hospital. She had been gone for three months. Daddy said she had a nervous breakdown. I didn't know what that was. She cried a lot and took a lot of naps with a pillow over her head. There were no child protective services, no social services. My little body was frequently covered in red welts from daddy's belt. Sometimes mama would spank me too because I was so bad. I am a product of generational dysfunction, born to a fragile mother and an abusive father.

My parents married out of high school. She was an intelligent beauty and he was on the football team. My mother came from a broken family. Her father had gone to WW2 and returned as a different man. Her mother became an alcoholic and left her family to be with another man when my mother was 11 years old. My mother endured abuse from her emotionally stunted father. She became the surrogate mother and homemaker for her two brothers and father. My father had been abandoned by his mother at 6 years old. It has been said that she was bipolar. He was the eldest of three children and his father was also an alcoholic. His grandmother stepped in to raise the children, as so many grandmothers in this world have done. Both my parents wanted to escape their childhood homes and getting married seemed the only way to escape. My sister and I learned to adapt to our parents' emotional pathology.

One time my father came home drunk and hurt mama really bad. He called her a lot of bad names and threw things at her and even broke furniture. I grabbed my sister, and we hid in the closet. We covered up with toys and blankets so that he wouldn't find us. Most of the time this worked. I only peeked out a few times to see if mama was safe. Mama cried and cried. Daddy told mama she was stupid and an idiot. I was afraid that daddy would kill mama. Mama begged daddy to stop. The trauma of this type of abuse is overwhelmingly everlasting in so many ways. Hoping to change the horror in my life I tried to run away when I was 9 years old. When daddy found me, he almost beat me to death. He pulled off my pants and beat me with his belt for a long time. He shook me and shook me. He was very mad. I just wanted to die after that

Daddy seemed like a nice man to everyone else. He had lots of friends. One time Daddy's secretary called mama and told her that daddy had a girlfriend that was a prostitute. I didn't know what that was, but my mama was furious.

Mama had gotten a job at an airline company making reservations so we would have a little money to get by on. After her nervous breakdown the doctors had encouraged her to get a job and get out of the house on a regular basis.

Daddy got drunk a lot, almost every night. Sometimes he got drunk at home and sometimes he went to the bar and got drunk. One night mama was so mad because, once again we had no food. She put my sister and I in the car and drove us to the bar. We marched right into that bar in our pajamas to ask daddy to come home. Daddy was drunk and he told mama to get out and stop embarrassing him. Daddy was very scary when he was drunk. I knew we would all pay for this impromptu visit, and we did.

Mama woke me and my sister one night telling us to pack a few things and we snuck out of the house after daddy passed out. We never went back there. We moved to government housing because we were poor enough to qualify. Mama was excited because there was a bedroom for each of us. My sister cried every night because she had so many bad dreams. Mama spent a lot of time sitting by my sister's bed so that she could sleep. Daddy had really hurt my sister and I on our bodies. He terrorized us and he sexually abused us, which made us have bad dreams. My sister had the worst dreams. She was so scared at night. For some reason I was better at dissociating, forgetting, and blocking. However, there is a specific cry that I occasionally hear from a small child that touches the depths of my soul and brings back immediate memories of extreme fear and hopelessness.

I grew into a teenager and discovered boys and drugs. The combination took my mind off my abusive past, the emotional pain that never seemed to abate. My father had instilled the fact that, as a girl, I would never make it on my own. I had no power. I had no confidence. I was promiscuous at a young age, which can happen with a history of sexual abuse. Sexual abuse has been studied extensively and we now understand the shame and guilt that result. I wanted to be loved and valued and I mistakenly felt those feelings from sexual relationships and accompanying mind-altering drugs. Sadly, many of us who endured childhood abuse gravitate to substances to quiet the disastrous life that echoes in our memories. The substances work well to squelch the memories and feelings, but they lead to a whole new bundle of troubles including the potential destruction of yet another family. Alcoholism, opiates, and other mind-altering substances have destroyed millions of families, left children orphans, spouses abandoned, and parents devastated. During my teens I was steeped in substances because I needed to escape the craziness I was living through. I woke one day, after doing white powder lines of who knows what and discovered that I had lost the prior 36 hours. I had an extraordinarily strong impression that said to me, "Stop this activity, this is not your destiny. You are damaging yourself and you need to stop." I was 16 years old. I had no way of knowing what that destiny was, but there was a tiny sparkle of hope in me that dreamed of a better life.

At 25 years of age, I had given birth to my fifth baby. My husband had become chronically ill and I was afraid that he could die. I would be left with five children to take care of and no way to make money. I wondered if I should go to school, but I remembered when I dropped out of high school the principal told me I would never amount to anything. I had my GED so I thought I would be able to at least go to community college. I decided to give it a try. I was terrified to go to the big college where all the smart people were, to put it mildly. Echoing in my mind was my father's voice telling me you are bad, you are just not good enough. I decided to try anyway. I was sitting in the parking lot outside the local community college trying to avoid the panic attack that was looming all around me. The last time I was in school was the 10th grade. I went through about half of my 10th grade year and here I was, in the parking lot, in front of the administration building ready to go in, but frozen in the seat of my car. I watched all the students walking on the campus with their backpacks filled with educational things, books, papers, etc. I was frozen because I had been told too many times that I would never amount to anything. I wasn't smart and I was just an uneducated girl. After a heartfelt prayer I made myself go in and register.

Five years and two more children later, I graduated with an associate's degree with a 4.0 GPA. I discovered that the college could be paid for through financial aid and I kept getting good grades and scholarships, which surprised me. I moved on to a regular university and majored in nursing. I decided that I could get a good paying job as a nurse. Two years later I was a real nurse and landed a job in labor and delivery in a brand-new hospital. I graduated with honors, but I still thought it may have been an accident. I still didn't think I was very smart. One of the side effects of abuse is thinking that someone will find out that you are a fake, that you really are worthless.

Three years later I went back to school for my master's degree. I was a keen observer of people and I had observed that doctors were frequently interventive and aggressive during childbirth. There were inductions scheduled where the outcome was surely a cesarean, but the patient did not know the risks. There were cesareans and inductions performed for doctor's scheduling needs. Babies were pulled out with forceps and vacuums before it was medically necessary. Internal monitoring had become common, which kept a woman from moving out of the bed and impeded the labor process. I was frustrated at these seemingly unknown injustices to women. I wanted to do something about it and I realized that I could.

I became a Family Nurse Practitioner and obtained a post master's degree as a Certified Nurse Midwife. This allowed me to make the decisions instead of following someone else's orders. My professional life was well on its way. My home life was incredibly busy with seven children. My husband's chronic illness turned out to be an unidentifiable pathogen that caused small bowel blockages and he had several surgeries to remove the affected parts. I'm not sure we ever would have found this out if I hadn't become a nurse.

My husband was my biggest supporter. He told me I could do anything. I had been a women's health provider for many years. Even before I was a nurse, I had been an advocate for natural childbirth, breastfeeding, and loving your babies to bits. I learned physical touch was vital to babies' and children's development of self-worth. I loved my children so much. I never talked to them like they were little children that didn't understand adult talk. I just talked to them like I would a friend. I believe children have grown up souls inside of them.

As I grew in my career I kept achieving more and more. I discovered that I wasn't as bad as I was led to believe as a child. I spent many years trying to recover from the abusive childhood that had affected me so dramatically. As with all experiences there were many opportunities for growth and understanding.

My mother was unempowered and vulnerable because she was uneducated and because she was a victim of that time in history. I believe she did her best and my sister and I are grateful that she got us away from our father.

Becoming empowered, I began to empower other women, especially in birth. Women are powerful when it comes to creating new life. It changes them. There is nothing quite like the experience of 40 weeks of pregnancy along with the body's changes and ultimately giving birth. I have been incredibly fortunate to be a part of thousands of births. I have made wonderful friends and have been a participant in miracles. I have always seen myself as a buffer between the doctor and the patient. I had a patient that, at 20 week's gestation, discovered her baby had spina bifida. The specialist told her to abort, that it was best for the baby and that the baby wouldn't have a good quality of life. This patient didn't want to abort so we set out to find other options. This led to one of the most miraculous events I have ever witnessed.

A group of doctors operated on her baby while she was pregnant. I was able to witness something that seemed like science fiction only a few years earlier. It was utterly remarkable to witness, as the team opened the mother's abdomen and carefully operated on the tiny fetus. A baby that would have been discarded because it wasn't perfect is now having a wonderful, impactful life and I know the mother is so happy that she was able to find another option.

I have opened birth centers and I've also been able to witness incredible water births. Most people are unaware that a baby can be delivered in its bag of water in a tub filled with water and that the experience is serene and spiritual.

I must reference my higher power, my guardian angels, all those ministering angels that comfort and inspire us. I'm lucky that I have always believed in these unseen beings. As a child I recall one night in my bed when I was crying alone, again. In my child-like faith I prayed for Jesus to help me, to be my friend. I felt a warmth that I had never felt before. I felt comforted.

Many people who start out life as I did struggle their entire lives to find the why and the how to overcome their fear, doubt, and shame. They seek to escape the complete devastation that can ensue after abusive trauma. I believe that education can change a woman's path. Women can achieve greatness despite their early circumstances. Too many women are victimized because they believe they have no options for survival. If you have a story like mine, I can promise and assure you that you can be independent and successful. It isn't easy, but you are already acquainted with difficulty.

My message is one of hope through education. It is universally understood that when women are given the opportunity to obtain an education, future possibilities soar and societies improve. Everyone is blessed when a woman can go to college. I didn't know about grants and scholarships when I first started. As I continued my educational path, I learned that there are many ways to navigate the educational system. I believe that it is never too late to go to school. If you are breathing, you can continue to learn and progress. Our progression is dynamic, always changing and growing.

My plate has always been full. Rarely did I have a chance to rest and recover. My husband was self-employed and had health problems. My sister had struggles because of our disastrous upbringing. At one point I had her six children, as well as my six children, while I was pregnant with my seventh. This was only for a few months, but I continued with school. My sister also became a nurse. We are survivors. We survived physical, emotional, mental, and sexual abuse. We came out on the other side of abuse tattered and torn, but still alive with additional life to live and more experiences to learn from.

Things did not change immediately, but over time, day by day, week by week, month by month, and year by year they did change. There was nothing easy about the steps I took to change my future. To say it was hard is a gross understatement. I look back now and see that, while I was working hard to change my future from my past and to climb from darkness to light, I was given many thoughts and situations that directed me to a new way of life. A life free of substance abuse and free of violence and shame. My children grew up much differently than I did, and I see this as tremendous progress. There are long generations of abuse that never seem to change until someone stands up and says enough. You can be that person. Stand up, engage, and make changes and you will be pleasantly surprised at the amazing and miraculous events that naturally follow. You are more powerful than you know!

ABOUT DIANA BUCKWALTER

Diana worked as a Registered Nurse in Labor and Delivery for four years and as an Advanced Practice Nurse and Midwife for over 25 years in Obstetrics and Gynecology. She has been a pioneer in her field, championing the rights of women to have a voice in their procreative abilities. She has worked diligently for midwifery to be present in hospitals. She built one of the most beautiful in-hospital birth centers in the country. Diana has traveled internationally to learn the customs of other cultures as it relates to women's health. She has worked with women who, for generations, have been oppressed and abused through experiences such as female genital mutilation, rape, violence, and significant emotional and physical pain. Diana has extensive experience counseling women and couples about sexual fulfillment when women and couples thought all was hopeless. She has experienced physical and sexual abuse, which has helped her to understand the trauma and subsequent emotional, physical, and spiritual sequela which frequently accompanies these events. Diana is a strong proponent for education because of the opportunities that show up when you make that choice. Diana lives in Colorado and has 7 children, 5 daughters and 2 sons, and 34 grandchildren.

Contact Diana at hello@intimate-knowledge.com or dianabuckwalter@gmail.com

Website: www.intimate-knowledge.com
Facebook: Intimate knowledge
LinkedIn: Diana Buckwalter

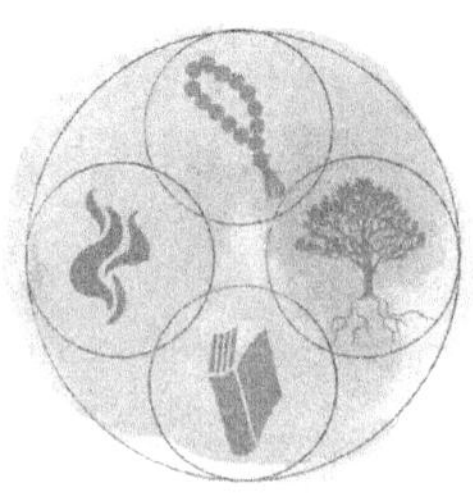

IGNITE YOUR INNER SPARK

Stacy Kuhen

"Just QUIT! No one will hold it against you." That's what my family and friends told me when I was immersed in a spiral of self-doubt during my first year of teaching. I know they didn't really want me to quit teaching; they just didn't want to watch me beat myself up anymore. Even though I began each day by reminding my students that they could accomplish anything as long as they believed in themselves, I wasn't following my own advice. I was letting my inner critic get the best of me and I felt like a failure. I became a teacher to make a difference in the lives of my students, yet I felt like I wasn't even connecting with them.

As I reflect back on my first year in the classroom, there are so many experiences that I am grateful for, but at the time, I felt like a lost soul without a purpose. The initial excitement of being a new teacher was overshadowed by my insecurities. I was eager to work with middle schoolers, but I soon realized they viewed me more as their peer than their teacher, so they didn't always show me the appropriate respect. Most days my head was spinning as I was scrambling to figure out what to do next. I was disappointed in myself for feeling out of control. I was showing up to work each day with a smile on my face, but the feeling of not having a purpose continued to build inside of me. I was spending hours developing lessons and trying new strategies to motivate my students, but something seemed to be missing. The shame of feeling like a failure was sucking the life out of me and making me question whether I had chosen the right career.

I remember telling myself, "You can't give up. What will your students think? Will they feel like you abandoned them? You don't ever want them to feel that way because you would never give up on them. You know you can do this. Just take it one day at a time. Focus on the positive moments and be grateful for the opportunity to make a difference in their lives. As long as they know you are there for them, everything will be okay."

And everything was okay because I made the choice to get out of my head and I started listening to my heart. My heart told me to focus on **gratitude.** I began appreciating the moments each day that I was grateful for and in doing so, my relationships with my students began to flourish. We established core values in our classroom, supported each other's strengths, worked through challenges as a team, and learned to believe in ourselves. We became a supportive community where each person was valued and appreciated. We began showing up for ourselves and each other and as a result, our confidence began to shine brightly. Having gratitude positively shifted our class dynamic; it was the little spark we needed to light a fire within each of us.

I am proud that I did not give up on myself and my teaching ability. It's now 16 years later, and I am a better version of myself because I chose to be grateful for my experiences rather than stay stuck in a spiral of self-pity. Gratitude allowed me to spark a light inside of myself and share that light with others. I knew I could make a positive impact as a teacher, but I didn't know how much my life would be impacted by my students. My students are my children, and I would do anything for them. They bring me so much joy and I am grateful for the opportunity to work alongside them. We have taught each other to believe in ourselves and to grow from our experiences in pursuit of our passions. I am eternally grateful for every student I have taught throughout my career. Each one of them holds a special place in my heart and has inspired me to become a better version of myself.

When we are passionate about our career, it often becomes who we are. Being a teacher has become my identity. My experiences as an educator have shaped me into the person I am today, but my career is not the only thing that defines me.

How do you connect to the word *identity*?

Is your identity shaped by the roles you have been given by others?

- Mother. Daughter. Granddaughter. Sister. Aunt. Niece. Cousin. Wife. Girlfriend. Partner. Friend. Teammate. Colleague.

Or is your identity shaped by the roles you have created for yourself?

- *Loving* Family Member. *Loyal* Friend. *Supportive* Colleague. *Encouraging* Teacher.
- Adventure Seeker. Motivational Leader. World Traveler. Philanthropist. Entrepreneur.
- Perfectionist. Workaholic. People Pleaser. Procrastinator.

When I reflect back on my first year in the classroom, why was I allowing myself to feel like a failure? I realize now that I was allowing the part of me that identifies as a *perfectionist* and a *people pleaser* to control me and in doing so, it dimmed my confidence.

We all know that there is no such thing as perfection, so why do we strive so hard to attain it? How did I become a perfectionist?

Maybe my desire to be perfect began in elementary school

when I received recognition for perfect attendance, earning straight A's, and winning first place in the Halloween costume contest every year. (I can thank my mom and dad's creativity and sewing skills for that honor!) Maybe my desire to be perfect is connected to my fear of letting down my family, friends, students, and colleagues if I am not able to be there for them. Maybe my desire to be perfect is connected to my fear of failure if I do not accomplish a goal that I set for myself.

I don't know how this desire to be perfect began, but I am working on letting go of perfectionism and the stress and anxiety that accompanies it. There is no such thing as perfect. Everyone makes mistakes and everyone experiences failure. Our mistakes and our failures provide us with the opportunity to learn and grow from our experiences. I am grateful for the lessons I have learned from both my positive and negative experiences and I remind myself daily to strive for growth rather than perfection as I work towards becoming a better version of myself.

Letting go of perfectionism starts with self-compassion. Set an intention to begin each day by looking in the mirror and sharing at least one thing that you love about yourself: *I love my ability to make others smile and my sense of adventure.* Then repeat several positive affirmations to yourself: *I am strong. I am beautiful. I am kind. I am worthy. I am loved. I accept myself for who I am. I am proud of myself for all I've accomplished. I believe in myself and know I can do anything I put my mind to. I am open to learning from my experiences and will give myself grace if things do not go as planned.* Finish up by expressing your gratitude for at least two things: *I am grateful to have a loving and supportive family and I am grateful to have a healthy mind, body, and soul.* Establishing this daily practice of reflecting on what you love about yourself, repeating positive affirmations, and focusing on gratitude will create a foundation for self-acceptance, allowing you to let go of perfectionism and love yourself for who you are.

Another part of me that I have allowed to control my

life is being a *people pleaser*. Being a *people pleaser* is a form of *perfectionism* that can dim the light within you if you let it. We all know that *you can't please everyone*, so why do we try so hard to make others happy? How did I become a *people pleaser*?

Maybe it began in my childhood when I wanted to please my parents. Maybe it continued during school when I wanted to please my teachers. Maybe it showed up in my friendships because I wanted my friends to be happy. Maybe I am a people pleaser because it is easier than confrontation. Maybe it is associated with my fear of disappointing others.

I'm not sure how I decided to be a people pleaser, but honestly it can be exhausting. I know I do not need approval from others in order to live my life, yet I have created a life that focuses on making others happy. Making people happy brings me joy. It is part of who I am. But I've recently learned that it is also important to make myself a priority. Self-care is essential and finding a healthy balance between doing for others and setting aside time for myself is what I strive for now. When you make yourself a priority, you are actually able to do more for those around you.

The expectations and opinions of others don't matter. The only expectations that you should try to live up to are the ones that you set for yourself. You have control of the way you view yourself so start shifting your perspective and focus on things that spark a light within you. Growth is a continual process that requires you to give yourself grace. When you embrace growth, you are allowing yourself to shine in all areas of your life—mindset, health, family, friendships, relationships, career, dreams, and aspirations.

When you are afraid to push outside of your comfort zone, you are limiting yourself and your potential by allowing your fear to dim the light that shines brightly within you. The light that is longing for you to embark on a new path in pursuit of your passions and dreams. Listen to your intuition and allow your inner light to guide you through your fears as you step into a better version of yourself. Believe in yourself and your ability to become anything that you want to become, and you will accomplish everything your heart desires.

Pursuing your dreams does not have to feel like work. But many of us have been conditioned to believe that the more we work, the more successful we will be.

Have you ever felt like you were married to your job?

That's me—I am a self-proclaimed *workaholic* and I used to be proud of it. But over the years, that pride has turned into burnout and exhaustion.

I never understood why asking someone what they do for work has become a go-to question when striking up a conversation with someone new. Is our society so obsessed with our careers that we have become what we do? Work is a big part of who we are because we spend most of our days committed to our work, but we do not have to be defined by our careers. Why have I chosen to be a *workaholic*?

Maybe it is because my job is connected to my purpose. Maybe it is because my work brings me joy. Maybe it is because being busy makes me feel accomplished.

My workaholic tendencies often have me taking on too much, doing everything by myself, living my life by a list, and living to work rather than working to live. I can admit that delegating is not one of my strengths, so I always end up adding more to my own plate. When it comes to living my life by a list, I focus on what must get done in order to feel accomplished. I feel satisfaction in crossing items off my list, but if I do not accomplish everything, I feel anxious and stressed. I feel guilty when I think about taking a day off, so I rarely do. But not taking days off can lead to feeling burnt-out and exhausted and feeling that way does not allow me to be the best version of myself or give the best of myself to others. Mindset and mental health are so important. Everyone deserves to take days off without feeling guilty because in doing so, you are making yourself and your mental health a priority. When you make your mental health a priority, you are able to show up as your best self and share the best of yourself with others. I am doing my best to let go of the workaholic mindset as I shift towards a better work/life balance. I am passionate about my work, and it is a part of who I am, but it should not be the only thing that defines me.

Our identities are shaped by our experiences; therefore, our identities are constantly evolving. Who we are is often a reflection of how we see ourselves. Sometimes we are our biggest fan and other times we are our biggest critic. We must learn to *fuel our inner spark* by seeing our "light dimmers" as *opportunities for growth*.

Over the past two years I have done my best to allow my light dimmers to become a spark that has ignited a fire within my soul.

By focusing on self-love and self-care, I am letting go of perfectionism and doing my best to be present each day. I am talking to myself the way that I have always talked to my students—in a loving, encouraging, and supportive way. I am giving myself grace when things do not go as I planned, learning from my mistakes and my experiences, and embarking on new opportunities. I am focusing on my mindset and my health, and I am living in alignment with my core values.

Gratitude has provided a spark for strengthening my relationships. I value and appreciate each person that I have in my life, and I try my best to show my appreciation. By focusing on gratitude, I am releasing the part of me that is a people pleaser to find a healthy balance between being there for others and being there for myself.

Releasing control and establishing boundaries has allowed me to work towards creating a healthy balance between my professional and personal life. I have tried my best to establish "me time" each day where I focus on things unrelated to work that bring me joy. I have incorporated exercise, listening to music, listening to podcasts, going for walks, reading, photography, and journaling into my "me time." I am also trying my best not to spread myself too thin and to allow others to help when they offer. I am letting go of my identity that is connected to being a workaholic and I am creating a healthy and balanced lifestyle.

When you think of your identity, think of what ignites a spark within your soul, as well as the challenges you have faced that have extinguished that spark. Then focus on how you have overcome those challenges to reignite the spark within you.

Although there have been many times throughout my career when I have questioned myself and my purpose, the one thing that has always remained the same is the love that I have for my students. The love that I have for my students has allowed me to push through challenges and to learn from my experiences. It has also inspired me to strive for growth in pursuit of my passions. It has ignited a spark within me that is determined to impact the lives of others on another level. I have always felt that my most important role as a teacher has been to instill core values, confidence, and character in my students while encouraging them to follow their dreams and pursue their passions. And now I am inspired to share these lessons on a greater scale.

Although being a teacher will always be a part of who I am, I have decided to step outside of the classroom to pursue my passion in a new way. Through my company, *With Gratitude*, and my new role as an educational consultant, mindset coach, and motivational speaker, I am dedicated to sparking a light within others and empowering them to work towards being the best version of themselves.

I am filled with gratitude for the relationships, experiences, colleagues, mentors, friends, families, and students that have been part of my journey over the past 16 years. They have helped me grow into a better version of myself, which has inspired me to embark on a new path as an entrepreneur. I am dedicated to pursuing my passions and to living out my purpose in a new way. As I reflect on the experiences that have brought me to this point, I am grateful for my family and friends who have always supported me and encouraged me to follow my dreams.

I am also grateful that I did not give up on myself when I felt like a lost soul without a purpose. I know I was put on this earth to help others, and as I take a leap of faith into this new chapter, I am reigniting the spark within me that believes in myself and my ability to make a difference in the world.

You have the power to start a new chapter. Embrace growth through gratitude in pursuit of your passions. Believe in yourself and your ability to accomplish anything your heart desires. Shift your perspective and allow your light dimmers to become opportunities for growth. With gratitude in your heart, *ignite your inner spark* and allow your light to shine brightly.

ABOUT STACY KUHEN

Stacy Kuhen is an educator, mindset coach, motivational speaker, New Jersey realtor, and #1 International best-selling author of *Women Who Empower.* She is dedicated to empowering others to become the best version of themselves. Stacy has developed programs that instill confidence, promote acceptance, and inspire children and adults to embrace growth through gratitude. Her areas of expertise include promoting positive relationships, fostering social-emotional learning, and teaching effective leadership and communication skills.

Stacy is also passionate about service learning and philanthropy and has partnered with many nonprofit organizations both locally and nationally. In 2014, she embarked on a 7-month volunteer journey, traveling to 14 countries with a mission to support communities around the world. This experience inspired her to create her company, *With Gratitude.*

As the founder and CEO of *With Gratitude*, Stacy offers personal development courses on experiencing growth through gratitude, finding joy in the journey, becoming the best version of yourself, and igniting your inner spark. In addition, she provides motivational trainings and leadership workshops for individuals, organizations, schools, and businesses. Her programs focus on promoting positivity and cultivating collaborative communities where every person feels valued and appreciated. She is currently working on her first children's book which focuses on the power of positivity and believing in yourself. Stacy hopes her message will inspire children to embody a growth mindset, persevere through challenges, learn from their experiences, and always believe in themselves.

To learn more about the programs and training that Stacy offers, please visit www.stacykuhen.com and become a part of her community on social media.

Learn more about Stacy Kuhen:

Website: www.stacykuhen.com
Email: stacy@stacykuhen.com
Facebook: Ms. With Gratitude
Instagram: @mswithgratitude

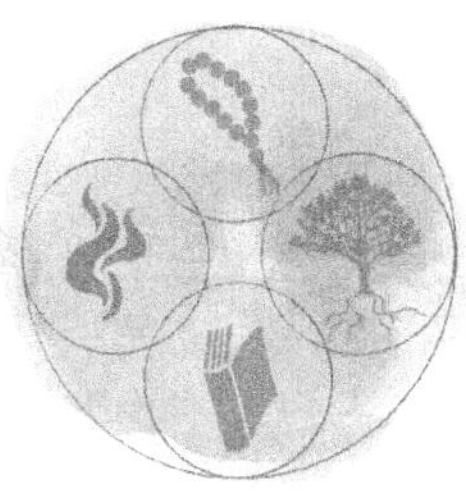

STARS CAN'T SHINE WITHOUT DARKNESS

Christine Lavulo

Darkness is something I'm familiar with. Adversity has been my life's journey. And yet, I always felt this spark within me, even at a young age. I didn't really understand what it was or what to do with it, so I hid it. As a matter of fact, for the better part of my life, I felt that I was made for something greater, but it seemed the world was telling me I was nothing, no good, not enough, and totally unworthy of greatness.

I'm sure it was just my own false beliefs, rooted in experience from my childhood. From the time I was about 10 years old I was told there was someone better than me in every love and pursuit that I desired. I felt I couldn't compete, so I stopped trying to even pursue things. At that time, I didn't realize that we each have a uniqueness about us. There is no such thing as better than or less than, just different. However, I didn't understand abundance mentality and that there is truly enough to go around. There is more than enough talent, opportunity, and love.

When I was a little girl, it always felt like something was missing from me. It seemed as if nothing I did was ever quite good enough and at times I wondered if I would ever measure up to those around me. I loved to sing and thought I was pretty good, but never as good as my best friend, Shauna. When I would sing a duet with her at church, everyone would come up and tell me how well we did and then go on and on about Shauna's voice.

I really wanted to be a professional singer from the time I was little. I always saw myself on stage, microphone in hand, a large crowd in front of me, and a spotlight on me. Then, during my sophomore year of high school , when I didn't make our high school musical or the chorus, I realized maybe this was just a dream and I needed a back-up plan like my parents always suggested. Maybe I really wasn't good enough and had to start thinking realistically.

Before I had a chance to really focus on a new career path (although dance was my next move), I found myself pregnant and alone in my senior year of high school. I saw all my future hopes and dreams fade away as I took on a new adventure, motherhood. I knew there was joy in motherhood and I had wanted to keep my son. Adoption wasn't an option, even though I knew that would be an easier path in some ways. As I went into the real world, living paycheck to paycheck, trying to survive, I started to wonder if I had what it took to really do more with my life. There seemed to be plenty of messages from the world about how I'd never amount to anything. Yet, somehow there was this fire inside me that kept telling me there was something better out there; that I was meant for more. I just couldn't figure out what it was or how to achieve it. How could someone so low, so unworthy, untalented, average and basic have anything more to offer this world?

For most of my life I felt I was being given this subliminal message of not being enough. Not being smart enough, pretty enough, skinny enough, talented enough, rich enough, popular enough. Just a lot of not enoughness and not much encouragement and building up. I realize that it was the way I chose to perceive things and not a true reality, but at the time, it felt like each comment that wasn't cheering me on was burying me alive.

Don't get me wrong, things weren't always bad and hard during those years. I did have some good moments, times where I seemed like I was doing well. There were times where I felt confident in my abilities and the future seemed bright. Then things would shift, get harder, and all the negative voices from the past would flood in and take me back to a dark place. There were times when the mist of darkness was all around me. There was no light shining before me. I had to rely on the light within me. That burning inside me that remained strong, telling me I was born to shine.

What does it mean to shine? Merriam-Webster Dictionary writes that, to shine "to emit rays of light; to be eminent, conspicuous, or distinguished; to have a bright glowing appearance; BRILLIANCE, SPLENDOR." These are just a few of the possible definitions and these are the ones I want to focus on.

Each one of us has a light inside of us. It's just a part of the spirit that makes up who we are. We all have a light. I know that when I'm feeling really good, physically, mentally, and emotionally, that it is really easy for my light to shine bright. When I'm not feeling really good, it is definitely harder for that light to shine. I can either draw people to me or push them away, just by how I'm feeling inside.

I used to look to other people to determine how I felt about myself. Anything that I perceived as a dig or an insult, I would use as ammunition against myself to prove to myself just how little I had inside me that was of value. I'm not sure why that always seemed to be my default pattern. To be honest, I think it's part of our human nature and something most of us have to strive to overcome. However, one day while I was sitting in a workshop that was being put on by Jack Canfield, I realized I have the power to choose what I feel. I have the power to choose what I think. I have the power to choose who I am going to be.

And so do you.

Just like me, you were born to shine.

Every single person that has ever lived has possessed a unique purpose that only they can fulfill in their own unique way, with their own unique gifts and talents. We all have something special inside of us that makes us who we are. We may have similarities with others, but no one is exactly the same.

It has taken me a long time to overcome comparisons and using other people to measure myself, my worth, and my successes. Truthfully, I still have to work on it daily, because I believe it's naturally a part of our human nature to compare ourselves, and others, in an effort to determine how we measure up. But no one is better than or less than anyone else, just different. We have different circumstances, different obstacles, and different abilities. That doesn't make anyone better, just uniquely themselves.

As I've stepped into my true purpose of becoming a speaker, author and coach, it is easy for me to look at other people in my field and wonder why they seem to get more people to their events, sell more books, or get more clients. Then I realize that they've been working on this much longer than I have. They may also have a different set of circumstances in regards to their other obligations and what fills their time.

There's a difference between someone who is single with no kids and someone who is married with five kids or even a single mom with any number of kids. Life isn't the same for everyone. It's okay to be on your own journey and not worry about other people's journeys. That's really what it's all about. Focus on you. If you don't already know what makes you unique, take action to discover it. Ask people to tell you the two things that first come to mind when they think of you. What makes you unique? What qualities do they see in you? Don't worry about the answer. Just look at the majority and discover yourself through other people's eyes in a delightful way.

Explore the things you're passionate about. Make a joy list and do something daily that brings you joy. It could be as simple as a long, hot bubble bath or a hike some place that makes you feel connected to the earth. It could be going to a favorite restaurant, watching a movie with a loved one, or writing in your journal. There are no wrong answers to what brings you true joy.

Your purpose is typically found in what brings you the most joy and what you are most passionate about. It is usually the thing that lights you up when you think about it and makes you feel great when you're doing it. It may be something you've shut down. I have found that life comes along and tends to stifle our dreams. Give yourself a moment to close your eyes, breathe in deeply, and consider what you love to do the most. What were your dreams when you were growing up? What happened that made you shift away from that? Dreams can change and that's totally okay, but we should always have a dream. If you've stopped dreaming, it's time to start again!

Dare to dream big! Dare to BELIEVE in yourself! Consider that everyone you see shining is just reflecting who you are inside. When you look at all those women you may be comparing yourself to know that you wouldn't recognize the qualities in them unless you had those qualities yourself. They are just further along in their journey, and actually, they may be on a completely different road. It's okay to be where you are. It's okay to give yourself permission to pursue something more and to truly become all you were created to become. You are wonderful and magnificent and the world needs all that you have to offer!

I remember participating in a meditation at that same Jack Canfield event. I had realized I had my own journey and life purpose after an experience in 2011, however, the life purpose meditation we did at that particular event brought everything home for me. During the meditation, I saw clearly I was given a gift of a microphone and angel wings. I realized at that moment that the vision I had since I was young wasn't for me to be singing, but to be on stage speaking, teaching people how they can live a higher life, have greater relationships, and truly fulfill the measure of their worth!

I love what Jim Carrey had to say about this. "Your need for acceptance can make you invisible in this world. Don't let anything stand in the way of the light that shines through this form. Risk being seen in all of your glory."

Be willing to take the risk and let your light shine. Let it shine even brighter.

ABOUT CHRISTINE LAVULO, CPSC

Christine Lavulo is a Certified Professional Success Coach, Best Selling Author, Motivational Speaker and Success Principles Trainer. Christine has had a successful corporate career, as well as her own business ventures, but Christine's biggest passion lies in helping women reclaim their true identity, find their life purpose, and create a beautiful life, founded on her Relationship Formula—because the most important thing in life is our relationships with self, higher power, family and friends. This is where Christine truly shines.

Christine has an extensive tool belt. She has worked with legends such as Jack Canfield and John Maxwell and has been employed by Franklin Covey. She is a firm believer in personal development as a part of her self-care routine. Life is all about progress, not perfection.

Christine has been married to her husband, Clawson for over 23 years. She has 5 sons, 1 daughter-in-law, 2 grandsons, 3 granddaughters and 2 grand-dogs to date. She loves to dance and dances as often as she can, especially enjoying the opportunities to dance with her high school alumni drill team.

To find out more about hiring Christine to speak at your event or to learn more about her coaching, visit her website at www.christinelavulo.com or find her on LinkedIn, Facebook or Instagram. She would love to connect with you!

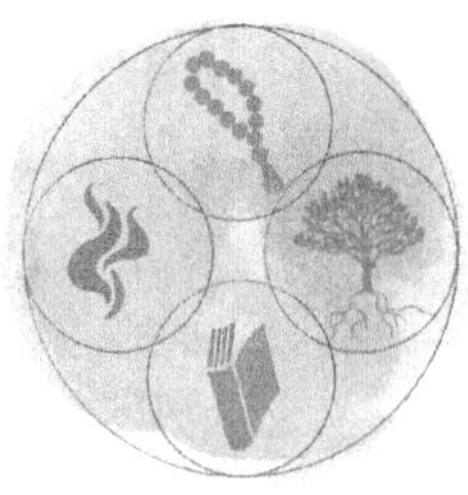

BECOMING YOUR BEST

Laurie Maddalena

"None of us can change our yesterdays, but all of us can change our tomorrows."

~Colin Powell

Two years ago, I was invited to facilitate a workshop on creating success for a small group of teachers at my old high school in upstate New York. During the workshop, I shared how I overcame disadvantages in my childhood and used those experiences to create positive change and success in my life. I have a beautiful life. I am happily married with three wonderful children. I am an entrepreneur, professional speaker, success coach, and leadership consultant. I run a growing and thriving consulting business where I help leaders create more personal and professional success, and help organizations create exceptional cultures where people love to come to work. My life is fulfilling, and I am constantly growing and expanding my potential. I have a business and a life that I love. I am confident in my abilities and feel excited to engage with life.

It wasn't always this way.

You know those kids who peaked in high school? The ones who had it all together? They were smart, pretty, great at sports and seemed to have unbounding confidence? Yeah, that wasn't me. For many years, I struggled with low self-esteem and never felt good enough. I compared myself to others and felt like I never measured up. I was a follower, not a leader. I was conditioned to follow authority and I let others influence how I felt about myself. I lacked the confidence to stand up to others and I was desperate to be liked.

My story isn't very unique or unusual. Most of us have moments or interactions in our childhood that shape who we believe we can be. For me, there were several key moments that took root in my self-image and created a belief system that limited my potential and my own personal power. It took me years to break through the negative beliefs that took root in my self-concept early in my life. This negative belief system was like a low-grade fever holding me back from ever feeling my best.

My earliest negative memory was in kindergarten when my best friend, Tonya, and I were coloring at a group table. We were learning the letter "Z." Tonya was coloring a zipper and I was coloring a zebra. As we were finishing up our work, the teacher's assistant called us into the kitchen (in my town kindergarten was in a schoolhouse at that time!) and scolded us for coloring outside the lines. I remember feeling ashamed and embarrassed. At only five years old, I was being scolded for not being perfect. I froze in that moment. I was so terrified of being singled out that I wanted to be invisible. From that point on, I stayed quiet and tried to do the right thing by fitting in to avoid criticism. I was scared of being wrong and not meeting my teacher's expectations. I was a good kid, and getting in trouble was mortifying for me. So, I did what good girls did, I followed the rules, did what I was told, and tried my hardest to please.

That same year, Tonya and I were in the daycare room while our moms bowled in their weekly bowling league. The daycare room was long and spacious and there was plenty of room to run around. There were about twelve of us running from one side of the room to the other when one of the girls tripped and fell. She started crying. When the teacher came over and asked what happened, she said that someone had tripped her. The teacher asked her who had tripped her. The girl turned around looking confused and she pointed to me. I was nowhere near her when we were running, but my guess is that she felt pressured in that moment to pick someone. The teacher yelled at me and told me to go sit down. My five-year-old self would never argue or defend myself, so I did what I was told. I sat down in the corner and cried.

I remember both of these incidents like they happened last week. In neither of those interactions did the teacher ask me what happened or engage me in a conversation. Both of them assumed the authority role and scolded me without question. I was young and impressionable, and I was conditioned to follow directions and comply with authority. I learned that it wasn't safe to disagree or stand up for myself.

Being an only child for the first seven and a half years of my life, I didn't have siblings to fight or compete with. I was mild mannered and quiet, and my early life was easy and calm. I didn't experience situations where I had to speak up or stand up for myself. I was young and naïve, and I wasn't prepared to handle difficult and uncomfortable situations. So, when I encountered negative words or actions from others, I internalized those negative feelings and let them chip away at my self-worth.

As I grew older, I encountered more situations that I didn't know how to handle. A popular game in my neighborhood as a kid was called "Cootie." If you were the Cootie, you had to try and tag another kid to become the Cootie so you could be safe. I felt like I was always picked to be the Cootie first because I had a hard time keeping up with the older kids and catching someone else to be the Cootie. I hated that game, and I remember neighborhood kids teasing me as I tried and failed to catch up to them. Of course, that is the whole point of the game, but as a young self-conscious girl, I took it to heart. I was always the Cootie and the child who others would tease and laugh at.

One day when, I was about seven or eight years old, I came home crying to my mom that the other kids were teasing me. My mom told me that they wouldn't tease me unless I let them. I had no idea at the time what she meant. My young mind couldn't understand how I was letting kids tease me. I just wanted to be liked and accepted. I didn't know how to stand up for myself. I was allowing these kids to take advantage of me and to tease me, and I felt powerless.

As I progressed through elementary school, I did well academically, but struggled with confidence. Those instances from my early childhood took root in my belief system and continued to chip away at the natural confidence I had. I wasn't good under pressure, and I didn't want to stand out. One day in fourth grade, my teacher told me to go to the blackboard and solve a long division problem. I stood at the blackboard, frozen in fear, afraid to get the problem wrong. She yelled at me in front of the class for not being able to solve the problem. These moments were conditioning me to not take chances. Don't stand out. Fade into the background and try not to be noticed. Just try to fit in.

My story is not uncommon. Lots of kids get teased when they are young. There were certainly great moments in my childhood too. I remember glimpses of feeling good about myself, like when I won an academic award in fifth grade or performed in the high school musical. There were times that I could envision myself doing something great or impactful in the world. Yet the negative experiences shaped how I thought about myself. I let those painful experiences take root in my self-concept. I created a limiting belief that I wasn't good enough and that I should stay in the shadows where it was safe. Whenever I felt my inner light start to shine, my doubts and fears would dim it. I was afraid of failure, so I played safe and blended in.

Because of my academic success in sixth grade, I was placed in advanced classes for seventh grade. I was being stretched and challenged, and while this could have been a positive experience to stretch me toward my potential, my lack of confidence took hold and I struggled. Up until that point, good grades had come naturally to me. I rarely had to study, but these challenging classes required a different level of study and focus. I doubted myself and my potential, and chose to go back to regular classes the following year.

The stakes felt higher as I entered high school. I had a lot of friends in different groups, and for the most part, I enjoyed my classes. I was involved in band, theatre, softball, and choir, but always felt myself holding back from my true potential. I didn't excel in sports or activities. I felt average at best. I would compare myself to a few of my friends who were better at sports and academics than I was. While I felt self-conscious, quiet, and insecure, my best friend from childhood was the opposite. She appeared confident, bold, and smart. Focusing on how others were better than me just fueled my own discomfort and doubts.

When I was thirteen, one of my guy friends told me that he and the guys in our group of friends were sitting around one day rating the girls in our group on attractiveness. Apparently, the guys thought I had a nice body, but not a pretty face. I think he stupidly thought that hearing I had a nice body would make me feel good. Crazy, right?

By my senior year of high school, I was gaining confidence and feeling better about myself and my potential. I started studying more, and I found a class that I not only enjoyed but excelled at—writing. My grades reflected my effort, and when I put in the effort, I would see positive results. That year, one of my friends asked me to be co-editor of the yearbook, and I agreed. The teacher who was the advisor for the yearbook club was the head of the English department, and didn't want me as co-editor. He wanted a student of his from the advanced English class, but most of them were involved in sports and couldn't commit the time. My friend advocated for me, but the advisor was not happy. The advisor didn't speak to me once during the entire year I served as co-editor of the yearbook. He would speak to my co-editor, but would completely ignore me. Once again, I felt ashamed, unworthy, and inadequate.

It was around this time that I started reading personal development books. I was desperate to gain more confidence, so I read books on personal power and success. I had always been a hard worker at my summer jobs, but a turning point for me was when I was about nineteen years old. I had been working at an ice cream stand in my town every summer for a few years, and one of the owners was impressed with my work ethic. He also owned the restaurant next store, and asked if I was interested in bussing tables. I spent the summer juggling both jobs, working hard, and earning money. I remember one day the restaurant wasn't very busy and most of the employees were standing around. One of the owners, Vinny, came out and said, "If you can lean, you can clean." His comment really struck me, as I realized that he was looking for his employees to take ownership and not stand around with nothing to do. This was a big lesson for me, and one that I would carry with me to my future jobs. When I worked hard and put in effort beyond what was expected, I would be rewarded with accolades and more responsibility.

A year after I graduated college, I moved to Maryland and rented a townhouse with my best friend from college. I worked at Dave & Buster's as a server while I looked for a more permanent job. My work ethic and positive attitude earned me a promotion to assistant department head of the waitstaff after four months. I was selected for the travel team, a group of the best and most experienced employees who would travel to open new stores across the country. The following year, I was recognized by the management team with the annual "Shining Star" award.

A little over a year later, a coworker told me about a job at a credit union that she thought I might be interested in. The position was for the assistant manager of a call center, and I would manage twelve people. I was selected for the position. The best part of that job was managing people. I enjoyed the leadership part of that position, and I discovered I wanted to focus my career on helping others grow and develop. Within two years, I earned a promotion to the human resources department.

This was a pivotal time in my life. My confidence started to grow, and I realized that, although my past experiences impacted me, they didn't have to define my future. I continued to read books and visualize a future of abundance and success. The more I stepped out, took action, and experienced success, the more my confidence started to grow. I finally felt in control of my future, and I felt good about my life.

Over the next few years, I excelled in my position at work. I was promoted several times and given more responsibility. I worked hard to become indispensable to my boss. I volunteered to take projects off her plate and support her in any way I could. Four years after my move to the human resources department, my boss left the company because her husband's job was transferred to another state. Two weeks after I turned 30 years old, I was promoted to vice president of human resources. Over the next four years, the HR team worked to create a great place to work for the employees of our company. I started a coaching certification so I could bring those skills into our company and teach our managers how to effectively coach and develop employees. During the coaching certification, I was encouraged by other participants who had their own consulting firms. They didn't work for anyone else; they were in charge of their own futures and destinities. I yearned for the chance to make a bigger impact in the world and also continue to develop my own personal potential.

As I succeeded in my career, my confidence increased and I learned to not only like myself, but love myself. I realized that comparing myself to others was a confidence crusher. When we look at others' success, we are only seeing their front stage, the part of their experience that is visible to the outside world. We don't know what their backstage experience might be—the struggles, pain, and hardships they've had to overcome behind the scenes. Even the person you admire most who displays unshakeable confidence has insecurities and challenges too.

In July 2008, I left my executive job to start my own company, Envision Excellence. I have been in business for thirteen years, and although there are constantly new obstacles to deal with, I have developed the mindset, skills, and confidence necessary to deal with anything that comes my way. I am passionate about empowering leaders to create engaging cultures where employees love to come to work. I've worked with over a thousand leaders to help them elevate their leadership skills, confidence, and their lives.

In my work with leaders, I've found that many people have struggled in their life with a lack of self-confidence and self-worth. In fact, even the kids who seemingly peaked in high school had their own insecurities and challenges. It might not appear obvious on the outside, but no one is immune to self-doubt and comparison.

As I watch my own young children grow, I sometimes fear that they will let others dictate how they feel about themselves. I'm very conscious to instill positive messages and teach them to honor other people's talents and gifts while also honoring their own. We teach our children gratitude, kindness, and compassion, and my biggest hope is that my children love themselves enough to overcome any adversity, negativity, or challenge with grace and confidence. I think about my five-year-old self and how I wish I could go back and tell her to hang in there, speak up, believe in herself, and punch that friend who told me I had a great body but not a pretty face.☺ But most children don't have the emotional capacity at a young age to reason why others would say mean things. As adults, we have to be mindful that the words we speak to children have great impact. We have the opportunity to inspire their natural gifts and potential, or crush their spirit.

We are each a unique individual with our own strengths, talents, and life path. Every human being in this world is worthy of fulfillment and happiness, despite their personal challenges. There are still times when I compare myself to others and feel like I am behind where I want to be. When I catch myself doing this, I mentally say, "Beware of Compare!" and then I reframe the experience. Witnessing someone else's success inspires me to continue to reach for my potential and go after what I want in life. Instead of focusing on what others are doing, I look inward to my own desires and what will personally fulfill me.

I'm often asked in my leadership programs how to increase confidence. I believe it starts with instilling practices to caretake your mindset. Every year that I invested in myself, in my mindset, and my skills, I elevated my confidence and success. Don't get me wrong, this wasn't a fast shift for me, rather, a gradual process of working on myself year after year until my mindset was more positive than negative. Listening to uplifting podcasts and videos, reading personal development books, learning more about your strengths and talents, and seeking out constant growth and development are practices that will create a foundation for a positive self-concept.

I truly believe that we never reach our full potential in life. As we build skills and competence, our dreams and goals get bigger and bigger. We are constantly evolving, and what we are capable of evolves and grows too.

Confidence comes from taking action. You can't just think about what you want in your life, you have to take action on your dreams and goals. It can be challenging to step outside your comfort zone and take chances, but that's how you improve your skills and boost your belief in yourself.

I love this quote from Marianne Williamson:

> *"Our deepest fear is not that we are inadequate. Our deepest fear is that we are powerful beyond measure. It is our light, not our darkness that most frightens us. We ask ourselves, 'Who am I to be brilliant, gorgeous, talented, fabulous?' Actually, who are you not to be? You are a child of God. Your playing small does not serve the world. There is nothing enlightened about shrinking so that other people won't feel insecure around you. We are all meant to shine, as children do. We were born to make manifest the glory of God that is within us. It's not just in some of us; it's in everyone. And as we let our own light shine, we unconsciously give other people permission to do the same. As we are liberated from our own fear, our presence automatically liberates others."*

We all have beauty and light inside us. Perhaps you have let other people dim your light or you've compared yourself to others and let that crush your spirit. No matter what you have experienced in life, you can still become your best. Your peak life is waiting for you. It's *never* too late to let your light shine in the world.

ABOUT LAURIE MADDALENA

Laurie Maddalena is CEO and chief leadership consultant at Envision Excellence. She is a professional speaker, success coach and a Certified Speaking Professional (CSP)—a designation earned by less than 15% of speakers worldwide.

Laurie teaches modern leadership skills and works with leaders to increase their confidence and influence through workshops, onsite leadership programs, and transformational keynote speeches. Her vision is to create a world of engaging cultures where people love to come to work.

Laurie also offers an online leadership experience where leaders all over the world can elevate their life and leadership. She is known for her engaging and inspiring programs and has hundreds of testimonials from clients who were personally and professionally transformed by her programs.

Laurie lives in Maryland with her husband, Rino, and her three children, Olivia, Luca, and Clara. She is an avid reader and enjoys playing tennis. She loves good food and wine, cappuccinos, and a nice glass of Cabernet Sauvignon.

To learn more about Laurie's programs, or to work with Laurie, visit her website at:

www.envisionexcellence.net

You can also follow Laurie on social media:

https://www.linkedin.com/in/lauriemaddalena/
https://www.facebook.com/laurie.hackettmaddalena
https://www.instagram.com/lauriemaddalena/

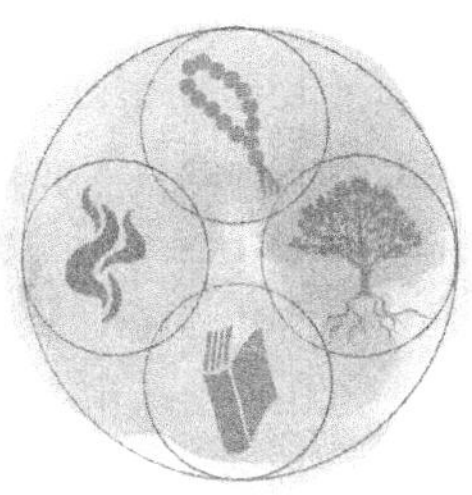

PLANTING SEEDS IN THE MIND TO SHINE

Denise McCormick

There is a defining moment in everyone's life when a traumatic event can either make you or break you. Here is my poem "for a time such as this" (Esther 4:14). These six simple words inspire us toward that one defining moment we all long for—our chance to make a difference. It also involves trusting God right where we are.

Gone Too Soon! Why Am I Left Behind?

A pristine summer's day golfing with friends.
Innocence intact, a life full of laughs.
Another friend appears; we all walk over to speak.
What takes place next shatters lives,
Our innocence no longer intact.
I race to the clubhouse, seek help for my friend.
Since Jeannie teed off, the ball hooking,
Then racing toward and hitting Kathy's head.
Confusion ensues, we all disembark.
An accident piercing a day now forever lost.

I leave for vacation, return the following week,
Not even aware of what havoc had ensued,
During that passing week.
I lie down in disbelief after calling a friend;
Kathy died the next morning from that blow to her head.
Too many questions, no one to talk to for answers.
God, why did you leave me and take her instead?
I was standing right beside her,
Why am I left behind?
Her family so loving,
Her goals indeed lofty.
What can I do now? Choices must be positive.

—*Denise McCormick*

The day that my family came home from vacation, I was questioning Kathy's death. Not a single person was to ask me how I felt about losing my good friend. There was no one to talk to for answers so I began a dialogue with God that day which has truly lasted a lifetime. The beauty of this sad event was that I learned to rely on God for help. My dysfunctional family life was to give me unbelievable strength for life's challenges ahead. That fateful day, I stayed alone all day up in my bedroom with a book of quotes and my prayer book. I was desperately trying to making sense and process all that had transpired that week, "for a time such as this" (Esther 4:14). I pleaded to God to understand what I was to do since I was left behind. I read page after page seeking solacc and a purpose for my life now. My angels were surrounding me that day for I felt from that moment on that I was never walking alone. From my hours of prayer and meditation came a dream to honor Kathy's life. One thought whispered to me from God's soothing voice, "Choices must be positive." God was planting a seed in my mind to shine.

As I reflect back on that day when I started embracing reading quotes and prayers daily, I realize my gift from God was a growth mindset. I began to make short and long-term goals, then visualized myself achieving them. I have done this every decade of my life for I have learned that what you say to your mind gives you the power to achieve anything. Years later, I am grateful that I had this difficult event and that I decided to react to it with love and a promise to be of service to others. The outcome was a definiteness of purpose for my life from that day forward.

Forty-five years later, there was to be another traumatic event that I called the dark night of my soul. With a broken heart and spirit, I traveled alone to a Breakthrough to Success training with Jack Canfield in Scottsdale, Arizona. It was August of 2014 following the sudden death of my mother on January 3rd and my nephew's suicide ten days later. It was the work I did with those 250 people from around the world with Jack's guidance that I realized that E+R=O (Event + Response = Outcome) had been my strategy of coping through all of life's challenges. With this new awareness, I pledged to commit to becoming a Certified Canfield Trainer so that I could be of service to others desiring a breakthrough to success in their lives.

At this training, I also realized that at thirteen, after the accident, I had discovered that taking 100% responsibility for my life was a way for me to honor the light of God inside of me. I wanted to continue to let it shine. And shine it did throughout my teenage years, for upon graduation from high school, I received the Danforth Outstanding Leadership Award. My journey of service was just beginning!

Planting Seeds in the Mind to Shine

Quotes plant a seed in the mind to shine.
When we're feeling down and don't know what to do,
Pick up a book of quotes and transport yourself to,
The land of strength, confidence, and courage,
Where all the seeds you plant in your mind,
Make dreams come true.

For what you say to your mind,
Your mind then says to you,
It all starts with your words
Which YOU have the power to choose.

—*Denise McCormick*

The journey through my 20s and 30s was a time of immense responsibility. I wrote my story of this time period in Kate Butler's book *Women Who Impact,* which became a #1 International Bestselling book in 2018. Our two wonderful daughters were born in my early 20s and John and I and Pat (John's brother and our business partner) worked for ten years to survive the 1980's Farm Crisis on our 4th generation farms. My chapter, From Surviving to Thriving, chronicles the goals we had to set and my quest to earn a teaching degree which were unarguably long-term goals. The song I wrote in 1983 for our family reunion, which we have every five years, praised the fortitude of my husband's great-great grandparents when they came over from Ireland seeking a better life. Michael and Margaret McCormick most certainly planted seeds in the mind to shine for subsequent generations by their example of hard work and perseverance. There stands in one field a sign that reads, Canaan Township. The Single Richest Township of Land in the World.

The Michael McCormick Song by Denise McCormick

Communion Song and Family Blessing

Michael sailed from Ireland
Across the deep blue sea;
Hoping for a better life,
More opportunity.
Michael married Margaret in 1864;
Rented sixty acres
Through hard work bought eighty more.

He built all of the fences and the buildings on the grounds;
Turned a tract of raw prairie
Into fertile farming ground.
In 1874 a privilege was bestowed on him,
Michael became a citizen of this
Great land he loved.
Four sons, four daughters were born to them,
Two boys they died so young,
Often epidemics took the children then so small.
And now on this day we pray for those who came before;
Since that time six generations
Now have been born.
We thank you Lord, for all our families
Gathered here,
To celebrate this heritage
That we all hold so dear;
We are all so grateful to those pioneers,
Who through their faith,
Began a new life here.

The seeds John and I and Pat planted in our minds to shine had finally taken root and produced much fruit. The farms were now very successful and we were enjoying the fruits of our labors. Our lives in our 40's were filled with many blessings and adventures.

But another traumatic event was again to happen to teach me more patience and life lessons. This story can be found in the book, *Ordinary Miracles -True Stories About Overcoming Obstacles & Surviving Catastrophes.* I wrote this story at the request of my occupational therapist, Joe Whalen. He knew that I was a writer and I submitted the story in gratitude to him for helping me to regain the use of my right hand after breaking my wrist from a fall in my classroom. I had been packing for a move to another school and a different grade level. I learned so much from the seven months it took me to regain the use of my hand with Joe's encouraging words and expertise. Again, I told my mind that I would have a complete recovery, did the agonizing work to make that happen, and planted seeds in my 3rd graders' minds as they watched me set goals to be able to make a fist and ultimately play the piano again. We said a poem every day in our classroom that helped to plant seeds in our minds to shine.

I AM Poem

I am who I am because of who I believe I am.
I am a winner if I start as a beginner because I think I am.
I can enter the Hall of Fame and win a gold medal in my name
because of who I think I am.
For it's not just my talents and it's not just my bank account,
That determines my destiny or how my life will turn out.
And it's not the school I go to or the color of my skin,
It's my attitude that determines who I am.
If I can dream it, I can achieve it,
And I won't be satisfied until that's who I am.
For it doesn't matter if I've lost before
or even made a very low score,
There's always a chance to try again,
Nothings over until it reaches the end.
What I believe I am, I am.
Yes, I know I can do it!

—*Denise McCormick*

Be prepared—For whenever you begin something new, you will begin to hear the subconscious monkey mind's negative chatter to you. Never mind the monkey mind. Just say delete!

—*Denise McCormick*

Learning to Read, Planting a Seed in the Mind to Shine and Other Miracles

Learning to read is like that. I taught children to read and university students to teach them to read for twenty-six years. I could teach children how to sound out words and to put the words together into sentences. But that isn't reading. Reading involves understanding the meaning behind the words and interacting with the reality of what those words mean.

I've never been able to explain how that miracle happens. One day a child is still struggling to sound out "ma-ma-ma-MONKEY!" and the next day, with a smile that lights up the room, the child is reading, really reading, and not just blurting out syllables.

Some children discover how to do this on their own, without anyone really teaching them. Others really struggle no matter how much instruction and extra help they receive. Some learn how to do it but never get the "why," the sheer joy reading can bring. For them it is work, a have-to and a never want to. I discovered an antidote for the children's limiting belief in themselves the year that Charles entered my 3rd grade room. He was a foster child who had been moved around from school to school and was unable to read when he walked into my classroom. During a one-on-one conference with him, I asked the question that was to forever change the trajectory for every student that I asked this question to from that day forward. I could scc his frustration during silent reading that first day. I quietly sauntered over to his table, bent down and with a smile coaxed him, "Charles, what would you love doing?" A smile came over his face as wide as the Grand Canyon. After a brief hesitation he quietly shared with me, "Mrs. McCormick, I would love to read a chapter book!" I returned his radiant smile with my own and with an immediate answer offered, "I'll have some chapter books here for you to read tomorrow." At recess time, I scoured the book shelves in my room finding all the *Frog and Toad* books I could find from my years of teaching 1st grade. I then headed for the school library where I checked out more *Adventures with Frog and Toad*. After school, I went to the Public Library and then called the AEA Library and his library of chapter books he could read on a 1st grade level were assembled. The next day, these books were sitting on his desk ready for silent reading time. During shared reading, I paired him with an amazing partner who I had worked with to have him assist Charles with a strategy to figure out new words. I always had individual conferences with students to set goals so that each was given the time to plant a seed in their minds to shine. One simple question had changed everything for Charles as his reading level skyrocketed that year.

Two years later at Open House, Charles now a 5th grader, proudly walked into my classroom carrying a very thick chapter book. With the same radiant smile, he rejoiced while declaring, "See what chapter books I am reading now! Mrs. McCormick, thank you! You were the first person to help me learn how to read!" With tears in my eyes, I thanked him and reminded him that all I did was ask him what he would love to do. He was the one who accomplished that extraordinary feat through his perseverance to accomplish the goal he set in his mind! As he proudly walked out the door that evening, I reflected that this is why I love what I do as an educator.

I can't tell you how Charles learned to read any more than I remember how I learned to read. All I know is that when you take the time to ask this life-changing question, "What would you love doing?", you empower children. You allow them to believe that what they would love doing is important and possible. With the seed planted, they then go to work to water, fertilize, and weed their own garden. They learn in that instance that they have the right to shine!

Teaching someone to read is nothing more than turning on the light switch of belief in the mind of a child. We as educators plant seeds in the mind to shine with our belief in the child's ability, which then illuminates that child's world for a lifetime! What an incredible miracle and responsibility we are entrusted with, shining the light of belief on the genius of a child.

—Denise McCormick

Planting seeds in the mind to shine takes deep fertile listening. Just ask the question, "What would you love doing?" Then just stay silent and listen. Notice that silent and listen are spelled with the same letters.

—Denise McCormick

My late 50s and early 60s have been a time of tremendous personal growth for me. I took the time to discover Denise. By working with coaches, reading hundreds of books, writing four published stories, taking trainings and receiving certifications from the world's best personal development educators, I have researched ways that I can coach and train others about the life transforming benefits of using a growth mindset in all aspects of a person's life. This has been the inspiration for writing the I Am Series of children's books. As a K-12 Reading Specialist, I have read thousands of books over the years with the dream of one day writing my own book with an original song to forever cement the lesson in the mind of a child. My first children's book, *Never Mind the Monkey Mind*, is indeed that dream and is autobiographical. Charles is the boy in the story and I am the mother he didn't have in his life at the time to answer his question. His journey is my journey through the years too. I shared with my illustrator, Chloe Helms, that I had recently accidentally bumped into Charles's class composite picture one day in a misplaced file. "Chloe, I exclaimed, the boy you drew looks just like Charles!" I put the pictures up side by side and we both smiled on our messenger call acknowledging that there are no accidents in the Universe.

Who I AM and Why It Matters

By Denise McCormick

- I AM a spiritual being having a human experience.
- There is only one like me.
- I was created in the image and likeness of God.
- I have a divine purpose in this world and the universe places people and knowledge into my life as I need them.
- All of my life experiences are a blessing because they have made me who I AM.
- I choose to look at traumatic events in my life as experiences to teach me the importance of forgiveness, not submitting to harsh judgment but compassion and a return to love.
- I AM a loving, compassionate, dependable, caring, and kind woman. I AM someone who values strength, confidence, and courage in facing my fears and talking down my ego. I do what I am afraid to do knowing that the wisdom of taking action will always dispel the darkness of disbelief.
- I AM an empathetic friend who realizes that when I judge other's faults, I am also judging my own.
- I AM someone who focuses on progress, not perfection. When I revert back to judging myself, I will laugh at the ego's mad ideas, forgive the thought, and choose one of the steps to return to love.

There exists inside each one of us the light of God just waiting for us to turn it on with our positive thoughts and words which in turn will dispel the darkness of disbelief with the shining light of love. It's our choice. We can all be Women Who Shine.

—*Denise McCormick*

ABOUT DENISE McCORMICK

Denise McCormick, M.A.E., is a State Awarded Educator, #1 International Bestselling Author, Inspirational Speaker, Certified Canfield Trainer and Success Mindset Coach. A former Elementary Educator, Education Lecturer and Reading Specialist at Iowa Wesleyan University and an Iowa Writing Project Instructor, Denise has over 26 years in education. She is a world traveler who believes that travel is fatal to prejudice, narrow-mindedness and bigotry. She became the Primary Delegation Leader for People to People Student Ambassadors for five summers taking SE Iowa middle school students to ten countries around the world. Denise believes that people don't care how much you know until they know how much you care.

Her expanded roles since 2014 have included working with coaches, becoming a Certified Canfield Trainer and Virtual Trainer in the Success Principles, Alum of the Brave Thinking Masters, Permission Granted and Momentum Masterminds, a graduate of Speak Your Way to Success and becoming a Licensed Worldwide WomanSpeak Circle Leader.

Denise's work as the Educator's Coach finds her coaching with both individuals and groups. Her programs are on her created Facebook groups, The Educator's Edge and her business page, Denise McCormick Success Mindset Mentorship LLC. She is passionate about supporting educators around their self-care and personal development, areas she felt were lacking in her 26 years of teaching elementary, university, and graduate school classrooms. Denise meets someone where they are by asking one question, which moves them beyond their fears into the loving strength and power of who they are. She is currently publishing her first children's book in the I AM Series, *Never Mind the Monkey Mind* and is a legacy author (Women Who Impact) and now a featured author in *Women Who Shine.*

Denise and her husband John have been married for forty-five years and reside in their restored farmhouse in Iowa with their collie Polly. Together they have 2 daughters and 5 grandchildren who live in Colorado and Australia.

You can connect with Denise at:
www.denisemccormick.com

Email: denise@denisemccormick.com
LinkedIn: www.linkedin.com/denisemccormick
Instagram: deniseamccormick

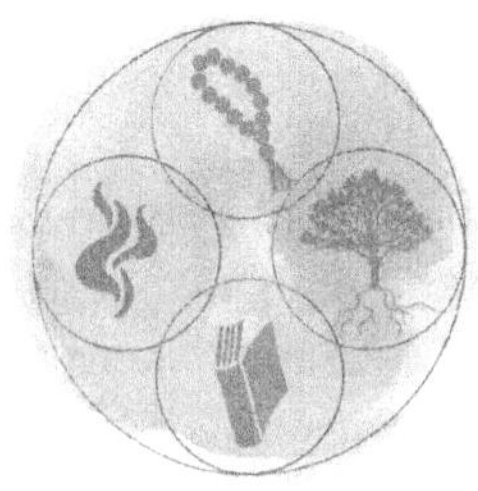

VIA COMBUSTA: A SACRED JOURNEY

Tatjana Obradovic

If you bring forth what is in you, what is in you will save you.

~Gospel of Thomas

I absolutely love to travel, that is how I recharge, grow, transform and heal. Secluded, little known places were always far more attractive destinations for me than very popular, crowded places. In my natal chart on seven degrees of Aries in the ninth house I have Mars, who rules Aries. The ninth house indicates higher education and far travels, both physical and metaphysical and placing Mars there is a strong indication that my soul and my body yearns to travel.

Some years ago my spouse had expressed a desire to travel from New York, where we live, to Belgrade, Serbia. He wanted to travel on his own to spend time with his friends and family. This was an unusual request because, until that point, we had always traveled together. No matter where we went, it was always our son, our daughter and the two of us. The Four Musketeers, always inseparable. This request came during a sensitive moment in our lives. It was the beginning of September and both children were in two different and new schools. I needed to drive them there every day, go to work, attend Open house nights and still maintain our typical daily flow, only this time it meant doing these tasks all by myself. I felt my husband really needed time on his own and I wanted to be supportive, so I agreed.

Somehow, I managed to achieve all my tasks successfully. My spouse had a beautiful time away and when he returned from his trip he was rested and in a good mood. He was so grateful to me that he suggested that I go by myself on a trip of my choice. This way I could experience how wonderful an individual voyage could be. At that moment, my teachers were traveling to Bhutan and my friends were about to embark on a journey to Egypt. Both journeys were to start within two weeks and I didn't have much time to process, analyze and prepare. Although I truly wanted to spend more time with my mentors and teachers, I would get a throbbing sensation every time I thought of Egypt, which proved to be a deep longing of my heart. Cognitively, a trip to Jerusalem, which was included in the voyage to Egypt, was an incentive that couldn't be overlooked. I was born and raised in a Christian orthodox atmosphere and I've spent countless days in churches and monasteries. My closest friends, godfather and spiritual mentors were from the highest realms of priesthood and monasticism in Serbia. Visiting Jerusalem and all the holy, Christian places, walking in Jesus's steps and receiving a prefix 'Hadzi' is a prestigious and highly sought after title. As a true Christian lady, I thought I would tolerate Egypt and truly enjoy my journey once we reached Jerusalem. As a result of that mindset, I was very relaxed, open, off guard and not expecting much of Egypt. I was just there for the ride.

Upon arriving in Egypt, our group checked into Mena House in Giza, which was originally a royal palace and to this day, my favorite place to stay while in Egypt. That first night our group had a private visit to the Great pyramid, the most mysterious structure and last standing Wonder of the ancient world. Our tour began at 3am. I was suffering from physical exhaustion, jet leg, sleeplessness, claustrophobia, an influx of new energies, and I missed my family. All these feelings were competing against each other and taking precedence within me during the long two hours in the Great pyramid. I had promised myself that I would not let my fears stop me from fully experiencing every aspect of this journey. I stoically followed the group step by step. I climbed a long corridor to meditate in the King's chamber, descended on my knees 150 ft in a long, narrow, dusty passage to what seemed like the center of the Earth into the so called Queen's chamber, and reemerged back into the light as the first rays of sun appeared on that warm October morning. I conquered my fear of small, closed spaces simply by taking one step at a time, trusting that eventually I would, like to rest of my group, emerge victorious from the heart of the pyramid.

As our journey progressed, I frequently felt deep sadness and I cried silently, shedding tears that were not always mine. I felt a deep compassion for everyone in our group, most likely identifying with the Egregor of Mother Mary. I was processing everyone's emotions around me and releasing their collective tears. This feeling was especially strong in Hathor's Temple in Dendera, where Goddess Isis hid her son Horus from his uncle Set who was trying to murder him. I felt Isis's agony when she needed to give up her beloved son in order to preserve his life. I felt a connection with my own children, released my own feelings of guilt for leaving them for two weeks for the first time in their lives. Although my children were 11 and 14 at the time, I felt that I broke our tradition by separating from them. All these great mother figures were bubbling up in me. Isis toughened up and gathered her courage to give up Horus in order to protect him. Mother Mary observed her son sacrificing himself for the benefit of humanity. I left my children for the first time ever to allow myself to embark on a spiritual journey of awakening, which was intended to make me a better person and ultimately a better mother. To this day, I remember the intensity of those tears and the great sense of release and acceptance that followed later that day. I understood why, the cure for the pain is in the pain, in facing it, seeing it, feeling it and still staying, not in running away from it, not masking it.

Several days into the journey we visited the Sobek Temple, dedicated to the Crocodile God. In ancient Egypt, crocodiles symbolized fertility, provided protection from evil spirits and assisted in conquering fears. Even today in some Nubian villages near Aswan on the banks of the Nile, some families have backyard pools where they raise crocodiles until they reach maturity. This is when it is safe to release them into a nearby lake. On this journey we had a fear releasing ceremony where we held a crocodile and quieted our emotions so that we could peacefully connect to our fear and let it go.

When we walked through the seven gates of the Sobek Temple we entered a sacred place where only high priests and pharaohs could stand. The group spent some time in silence as we sought connection and release of all the fears that we were aware off. While I was standing in that holy place I began releasing the fears I had at that time. Fears of closed spaces, loneliness, heights, scarcity, lovelessness, and for the first time in my life I heard a voice. That voice agreed to take away all listed fears if I was ready to release my biggest fear! Now, I am not a clairaudient person, I am clairvoyant. I see visions when I meditate. I never hear voices. But this time, there was a voice within me, vibrating and asking if I was ready to release my biggest fear, FEAR OF CHANGE! I literarily felt the ground beneath me shake, tectonic plates moved and it felt like my ground, my core was being changed, restructured. That was my breaking point, my cracking, my opening to the light, my awakening. It was my acceptance of the path and the changes that I was about to embark on during that journey. It was the end of an era as I knew it. For the third time!

In an earlier book from the Inspired Impact series, *Women*

Who Rise, I had shared a story that signified the first part of my life back home in Belgrade, Serbia. That story resembled the tale of Cinderella and Oliver Twist to a certain extent. The second part of my life, after I moved to New York, mainly portrayed the life of a responsible adult who tried to make it in a new country, on a new continent. It revolved around the struggles of finishing school, raising children, having a successful career, making sure the children have a good education and a loving home, bringing them up in a Christian atmosphere, and finally reaching a point of comfort. Reaching a comfort zone. That moment when you achieve everything a mother could strive for and dream off. It's the moment when I could finally relax. Many of us, once we reach this point, don't strive for more. I didn't strive for more, at least not consciously. This trip to Egypt was supposed to be a nice journey with my group of friends that completely catered to our wishes and needs. I thought I was happy and fully satisfied. I thought I finally had a perfect life and there was nothing missing.

Then the Sobek Temple event occurred. Suddenly, I saw my life in a very different light. I realized that cognitive-behavioral therapy was not giving me the answers nor the healing I needed. I admitted to myself that my soul had complex needs and that I would need to search for modalities that would take into consideration not only my mind, but also my emotions, my soul and my body. I acknowledged many subconscious processes still brewing within me, even after years of therapy. Mechanisms were at work within me whose roots were much deeper than I dared to look until that day at the temple. I knew that I would be working with these crocodiles for months to come, facing them with grace and the gratitude that I get to release the fears and trauma that was, until then, unknown to me.

As our journey was nearing the end, we have arrived to Aswan. One early, sunny morning we found ourselves on a motor boat headed to a small island nearby. The moment I stepped onto the grounds of the Isis Temple in Philae, Egypt, I felt a resurgence of a deep longing, one that I've had in my heart for years. A Welsh word, Hiraeth, best describes this phenomenon. It is the longing for a place you've never been to or a life that you've never lived. It's a home that you miss, but have never had. A person you've never met, but you yearn for. Tears of joy, recognition and satisfaction fluctuated within me. I found something I never knew I've missed. My reaction was a mix of happiness, laughter and childlike bliss. From that moment on, Isis, Auset, Goddess of Love, Beauty and Healing, the ultimate Mother of Egypt, became my source of inspiration, devotion and motivation to persist on this inspired journey of a healer.

One of the final destinations in Egypt was Mt. Sinai, where we hiked throughout the starry night to reach the summit by morning and watch the longest sunrise in the world. For 45 minutes we witnessed an enormous rose-colored sea of granite mountains basking in a glorious golden, liquid sunlight. This was the place where Moses had received the Ten commandments and where my spirit flew high every time we reached the top. In the beginning of my spiritual journey I was afraid that if I meditated or worked with energy to cleanse my chakras I would be breaking one of those very commandments. Then I realized that my God is not one that operates from fear, he is the God of Love, the strongest force in the Universe. Despite what I believed all my life, I learned that there are no written human rules which will mandate me to pray, meditate or connect to God in any specific or prescribed way. It doesn't make me a non-believer if I break the rules because I feel a pull and or a calling to communicate with the higher power in an unconventional way. My free will allows me to choose the approach I take when embarking on any type of spiritual work. I realized that an awakened person carries on in her life feeling that everything she does is a conscious ritual.

When we finally made it to Jerusalem, I wanted to literarily walk in the footsteps of Christ. I wanted to walk to Golgotha, to all the churches, to the river Jordan, to the Olive garden where

Jesus was betrayed. I wanted to feel and connect with the energies in each of these historic places. Stepping on the polished stones that make the foundation of our modern world history didn't have the impact on me that I had expected. I was torn apart in four different directions. I experienced a confusing, mixed feelings and I couldn't find my peace. The pull was baffling and intense, until I came to the realization that all three main religions were from this area. All three nations of "the people of the book" are rooted in ancient Egyptian spiritualty. From there, each group embellished their beliefs and made them different. However, the intention of the ancient Egyptian pantheon was to keep us all connected by our similarities. This revelation was very important to me. I was able to rely one of the main teachings of Christianity, love and acceptance for all, and build upon that to expand my horizon. I released the dogma that kept me captive and limited for decades. Jesus, God, Universe, higher self, however we intend to call the force that holds our realities together, found a place in my heart and gave me peace.

From that moment on I stepped on an accelerated spiritual growth path. I started to transmute energy, identities and former versions of myself very quickly. Some moments were heavy, deep, excavating, followed by the moments when I was transmuting my shadows I've excavated into transformation. As I continued to release limiting beliefs, obstacles or old ways of thinking, I've made space for more conscious joy, gratitude, peace, play and bliss in my life.

Goddess Isis, Aset, was with me every step of the way to remind me to trust that we have the power to heal the world with our intuition and divine feminine wisdom. She was there to remind me that now is time we reclaim that power, connect to our truths and expand our creative healing out into the world through reviving sacred sisterhoods. When women get together –magic happens.

When I returned to New York City, I felt that working as

a behavioral psychologist was not fulfilling anymore. I left a company where I was working for fourteen years and did some soul searching for a while. I looked for ways to align my work with my soul's purpose. With each day I became more empowered. I purchased a shiny red car and drove it to places I never dared to go before. I overcame my phobia of dentists and had my teeth repaired. I purified my eating habits, stepped into the light and demonstrated some of my latent skills. I shared my talents with the world, showering my clients with gentleness and love. I concurred my fear of heights while skydiving on my birthday during an eclipse. It's not that I wasn't scared anymore, I still was, but I had a new found courage and motivation to do things, despite my fears. I was able to find stillness and carefully depict every obstacle life presented to me with an understanding that it's a source of great power when we're brave enough to be vulnerable. The cure for the fear is in the fear itself. That initial journey to Egypt had a profound and lasting effect on my life. The changes were coming in waves and many of the things that I postponed, waiting to do one day when I gather some courage, became things that I was able to do within a month or two after returning from Egypt. The energies of Egypt ignited the light within me. The acceptance, love and support I felt there motivated me to dare and finally complete many of my "someday when I am brave enough" things. Most importantly, I was able to find peace with the life I dreamed of and strove to create, but could never have. I accepted the direction life was guiding me to go. A part of my heart was healed in Egypt, that part which I had already given up on, the part I thought had atrophied. That part of my heart resurrected like Osiris from the underworld, under the tender, loving care of his bellowed Isis.

I created the company called The Key of Love, which resembles an Ankh, the ancient Egyptian Key of Life. This is where I lead my clients who are in transition on inner and outer journeys of self-discovery, awakening and healing. I do this through individual consultations, virtual group workshops, online programs and luxury spiritual retreats to the place that inspired me to, despite my fear of change, align my life with my soul's mission. Since that first journey, I returned to Egypt every six months to refresh and recharge my connection with that powerful energy. My mentor, Dr. Nicky Scully, was the first who created spiritual journeys to the ancient Egyptian realm in 1970. After studding with her, reading about the energies of each temple and experiencing it on my own, I finally understood what the energy in these places really does to us, how each temple is connected to one of the energy centers and endocrine glands in our body and how, when we offer those centers to be harmonized, we experience pure bliss.

Every place in the world is governed by a planet from our Solar system. New York is governed by Mercury, Serbia by Saturn and Egypt happens to be on a very specific degree of the Zodiac, from 15' of Libra to 15' of Scorpio, so called Via Combusta, Fiery Road or Combust Way. According to an ancient aphorism, Libra and Scorpio are not congenial to the Sun and the Moon on the account of the obscurity and ill-luck connected with them and because each of them is the fall of one of the luminaries. Via Combusta, the dark night of the soul, that Burning Pathway Isis embarked on while collecting pieces of her husband, her Twin Flame, Osiris, while at the same time collecting fragments of her own heart and soul, making Osiris's body whole again and making her own heart (w)holy. All the deepest wounds and trauma are exposed to the light during this voyage. Pain that created blocks that were left unattended for a very long time created suffering and locks. The enormous amount of energy that was locked within those wounds is released as we lovingly accept those unwanted parts of ourselves. That trauma, that pain, becomes our remedy when we see it, understand it, and accept it as it is. Our potential for self-healing gets unlocked and the key that opens that lock is Love.

ABOUT TATJANA OBRADOVIC

Tatjana Obradovic is a holistic psychologist and creativity coach who helps people who go through major life transitions find clarity, direction and purpose in their lives again. She does this using synergy of techniques from traditional psychology, homeopathy, energy psychology and astrology during individual consultations, group therapy and especially during spiritual retreats in Egypt which she leads semi-annually.

Tatjana Obradovic is the founder of The Key of Love, LLC. Tatjana is a mom of two wonderful teenage children, and she has over 15 years of experience supporting people with autism while working as a Behavioral Psychologist.

Besides Cognitive Behavioral Therapy, Tatjana is versed in and has a passion for energy psychology, karmic astrology and integration through shadow/inner child journey, healing with doTerra essential oils, Astro-healing with planetary, gem and flower vibrational essences, which she absolutely loves to create and personalize for her clients, Astro-meridians therapy, Twin Flames journey programs to remove all obstacles which prevent one from attracting their soul mate, meditation, signature program Via Combusta which takes women who are in transition on a Journey to discover how to truly Awaken and Heal their Divine Feminine energy, Timeline Healing, Deep PEAT and Usui Reiki.

In her integrative psychology approach, Tatjana utilizes over 50 techniques and healing modalities including Ancient Egyptian Shamanic Journeys along with the most advanced healing devices, such as LuchaT8, an impulse for life, which combines Schumann resonances and an infrared light to maximize one's natural ability to achieve equilibrium.

Tatjana is a certified Intuitive and Success Coach who trained under Dr. Lea Imsiragic, Jack Canfield, and Kate Butler. She believes that healing is a natural gift of all people. Tatjana is a therapist, healer and a coach who lovingly guides her clients to remember that gift. Tatjana enjoys awakening unconditional love in her clients. She strongly believes that LOVE is the most powerful force in the Universe. She absolutely loves to ignite a light and passion for life, love and healing in her clients, not by making them realize that she is an excellent therapist, but rather, empowering her clients to recognize they are beautiful and skilled self-healers. She does this through one-on-one counseling, group workshops, live events, luxury retreats on main energy centers of the world, especially Egypt, and online programs.

Tatjana is able to integrate multiple facets of healing work in a very personalized manner. She is highly knowledgeable in psychology, astrology, vibrational and herbal medicine, and doTerra essential oils, therefore sessions are informative and provide clients with a plethora of useful and applicable knowledge. Aside from creating Personalized Flower and Vibrational Essences, she sends clients home with helpful tips and practical plans, which should be utilized until the next session. Tatjana is fully dedicated to her clients and their emotional, spiritual, mental, and physical advancement.

Tatjana is an avid world-traveler, a leader of Spiritual Journeys to Magical and Sacred Egypt where Isis, Goddess of Love and Magic became her source of inspiration, devotion and motivation to persist on this transformational path of a healer. Tatjana is a graduate of the University of Belgrade and Marymount Manhattan College, where she majored in psychology. She received her master's from the School of Professional Studies in New York City. To learn more about how you can connect and work with Tatjana, please visit her website at www.TheKeyofLove.org, where you can find complimentary resources, including a complimentary Chakra test and information about her programs.

W: www.thekeyoflove.org

FB: Tatjana Obradovic& The Key of love

IG: thekeyoflove_

E: Tatjana@thekeyoflove.org

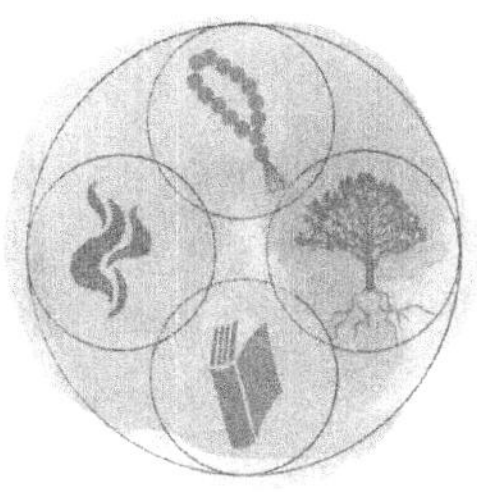

YOU LIGHT UP MY LIFE

Kristi Ann Pawlowski

From the time I was born, my mom referred to me as her "sunshine child." I could never really understand why, but as time passed, I began to. She said I was always happy, singing, dancing. People would stop her in awe of my external and internal beauty, bright smile, bright eyes, and joy in my heart. Certain people are born with a unique light that attracts others. I was fortunate to be one of those people. However, one must be cautious when having this gift. Aside from everyone telling you their life stories, personal information, and hardships, I also had to be cautious because I tended to see others as good people when they were not. I am a good person and expect that most others have a pure heart with good intentions as well. However, the truth is, there are people out there that emit false light or as I like to refer to it, luciferian light. With age and each passing hardship that I had been faced with, I got better at identifying which individuals' lights were false and which ones were pure.

The word "photon" is derived from the Greek word for light. There are many different types of light in this world. There are radio waves, gamma rays, radiation, visible light, x-rays, etc. However, the brightest form of light is a laser beam, which was created in a lab and is one billion times brighter than the sun. Prior to 2020, I felt like this was the light I was exuding onto others.

Shortly after my dad's passing on January 2, 2020, I had noticed God sent me gifts or God winks as my friend and I like to refer to them. I didn't even know these gifts were present until later. One morning in late January 2020, while serving at church, a gentleman came in and he passed me. I greeted him with a smile and said, "Hi Good Morning." A good 5 to 10 minutes had passed and he came back to me. I was at the front door of the church, and he passed at least 25 other volunteers at that time, but the person that he stopped to talk to was me. The only reason I can think of is that he saw my light and he said, "I need your help." I responded back saying, "OK, what can I assist you with." I thought he was going to ask me where the bathroom was or the complimentary coffee. However, I did not expect what was coming next. He began to explain that he needed my help because he was suffering from depression and anxiety. He said his wife was suffering from anxiety too, so much so that she could not get out of the car. Without any hesitation, I said, "ok let me help you," but in my mind, I was thinking, "me help you with this? This is out of my wheelhouse." I calmly and immediately took charge and looked at him and said, "I am going to get you the support that you need." I went searching like a wild woman and found one of the pastors who immediately went out to the car and tried to talk to the wife and prayed with her. The gentleman decided to come in and attend the service alone. During that time, I felt something in my heart nagging me to ask the gentleman if I could give him a hug. He said, "sure that would be great." I hugged him and he walked away. I felt the nagging feeling inside of me again and I heard a voice in my head saying, "you're not done with him yet. Don't leave him, he needs you."

I went to find my seat in church, sat my bottom in the chair, and then stood right back up again. It was as if I sat on a spring, that's how quickly I got up. I was on a mission now. I searched in the dark church for this gentleman, and I couldn't find him, so I went to the pastor and said, "Do you know where that man sat? I'm trying to find him." He looked and looked with me and then suddenly said, "there. There he is." I sat in between the husband and another young guy. Keep in mind that when I go to church I sit on the end because I'm a little claustrophobic and I need my space to praise during worship. However, I was determined to sit next to this gentleman no matter what. I wiggled my way through the people and into the middle of the row of chairs and sat with him. The husband was inches to the right of me and the young, buff guy inches to the left. Even though I was squished like a sardine and completely uncomfortable I sat with him the whole time. When the service ended, I had to leave him because I had to say goodbye to everyone exiting the church. On his way out the door, he found me and said, "thank you, you don't know how much you sitting next to me meant to me. I appreciate you." I saw him by himself the following week and I was so joyful that he had returned! A few months passed and I was volunteering on opening day, which was the very first service in our new building. I saw a lot of familiar faces. Then, I saw him too. The amazing thing was that he wasn't there alone. His wife was with him this time. I felt such joy in my heart. I felt like it was such a gift from God. When I was driving home, I reflected back to this man's name. Tears started streaming down my face as I realized the man's name was my dad's initials. Since I gave my gift of time, love, and compassion to this man God gave me a gift in return. Had this gentleman not seen my light I would have never been granted that experience.

I would love to say that this light remained with me for the rest of the year. However, shortly after I received the opportunity to help this gentleman the Covid-19 Pandemic hit. Who knew my life and the lives of other therapists/educators worldwide would be flipped upside down and inside out in a matter of months? It was a real battle trying to stay afloat during these trying times.

Within a matter of a few days into 2020, my dad passed away, 2 months later my sister was diagnosed with breast cancer, and 3 months later I was faced with juggling my responsibilities as a Speech/Language Pathologist, while at the same time struggling to care for and educate my own two children while being on lockdown. My heavy workload made me feel extremely guilty because I felt I was abandoning my own kids' academic, physical, and emotional needs. I also missed hugging my kids at school, lifting them up when they were down, and interacting with them in person. The struggle was REAL, and things became very dark for me during this season. It was extremely challenging and stressful managing a higher caseload during this time, trying to figure out a new way to provide services to my students, finding the time and/or a solution to provide my own children with the best education they deserved, and still take care of my household responsibilities. My work schedule was no longer Monday through Friday 8:00 AM-3:15 PM. It was now 7:30 AM to 8:00 PM and included late nights and weekends.

Just when I thought things could not get worse, they in fact did. I was experiencing a situation that was sucking the life and the light out of me during my darkest of times. Remember that luciferian light I was referring to? Someone who I had trusted and considered a friend was trying to destroy my happiness, my reputation, and my positivity. The truth is, I always knew that bad light was present within this individual, but I chose to ignore the warnings and gave them the benefit of the doubt. My friend was being nice to my face, but behind the scenes was being very vindictive and sneaky. We need to be careful because sometimes "the brightest flame casts the darkest shadows" (George R.R Martin). I think jealousy played a huge part. I had just co-authored an amazing book, which was very successful. My true friends supported me, bought my book, commented on my posts, and praised me for my efforts. However, not this individual. They never congratulated me, purchased my book, nor were they anywhere within sight of my cheering section. This experience made me realize who was in my corner and who was not. It made me realize that jealousy is an ugly demon. Most of all it made me recognize who was in my life to build me up and who was in my life to tear me down. The way this person treated me and plotted against me left me feeling depressed and anxious for months. I truly felt my light diminishing more and more with each passing day.

I had been working remotely for most of the school year and had not gone anywhere but church really. I went to church and sat in my usual spot at the very top of the auditorium. There were hundreds of people spread throughout the church. While worshiping, I had a young boy who I had never seen before approach me, gaze into my eyes, and asked me if I could help him because he was lost. At that moment I felt the little ember of light remaining inside of me transform to LASER BEAM LIGHT pouring out of me. I directed him to where he needed to go. At that moment tears streamed down my face. As I was wiping them away, I realized that was my God wink, my reminder that my light was not gone. Out of the hundreds of people, this boy could have asked, he chose me. I was his light in the darkness and at this point, I realized that no person or situation could take my light away. Although it may have been dimmed by bad circumstances and cruel intentions, it was there all along. The problem was that I was allowing others the right to take that from me, to steal my joy, but God was so good. He took that luciferian light that was blinding me and replaced it with my own pure light that attracted that child to me.

I finally returned to in-person instruction in April 2021. At this time, my kids at the school were so welcoming and loving. One child said, "It is good to see your smiling, sparkly, rainbow face in person." Another student said, "I missed you so much. I just want to hug you right now." A third student said, "You are the best speech teacher ever." The positive responses I got from my students were validation again that my light was still shining bright.

Storms are going to happen, but the rainbow in this situation was realizing my authentic self was still there. When pure light and love are present, they cannot be destroyed by anyone or anything. Instead, the stronger the storm the brighter the rainbow becomes.

I have learned that it is ok not to feel joy all the time. If your light flickers it is alright as long as you don't let negative situations or people extinguish it for too long. The real tragedy occurs when we let one or two peoples' negative actions or beliefs become our beliefs. The enemy starts to make us think that all people see us the way the enemy does because that is what they want us to believe. If I continued to allow this person to win, to make me feel lesser of a person, and to not exude my gift of joy onto the world, then the rest of the world would suffer the consequences as well. I needed to continue to be the rainbow in the storm for my family, my students, and my friends. I wanted and needed to continue spreading my love, joy, and light to those around me because it fulfills my soul and is truly my God-given gift. The joy and positivity I was giving to others helped to restore my own light and in turn, was helping me get back to my normal self. I also needed to remind myself that as a child of God I am protected from evil. As usual, God took what the enemy meant for evil and turned it for good. I can confidently stand in my own light and know it is coming from a good place with only good intentions. I have been given a light to share with the world and I will not let anyone or anything destroy it ever again. My light will continue to shine bright not just today, tomorrow, next week, next month, or next year, but for eternity.

"You are the light of the world. A town built on a hill cannot be hidden. Neither do people light a lamp and put it under a bowl. Instead, they put it on its stand, and it gives light to everyone in the house. In the same way, let your light shine before others, that they may see your good deeds and glorify your father in heaven."
—Matthew 5:14-16 NI

ABOUT KRISTI ANN PAWLOWSKI

Kristi Ann Pawlowski has worked in the field of education for 22 years as a speech/language pathologist, kindergarten, and first grade teacher. She has also taught classes at local colleges and universities, was an Early Intervention Provider, and worked in the hospital setting. Kristi has an extensive background in performing arts and encourages others to find their true passion and purpose in life. Kristi's passion is helping people discover that negative things or difficult seasons that are occurring/occurred in their lives aren't really negative, but possibly gifts from God, that have not been discovered yet. Kristi helps people see the rainbow in their past and present storms through her workshops, Facebook page, and personal coaching. Kristi writes books that encourage kindness, promote empathy, embrace diversity, and motivate others. Kristi is a #1 International best-selling author of the Inspired Impact Series *Women Who Empower*. She has a true desire to make a positive difference in the lives of adults and children. Kristi resides in New Jersey with her two beautiful children and her husband, Jason. They say good things happen to good people. However, Kristi believes that unfortunate things happen to good people to make them better human beings.

To connect with Kristi, visit her Facebook page "Find Your Rainbow in the Storm" or connect with her via email at speechkp@yahoo.com

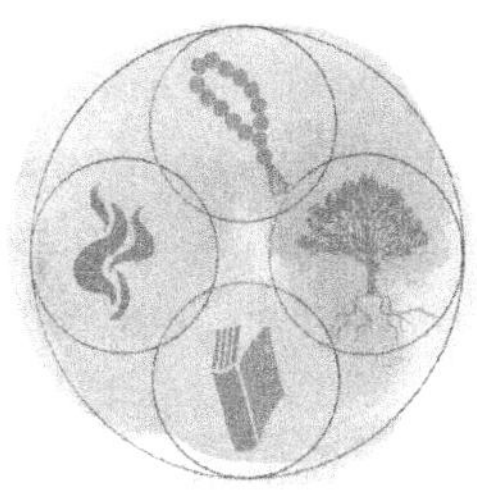

ASCEND WITH ME

Candice Shepard

Some stories are hard to tell. My story is hard to tell. It's not better or worse than anyone else's, but it's mine. I own it; the good, the bad, and the ugly. I've allowed God to work with it all and arrived at a beautiful ending that I never saw coming. My sincere hope, in sharing all of this with you, is that you'll feel the love of the Father and realize that you can have everything you want as well. The way you approach the awful things in your life will determine if you live in the valley or ascend to the top of the mountain.

I grew up in a very small town in the Midwest with a population of 1,200 people and graduated with mostly the same 28 kids I went to kindergarten with. I went to high school in the same building as my dad and grandparents, played basketball in the same gym, and was taught by some of their classmates. By most accounts it was an idyllic upbringing. Playing outside with friends until dark, chasing fireflies, night swimming, and riding bikes to the park, not a care in the world.

I was always a super high achiever, naturally, without being pushed. I learned to read at a very young age and soared past my peers in the academic realm without trying. As a result, I learned very early on that things would come easy to me. I needed to downplay that easiness so as not to offend and I needed to seek out other ways to experience challenges. I played every sport offered, learned every instrument I could, and pushed myself out of my comfort zone every chance I could get. Education, athletics, and cultural opportunities were difficult to come by in such a small town, but I looked for them.

I remember auditioning for a play when I was about 7 or 8 and getting the part because I looked the most, out of all the cast members, like a little Swedish girl. I was terrified at every play practice and when the time came to perform for an audience, I thought I was going to pass out. I made it through, somehow, and don't remember anything about the experience except the fear.

The first time I realized that the world viewed girls and boys differently was when I was in third grade. Our town, and several neighboring communities, put together a softball/baseball league. My dad sat me down to talk about it and asked if I wanted to play. Of course I did! Another challenge and something fun and new. I was quite excited. Girls in my age bracket were to play T-ball. I didn't know what that meant and when my dad explained that it was batting from a tee, instead of with a pitcher, I didn't want to do that. My friends and I had been playing baseball for years, Sandlot style, and I already knew how to hit a ball. I explained this to my dad, who agreed with me, and he said he'd sign me up for baseball instead. We went down to the hall for signups and got in line, ready to sign up. We got to the front of the line and my dad turned in my brother's and my forms to play baseball and the lady doing the signups told him no. "Sorry," she said, "she can't play baseball, she's a girl." My dad said, "no, she will be playing baseball because she's too advanced to play t-ball and will be bored." After a bit of back and forth, they signed me up for baseball and away we went. I asked my dad why there had been so much irritation by the lady. He told me that sometimes people don't think girls can do things that boys can do, but it's not true.

I ended up playing first base because, as my coach said, "I was the only one who could catch the ball." Honestly, I didn't even care. It was just fun. And I learned that someone having faith in you and supporting you can help you develop some of that same faith and confidence in yourself.

Childhood continued, fun and exciting and TV worthy, until middle school. My mom came to work at the school I attended and I couldn't get away with anything. She frequently knew I was in trouble before I did. Then everything changed. The rug was pulled out from under my entire family based on an untrue accusation, that led to criminal charges, court battles, fighting for justice and years of pain and shame and heartache. Have you ever experienced a pain so tremendous, a time where you hurt so bad, that your soul cried out to God, "WHY ME?" I think it's safe to say that we've all had that one experience. I don't know what yours is, but I see you and I feel your pain with you.

During that tumultuous time I was navigating the teenage years, which are so much fun without trauma. I was also being horrifically bullied in a way that defies what current culture defines as bullying. I was called all kinds of horrible names and people would shout profanities at me or behind my back, but always loud enough for me to hear and sometimes directly to my face. I was beat up and pushed down the stairs. I was sexually assaulted and then stalked by my rapist. Someone once spit in my face. My family was threatened. I was shunned and shamed and ridiculed. One of my classmates called a news crew to come to the school to attempt to put my shame on the news. I was blamed for all of the horrible things that other people were doing and blamed for some things that never happened. This went on for nearly five years. That's a lot of years to live in that. People can be very vicious. This was in the time when people couldn't hide behind a computer or phone screen, so I cannot even imagine what it's like for folks to experience something so traumatic in the public arena of Instagram and the like.

I should pause here and recognize that it wasn't awful all the time. I had amazing parents and a handful of really good friends. I had a brother who supported me unconditionally and fought my battles alongside me. I had coaches and teachers and mentors who regularly poured into me and propped me up when I felt like giving up. If you're right in the middle of your mess, and you have those people in your life, let them know how hard it is for you RIGHT NOW. And let them help. If you don't have those people, find them. They're out there and they will be more than willing to provide that for you. If you get a no, keep looking, because they are everywhere, your angels on earth who will help pull you through when you feel like giving up. Don't give up. Find your people. Find your tribe. Find your mentors and your helpers and let them help.

So, back to my story. In one of those soul crying "why me" moments, I had no more tears to shed, I was tired of fighting back, and I was exhausted from carrying around the pain. I lay on my bed just fighting to breathe. That's when something miraculous happened. I felt the pull of God telling me to hang on. That it would be ok. That he would take my pain and shame and trauma and something beautiful would come out of it.

As I shared earlier, I've always been a pretty high achiever. However, I also believe fully and sincerely, that God will give you the gifts, but you must be obedient to the call, and contribute the hustle and the grind. One of the things that he was impressing upon me in those moments was that I had to figure out how to get over the shyness and I had to get out of that environment. He had some work for me to do and he was going to use every tear, but I had to prepare for the work ahead of me. Not knowing any way to accomplish what He set out before me, I simply gave in. I said "Ok God, what do ya got? I'm all in. Just lead the way." Here's the spoiler. That was the moment that I recognized that my wisdom is irrelevant. It is HIS wisdom that needs to lead the way.

All of this led me to an "enough is enough" moment. I gave in to God and started seeking out ways to push past the situation I was in, in order to create the life I wanted. Even though education was always a priority in my house, a family value that was important, I wasn't certain there was any money for college after everything that had happened and I was really concerned that I wouldn't have the financial resources to continue my education. However, I knew being well educated would prove to be infinitely important to creating the life I wanted. I knew that was my best way out of the situation I was in and my best avenue for something different and better.

An Army recruiter came to my high school and a friend asked me to go with her. It was a way to skip third period so I said, "yeah, ok. I'll talk to them with you." One thing led to another. They said they'd pay for school and all the other things, and so I made the leap. I had never really been out of that small town and all of a sudden I found myself in basic training in New Jersey with a giant drill sergeant screaming in my face. I almost immediately regretted my decision to enlist, but it was too late. Since I had already sealed my commitment by signing a contract, there was no backing out. The drill sergeant confirmed that by yelling in my ear, "Private, we are the United States government, we own you for 6 years so you're going to do it whether you want to or not." Talk about "feel the fear and do it anyway!"

I got really good through all of the yuck in middle and high school at stuffing everything deep down, put your head down and plow through. It doesn't matter what you're going through, you get through the tough stuff. That's not an entirely healthy way to handle pain and shame, but it worked for me. Still, I was terribly shy and also very guarded after everything that happened. I kept praying about what I was going to do and God kept pushing me to get out of my own head. I was going to need to use my story someday and couldn't in my current condition. The Army helped, certainly. I became a communications major in college to try to get over my shyness. I became a litigator after law school. I found or created or faked internal grit and toughness. All things that prepared me for where I am right now.

The grit and the drive and the pull helped me get where I am now. The trauma could very well have broken me, but it didn't. I don't claim to take total ownership for that, but it started with the decision that "this will not break me." I now own a very successful business with many different facets. I have amazing children that I'm so grateful to get to parent. I've done a ton of cool things in my personal and professional life. You need to make that decision too and push through. Find help and keep hoping.

There came a point in time, just a few years ago, where I felt the culmination of all my preparations coming together. Now is the time to use this story, share my pain, put it out in the world (as scary as that is) and help others. First, though, I had to heal. The grit, the pushing the pain down and the pushing through, were making me less effective. And still causing wounds to reveal themselves.

Over the years I've spoken to many therapists and many people who were absolutely unhelpful and even sometimes harmful, in my healing journey. But I always had that baseline of God and family, people who loved and supported me. And now, almost 35 years past the starting point, I finally aggressively pursued healing, recognizing that it is time to lay down the burden of pain and shame and pick up the victorious ending that God had in store for me all along. Please, sister, lay your stuff down. Ascend to the top of the mountain with me.

ABOUT CANDICE SHEPARD

Candice wears many hats and loves them all. Jesus lover, Mama, sister, daughter, orphan advocate, animal rescuer, and friend are her favorites. She also proudly wears the hats of attorney, entrepreneur, thought leader, influencer, mentor, speaker, author, and servant leader.

Originally from the Midwest, Candice proudly calls North Carolina home now, along with her four children, and menagerie of fur babies. That Midwestern pragmatism is still very much present in her parenting style, daily living, and business.

Candice is the CEO and Managing Attorney of Shepard Law, PLLC, a law firm in the Charlotte, NC Metro area, which serves multiple counties in two locations. She is the Founder and President of the Board of Directors of Tribe 14:18 Ministries, a nonprofit that is being brought to fruition out of the desire of Candice and some of the most amazing mamas on the planet who seek to care for orphans and the families who love them. Finally, Candice is a certified Canfield Success Principles Trainer, coach, best-selling author and international speaker with The Athena Tribe. Candice seeks to empower others in all aspects of life and her diverse endeavors are driven by that desire.

Candice also loves to connect!

www.ShepardLawPLLC.com
www.Tribe1418.com
www.TheAthenaTribe.com

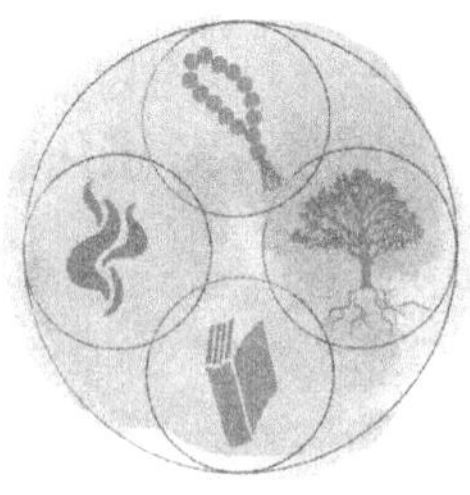

THE ART OF TRANSCENDING ABUNDANCE

Tara Truax

Have you ever been in line at checkout and had to put something back? Have you ever heard the embarrassing beep of a card being declined, while an irritated jury of your peers stand in line behind you? Have you ever had the payment go through, but you knew the impending overdraft fees were going to exceed your purchase of that $5 latte? Me too. All of them. The indescribable anxiety of looking at my bank account. Those tiny numbers, or lack thereof, defining my value to financial institutions. The minus in the front of that number a reflection of the cost to live in this world. My credit. My future goals of owning anything substantial. The overwhelming, hopeless anxiety. As a successful artist and entrepreneur I used to ignore those numbers. It was much easier than facing the truth, or so I believed.

In the fall of 2018, just minutes before heading to the store, I sat motionless with the glow of the computer screen on my face. How was I going to make it work this time? All of our credit cards were maxed out. If I paid only the minimums that were due, we wouldn't have enough cash left for food. How did

I get here? I was a strong, confident woman and a successful entrepreneur. Some of my friends even seemed envious of the lifestyle that we had. But behind closed doors I was burnt out, doubted every decision I made, and felt like a fake. I had retired from an incredible career in the entertainment industry and we lived in an affluent neighborhood surrounded by other successful people. Yet I was not sure of how I would be paying for groceries? To better understand how I had arrived at this reality, I would need to retrace the steps, thoughts and decisions on my journey. Luckily this money story had left breadcrumbs to follow, one step at a time.

As a child I witnessed my parent's successes and failures. One moment we had abundance, money, wealth, and security. The next it was gone. It was a spinning magic carpet of unexpectedness and it was all that I knew. I witnessed bankruptcy, divorce, having it all and having it all disappear. I made a decision at a young age to never trust money. When I needed it most, it was never there. I believed those with money let me down more than others, therefore money was not safe. It was also in that sentiment that I decided not to trust myself with money and ultimately not to trust myself at all.

At the age of 18, living in Los Angeles and barely able to afford groceries, I found myself needing a car. With zero credit and a full college schedule, I signed a lease for a ridiculous number of months so I could afford the payments. Every weekend I would drive to Northern CA, to see my family. Racking up the miles and the debt along the way. I was charging $5 lattes and living on ramen noodles. I had no plan in place. There was no future. Only the present moment existed. I was in survival mode with zero regard of the financial hole I was digging myself into. The only way out was by accident, literally. The blessing of the hit-and-run accident that threw my car into the side of a building, totaling the car, freed me of the financial chains I was locked in. No car meant no payment. The problem was, I also had no money, no savings, no plan, and now nothing to drive.

Further into my twenties I enlisted the help of a debt consolidation company to pull me from my financial ruin. They combined my credit cards and student loans, effectively tanking my credit score. But at least this time I had a plan and learned my lesson, right? Nope! One afternoon I answered the rotary phone in my 250sq ft. Hollywood apartment, to a timeshare telemarketer. I voluntarily paid $700, with my new CC that maxed at a $1000 limit. The senior girl's trip that I envisioned blurred my common sense. After college, the trip never happened and the timeshare expired. Money went down the drain and that $700 purchase cost me close to $2,000 with interest over time. The angry, abusive and self-destructive relationship I had with myself was showing up the same in my money story. I didn't like me. I was scared to be authentically me. I was triggered by other people's opinions of me and I was hiding the true me. Behind it all I was hiding my value to this world and my unconditional worth.

Years later in my dance career, I found protection in the starving artist badge that I wore with pride. I was limited in the belief that if I didn't work hard, I didn't deserve the reward. This became my money story and the epigenetic consciousness that I chose to activate and navigate my financial health from. Did you even know there is a thing called financial health? I was a physically healthy dancer with a thriving dance career and understood health on so many levels, but I couldn't afford food. Canned beans and black coffee were the daily menu. I became a master manipulator of money out of necessity. I would manifest just enough to get by 100% of the time. Always just enough. It became an addictive game that gave me an endorphin rush like no other. I hadn't figured out how to receive and keep all that I was worthy of, because I didn't own my worth. I could book the shows, perform on incredible stages, travel the world with platinum recording artists, but the bank still said I was unworthy.

The credit companies said I was unworthy. My friends, who I couldn't keep up with financially, said I was unworthy. I was the Houdini of my bank account, but the true illusion was my future. My external circumstances were reflecting my internal reality. And the ugly truth was that no one could face it but me.

In my search for hope I picked up a book. The words leapt off the page, "Money's not the problem, you are." I froze. Holy crap! What if every belief I had about money was the reason money wasn't showing up? I had to ask the question, "If I wasn't showing up for money, what would happen if I did?"

At the same time that the financial clouds began to thin, I had a sweet child that was swimming in anxiety. I too struggled daily to manage my own overwhelming feelings, as the pressure of life often paralyzed me. I was spinning every plate, trying to support his health, our family's health, and our family's future. Drowning I couldn't even focus two minutes in front of me, let alone two years into the future. Now how were we going to get out of this hole? I sat at the top of my stairs with my head in my hands while I listened to the crashes of thrown toys and tears of anger from my son's room. The blanket of hopelessness was heavy. Every last dime had evaporated from medical expenses. And everyone's health, the one thing I had an abundance of before, was disintegrating.

It was in my last ditch effort to find a holistic solution to my son's health that I found an unexpected business opportunity with a network marketing company. I'd had a bad taste in my mouth for the industry from a past experience, as so many do. It's a common theme in an industry with very little buy in, a lot of hype and very little business structure. It's also easy to get sidetracked without having a long term business plan that a traditional business would have. Many fail for this reason. Yet years before, even though I had failed, network marketing had brought me home from the dance studio and kept us financially afloat through the decline of our son's health. I knew there had to be hope for me in the industry long term. I was not ready to completely throw in the towel, but I did need to change the business model I was in. I had been stuck in the wrongness of me for years. For three years I had grown a business where no matter what I did, I couldn't help others win. I invested more of myself than the couple thousand dollars a month I was making and we were still swimming in debt. It all felt wrong. I found myself questioning, "If I did make the change, was I worthy of leading? Will people even follow me?" For most of my life I had a limiting belief that people didn't like me, so why would they like me enough now to partner with me? I questioned my son's health, I questioned my own validity. What if others thought I was a fraud? You name it, it went through my mind. But have you ever had that God Moment? That intuition or nudge that is so clear, if you don't listen to it, you are going to combust? That's what I heard that November evening. Clear as day, I heard "Go now." I closed my eyes, trusted, and surrendered to the possibility that this was the answer to our family's prayers. Then I got to work like my life depended on it.

Our first year in business, not only had we paid off all six figures of credit card debt, our son's health had massively improved. My own anxiety was a thing of the past. It became apparent that our family's physical health was impacting our financial health, which in turn was impacting our physical health. The cycle needed to be broken. What was unleashed was incredible. A debt free lifestyle, bringing in high six figures a year, while impacting thousands of lives globally and helping them find the solutions to what they were seeking.

Each trip to the grocery store became a moment to embrace the gratitude of our journey. I don't ever take for granted the freedom of not having to check my bank account before standing in line. In 2020 when the pandemic first hit, I found myself pondering my purpose, and the purpose of making so much money. Why should I build a business beyond what we were already blessed with? The overflow was there, so now how could I contribute more to this world? As I stood in the checkout line, super socially distanced and masked up, I overheard a couple in front of me. The fact I even heard the conversation was divine intervention itself. The couple didn't have enough money to buy their elderly family member, safely at home, the food that she needed. A flooding feeling of familiarity took over my thoughts as I flashed back to all of those similar cashier interactions from just a few years back. I could have easily been part of the irritated jury of peers. But instead, I felt the nudge in my gut again, that God Moment, and asked them if they would be okay with me helping with the remaining balance. The look of confused gratitude beamed from their eyes. Instantly I understood my bigger purpose and the motivation I needed to keep growing financially and giving unconditionally. We never know when we will be the answer to someone else's prayer, but if we don't show up, we can never be the solution. When I stepped into awareness and removed myself and my ego from the situation, I could show up and serve in unlimited abundance. My purpose finally had a path.

By the end of year two we had created over seven figures in earnings between my husband and I. Once again I found myself in my thoughts, questioning my authenticity, my purpose and the power of the impact we were creating. Even though we had helped thousands of families climb out of their own financial hole, shining light on their limiting beliefs while building our own financial foundation to freedom, here I was, questioning it all again. Sitting in a group of highly experienced conscious entrepreneurs with various business backgrounds, I felt shame emerge for the incredible abundance we had created. It was as if my money somehow held less value. My own hidden fears of what people would think of me as a Network Marketing Professional paralyzed me. I struggled to speak. As I walked the ledge, facing the fear of my own next level of leadership, I made the choice to become the bridge instead of shrinking. I had to use my voice.

I stepped onto the stage, in front of thousands, virtually and in person, and I publicly shared my temptation to hide. If I could find myself in this position, after making over a million dollars in this industry, I couldn't be the only person. The veil was lifted, and I realized money had no less value, regardless of where it came from, as long as I was showing up in service along the way. Right there, on that stage, I let the fear go like a balloon. I was a conscious, aligned Network Marketing Professional. I owned my voice and delivered the best training in my entire career up until that point. In my journey I have learned that resistance creates more resistance! It's in surrender that flow happens. The flow of money, the flow of community and the flow of a thriving business. I finally got to own that authentically as all parts of me came together and I showed up in totality as me.

Reflecting back on this adventure of life so far, I envision a giant heart. A heart is meant to beat. Beats are energy in motion and motion requires space. When I let my heart out of the box and allowed myself to be present, authentic and free in the exact vision and light the universe intended me to be in, the magic happened and the abundance flowed. And guess what? I am 100% worthy of it all. I not only found Light, Love and Abundance, I also found myself in the process, where money lives in the energetics of it all and in the frequency of me. Daily I now ask, "What energy space and consciousness could my body and I be to never have enough money, but always too much to spend for all eternity?" And daily I release anything blocking that from showing up with ease and joy. I've learned that safety is a paradigm that is pure illusion. The present moment is all we have and the choices we are making now, and continue to make every ten seconds, lay the foundation for our future self. The future is brighter with hope. It is brighter with possibility. It is brighter with choice. But most importantly, the future is brightest in faith. We shine bright because it's only within the darkness that the light can exist. The Divine calls us to find joy, not just in moments of light, but also in the moments of darkness, remembering that all is working for our growth inwardly. It is in that space that our humanness connects us all and compassion is created. We never know if sharing a part of our truth, or our story, may help another feel less alone and more accepted in becoming who they truly are. Within every story lies the potential to set someone free. Even our money story.

So whether it's in line at the grocery store or on a stage in front of thousands, I've found my solution by serving others and overflowing abundantly. What solution are you searching for? And what are you willing to receive to create that solution? The Universe is waiting for you to open your arms to receive infinitely, transcend abundance and SHINE.

ABOUT TARA TRUAX

Tara Truax is a creative entrepreneur and motivational coach, speaker and author who has reconstructed her financial reality from six figures of debt to seven figures of earnings at lightning speed. As a retired professional dancer, Board Certified Health and Wellness Coach (NBC-HWC) and Million Dollar Earner in the Network Marketing Industry, Tara has built an international business with tens of thousands of people and has spoken and trained on stages globally. Her desire to motivate others to unleash their limitless possibility fuels her as she inspires others to ascend in conscious, aligned business ownership. You can be an introvert, an empath and an authentic, successful entrepreneur.

If not seeking adventure in the world, Tara can be found in her backyard oasis in New Jersey with her husband Mike and their three children.

To learn more about how you can connect and work with Tara, please visit her website at:
www.Thebodywisedancer.com

Facebook: Tara Page Truax
Instagram: Thebodywisedancer

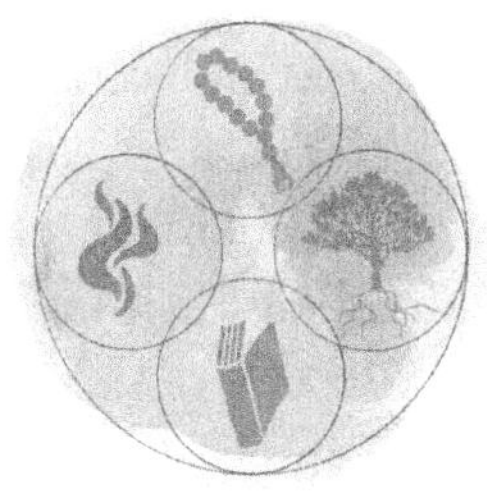

LUMINARY INSIGHTS

Ivanna Mann Thrower Anderson

Living through the divorce of my parents, my own divorce, years of Fibromyalgia and even a stroke were never as traumatic as being successful. That's not what you were expecting to read, was it? Most people think of trauma as coming from something awful, whether it's a terrible experience, a long-term illness or the sudden death of a loved one, but we never associate it with success.

I've always been a quick learner. I never thought of it as being unique, much less a threat to the success of others, until I started school. In elementary school, students were grouped by reading ability. This meant that some of the friends I had were no longer in my circle during class time. We could still play together, but as it became clear that we were somehow different, the dynamics of those friendships changed. I loved learning and I excelled at it. Finishing my work quickly often allowed me to work on bulletin boards and do other odd jobs for the teacher. Kids teased me for being the teacher's pet. I was proud to be valued by my teachers, but very hurt by the chastisement of my peers. I quickly learned that being myself and shining at the things I do best, could actually bring me pain.

The trend continued in the high school band when I decided to move from trumpet to French horn. The French horn section was thrilled to have a third member until the first monthly challenge, which determined rank within the group. I played the musical piece and placed first chair. At our next rehearsal I asked a question like I always did and was told, "Why should we help you? You already seem to know it all." Everything had changed. I realized I had a choice. I could continue to do my best or I could dim my light to fit in. I chose to shine, becoming a soloist and winning awards.

As I got older, the expectations of others and my own self-doubt began to creep in. I set huge goals for myself and I reached them all by the age of 23. This left me feeling empty and wondering what life was really all about. People expected me to keep reaching for the stars and shining among them, as if the success happened by magic or luck. I, too, expected myself to keep going at the same pace. And then I froze.

I couldn't dream about the future and I found it impossible to set long-term goals. I went through life following the flow, but it no longer held purpose. Based on my outward appearance, I continued to succeed in my career, but in reality, I was numb. I no longer knew who I was or what I wanted. My marriage ended in divorce and I was left alone to face the emptiness without the usual distractions. The alone time allowed me two things: time to concentrate on my career and time to grow new relationships with others and with myself.

I focused on my career. In less than six years, I moved from teaching English as a Second Language (ESL) at a local school, to working for the Central Office as an instructional coach, specializing in Sheltered Instruction (SIOP) and ESL for the district, and then to a position at the state. The pace of my professional advancement was rather quick, given that my earlier career iterations had been in adult education, as well as corporate consulting, in the US and in South Korea.

As I progressed in my career, I encountered the recurring pattern: a colleague purposefully tried to sabotage my work in order to bring theirs into the spotlight. Even though we had once been friends and productive colleagues, the energy had shifted into negativity. Now, I was at a loss. Without the goals to focus on, and with my empathic energy unprotected, I was unconsciously absorbing the negativity.

The impact of the negativity was gradual, but it was fierce. I began to feel achy, tired and I had trouble processing things. My usually quick brain was muddled, like sitting in a dense fog. I began to have trouble getting up in the morning, sleeping upwards of 20 hours a day and still struggling to function. Numerous tests and doctors led to a diagnosis of Fibromyalgia.

But I want to go back to the second opportunity that my time alone offered me, time for relationships. During the separation and divorce I had plenty of time to build relationships with others and myself. In my coaching position, I had the privilege of helping teachers tap into their strengths and those of their students. Each encounter allowed us to illuminate the steps in their pathways to success. I was successful here as well, seeing the things that others failed to recognize and helping them grow through it. Yet, I couldn't seem to do this for myself. So, God sent me a very special friend to help illuminate my path.

Ginny Tracy is the most positive person I have ever known. Anytime you ask how she is, she responds, "Wonderful!" Not only does she say this, but she lives it. As a multi-gold medalist and ambassador for the Special Olympics, a seasoned actor and skilled bull rider (the mechanical type), Ginny doesn't let her traumatic brain injury slow her down. I'd thought I could offer her some support after my divorce, during my new alone time, but it was she who supported me through her example of unbridled love for life, no matter the circumstances!

Being in her loving energy allowed new insights to be illuminated in my life. I began a journey of self-love and self-belief that brought me through the pain of divorce and the betrayal of friends. I tapped into my inner light in a way I never had before, but still, I couldn't set goals for myself. I remained in a fog of purpose intermixed with the fog of Fibromyalgia.

Somehow, I continued coaching and training others via my work with great success. It seemed I could illuminate the hidden genius whether the clients were struggling or seemingly on top of their game, yet this revelation was illusive for me. My hidden upper limits told me I couldn't shine. I couldn't be my best or I would be shunned or pushed for more at every turn. I could rest easy in what Gay Hendricks calls the Zone of Excellence, the place of success and comfort, just short of one's best, in his book *The Big Leap*. Yes, I was successful, but I was subconsciously scared to step into my true genius, into the Zone of Genius where each of us shines fully, offering to ourselves and to the world what only we can offer. This was where I truly wanted to be!

During the pandemic, I had another chance to have alone time, to slow down and search my inner thoughts. I took online courses from Natalie Ledwell, Mary Morrissey and Jack Canfield, gurus in the field of life coaching. I joined a book club designed to help us handle the stresses of Covid through positivity and understanding how the brain reacts to trauma. I was so excited to be reading for my own self-growth. I also found the discussions so impactful on my mental health and growth in personal healing. Then, the negative patterns surfaced again. Some of the things I shared about my work and my goals caused discomfort for the leader, perhaps a feeling of competition for the spotlight, and certainly a fear of proprietary materials being misused, and I was basically asked to step out. I was sad to lose this lifeline during the pandemic and, as in the past, a group I'd come to see as friends. Yet, through the life coaching, readings, and my own illuminated insights, I had a new set of skills and a firm belief that the universe was conspiring in my favor! I sent only love to the group as I left and waited to see what amazing thing would happen next!

I didn't have to wait very long. The next week, at the same time I would have been in the book study, I took a donation to a local thrift shop. I was drawn to the book section, an area I typically don't explore. I had an intuition, a gut feeling, that I was to find just the right book, and asked the universe for guidance. As I ran my fingers across the spines, I stopped on a hardback titled *Positivity*. I took it from the shelf and read the author's description which stated, "Among the most highly cited scholars in psychology, Barbara Fredrickson is most known for her broaden-and-build theory of positive emotions, foundational within Positive Psychology." I stood in awe. This book, this research, is exactly what I was looking for to support the less scientifically based life coaching techniques I had been learning. And, are you sitting down? Barbara Fredrickson, the neuroscientist who wrote the book, is right here in Chapel Hill, NC where I live!

Solidifying my commitment to work with Jack Canfield's *The Success Principles* and Barbara Fredrickson's *Positivity*, I made the decision to manifest my vision of creating a successful coaching business and brand, Luminary Insights. This decision led to me attracting and hiring an amazing business coach, Marla Diann, who guided me in putting the necessary structures, mindset and systems in place. I am now empowered and equipped to take a quantum leap in my growth and to help others grow as well. Isn't God amazing!

Finally, in my 50s, I understand that in order to be fulfilled, in order to help others shine, I must shine to my fullest. I must push past my fears, past my current success and into my calling, my Zone of Genius. I must be willing to always be wonderful, like Ginny, no matter the circumstances. I must be willing to push past my perceived limitations, set the audacious goals, reach them and then set some more! Only then can I be truly successful! I must continue to believe fully that the universe is conspiring for me. When things that seem negative, even as dire as chronic illness and divorce, enter my path, I must sit back and ask what gift is coming my way to take me to the next level of my journey. It is always more than I could have imagined!

I now understand that when others are bothered by my light, they aren't a part of my tribe. I know this is an abundant universe and that there is a place for each of us to flourish and to share our light with each other and with the world. I am still learning. I still contract into uncertainty, but now I have strategies for expansion and for turning up the dimmer switch to full illumination. I would love to tell you more about them!

ABOUT IVANNA MANN THROWER ANDERSON

Ivanna's passion is growing people! For over 30 years, she has been transforming lives, from the pre-K classroom through the offices of corporate presidents in the US, Korea, and China. As a NC State Education Consultant for English as a second language, past-president of the National Association of English Learner Program Administrators (NAELPA), and founder of Luminary Insights, Ivanna combines intuition, life experience and her formal education to expand creativity and productivity through core genius discovery and development. Ivanna moves fluidly among educators, government officials and business executives as she combines self-growth with intellectual pursuit and expansion of possibility.

Ivanna is a graduate of North Carolina State University and The School for International Training. She is a Certified Public Manager®, a Jack Canfield Success Principles® Certified Trainer, an accomplished speaker and writer and intuitive coach. Her work as an education coach is featured in the Pearson Publication entitled *Implementing the SIOP Model through Effective Professional Development and Coaching*.

Ivanna loves traveling, spending time in nature, and exploring creative ideas with her author husband, DB Anderson.

Work with Ivanna/Luminary Insights

Web: MyLuminaryInsights.com
Email: Ivanna@myluminaryinsights.com
FB: https://www.facebook.com/LuminaryInsights
Twitter: @LuminaryInsight

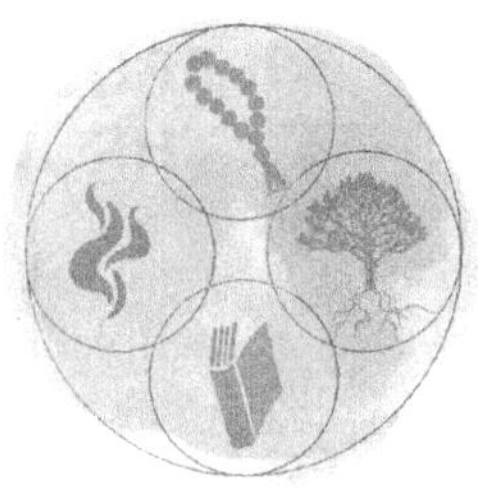

UNSTOPPABLE ME

Heather Beebe

Things happen to all of us. And as you sit here and read this today, know that you have survived the things you found to be difficult. I have too. This story was a game changer though. The loudest, most traumatic one yet. I'm sure you have a good story too. Let's take it back to January 2015. A positive pregnancy test after a fantastic vacation in Puerto Rico wasn't exactly the souvenir I had planned. Single, career driven, and already a mother of two; it just wasn't part of my plan.

It truly began in 2013. After some difficult times with the loss of my mother and my divorce, I was finally starting to see financial security again. I planned a surprise trip with my girls to Puerto Rico for some much needed vacation time and to meet up with close friends. It was our first trip post-divorce and it was special. To this day, the girls say it was the best vacation they ever had. I'm not sure I can put into words how amazing it was for me, but I can tell you that I was oblivious to what was in store.

There he was; intelligent and well-mannered with a wonderful family, and he was single. Most importantly, he was kind to my children and they simply adored him. When you see your children experience joy, you also experience great joy. We explored all over the island and when he could join us, he did. Holding their hands, attentive to their safety, and of course demonstrating gentleman-like behavior. Do you know how attractive it is when someone you're crushing on is kind to your children? Or any children for that matter! Returning back to my home in Upstate New York was an emotional drop. Something special was left behind. After an internal battle over the fear of rejection, I used my phone as a filtered way to express my vulnerability. One simple text to express my thoughts on how short life is and that I had a high school girl crush that consumed every moment since my return. I received an instant response, HE FELT THE SAME WAY! Oh, my heart. Full of wonder and confusion. Immediately, we planned a trip to Colorado to ski with family and friends and spend some time in the mountains together.

Planning the trip to the mountains was exciting. I was working in my corporate job at the time and even my boss was excited for this love story. I was so nervous. I am an introverted extrovert that has no clue how to approach people at times of high emotion. When I arrived at the airport, no one was there. Phew—I guess there would be no passionate hug with a physical confirmation of all these feelings. His brother finally arrived and we were on our way. Arriving at the house full of all of our friends eliminated the risk of being alone with him and talking about everything we had been texting about for two months. We skied, played cards, ate great food, flirted a bit, but mostly we enjoyed the entire week as if we never shared our feelings. It was not what I had expected. Each night, I would lie in my bed and wonder what it was. Was it our mutual awkwardness and lack of social skills? Was it because we were surrounded by others? I just went with the flow. Who was I to know what was right? Despite having these questions, I felt ok. I wasn't sure I even understood what love was supposed to feel like.

The last day came and he let me know that he wanted to talk to me before I went to bed. I was in my room and he came in to chat. Sitting on the edge of my bed, I could see that he was winded. So nervous and filled with anxiety that his words were weakened by his lack of breath. Fear tried to creep up but he sat and spoke his words regardless. "I don't know how this could ever work. You live in New York and I live in Puerto Rico," he shared. I was proud of him for doing that because I could visibly see that it was hard. We spoke about my children and his experience in medical school. It was all the truth. But so were our feelings. My response was just that. It all made sense that this shouldn't work, but that didn't take away from my feelings at that moment. As we stared at each other without a care in the world, I grabbed his face and kissed him. "I've been waiting for that for a long time," he responded. We barely slept that night. We laughed and held each other arm in arm ,wishing to stop the clock. This is what I was yearning for as I booked these tickets. This is what I wanted.

As morning arrived, I asked him to take me to the airport. The goodbye was so sad. The reality of the distance was like a brick to the face. After the tightest hug outside the airport, I walked away with one last wave. Will I ever see him again? While checking in at the counter, I was told that the flight was delayed and I would have to stay one more night. WHAT? What is the universe trying to do to me? An answered prayer; to see him again. He turned right around and came to pick me up. I don't understand why I felt the way I did. We both already agreed that logistically this was going to be impossible, but it felt so right. If it wasn't meant to be, why was this happening?

The following morning was the time he was actually scheduled to leave and we arrived at the airport together. After starting the check in process, we realized that we were on the same exact flight. Even the employee thought that was so sweet and gave us seats next to each other.

We flew to Chicago and that's where we had to part ways, which hit me hard. Airports are full of stories, some sad and some happy. In this moment, I was happy. Sitting in the airport by myself crying at the thought of the unknown. I truly felt as though I could love again.

The distance proved to be difficult over the next couple of months . As much as I wished for him to come visit me, the lack of action on his part was proof that I needed to be more realistic.

I began to date. Not long after, I found myself reconnecting with my long distance crush and I planned another trip to Puerto Rico. December of 2014 would change my life forever. Because of his ridiculous schedule as a medical student and the amount of people staying at the house I was given his room to sleep in. I didn't see much of him during the trip except for a few stolen adventures and moments spent without the family around. On my last night there, his friends invited us to go on a Parranda and I was so excited. Parranda is the Puerto Rican version of caroling, but with traditional instruments added. I realized that this wasn't for me when he went to sleep early instead of joining his friends. Things didn't feel right and I believe in listening to what your body is telling you.

I returned to New York confident that I was ready to move on. As the dating process often reveals, some people weren't meant to be together. I adored his family but that wasn't dependent on our secret rendezvous. Several weeks later, I began to feel ill. You guessed it. Pregnant and already a single mother of two at the height of my career. Tears instantly flowed. What was I going to do? I was so lost. Coming to grips with it, I texted him. "Please call me when you have a moment. I really need to talk to you." When he called I was in the car. I had to pull over because I was shaking so badly. First there was silence and then reassurance that this was going to be "difficult, but not impossible." This was the last time he was nice to me for months.

In fear, I began searching for clinics in the New York City area. As an avid supporter of pro-life, I knew everyone in my local clinic and couldn't bear the shame of facing them. I began to dig for clarity. What should I do? I had a week to make a decision. I had a note in my phone with a list of the pros and cons. The pros included God's will, a baby, life, excitement. I always wanted more children and being a mother is my favorite thing to do. For cons I wrote distance, doing it alone, explaining this story to traditionalists, and the father's anger. I listed some questions under "Uncertainties." Will I ever see him again? Will I completely lose the family over this? What lies ahead for my future as a single mother? The night before making my final decision, every bone in my body told me that driving to a clinic five hours away wasn't the right decision. I woke up in a night sweat and had to change my clothing. My body screamed for me to seek clarity. I needed to stop focusing on what others may say and think of me. And that was it. I could feel it again, so I kept the baby. It wasn't always easy to face myself in the mirror knowing how judgmental I was to women in my exact scenario. I wasn't reckless and irresponsible. We were both highly educated professionals having an unplanned baby.

Oh, my boy. I never had a boy and I had always wanted one. His name would be Mateo Gabriel, meaning "Gift from God with courage." He was a gift. A beautiful gift.

I spent the following two years going back and forth to Puerto Rico hoping that it would all work out. I wanted to relive the beautiful moments we had in Colorado. I learned Spanish. I learned to Salsa. I fell in love with his island. I did all these things in an attempt to be a woman he could love. He would be mean and say terrible things. He wouldn't spend a lot of time with his child, but I kept going back. The fear of failure pushed me to ignore what I knew felt so wrong in my heart. I deserved a man that was going to show up, but for that to happen I needed to let go of the shame that engrossed my mind. I, alone, was enough. I just hadn't realized it yet.

What the hell was I doing? I never felt further from my true self. Not once did I speak poorly of this man to people who didn't know the truth. I was so afraid that people wouldn't like him. I held it all in just as hard as I held on to the idea that it would all be ok. He would get better and we would have an incredible story of resilience and love. To those that did know the truth, I spent every moment with them sulking in my victim role. Eventually I was pushed into a dark space. I was infatuated with fixing the situation and presenting a perfect visual for outsiders. I ignored the unacceptable behavior so that our picture could be perfect. The feelings of shame pushed me to make choices I typically wouldn't make. I was desperately in need of help.

Intensive work was ahead for me. This is where my next chapter begins. Who was I to settle for anything less based on what others thought of me? I discovered why I do the things I do and it began to make sense. Protecting an image wasn't something I just came up with. It was deeply rooted in my upbringing. It's the original reason I wouldn't leave my marriage. Divorce "looks" bad. Having children by multiple men "looks" bad. None of this was true. They were stories I told myself because change is hard work. Sometimes we tell ourselves it's "just the way it is" because that's easier than looking in the mirror, speaking to yourself realistically, and taking responsibility for the changes you'd like to see. If I wanted love in my life then I needed to start loving myself first! I was responsible for the situation in my life and the happiness I was so desperately looking for.

In September of 2017, hurricane Maria devastated the island of Puerto Rico. It was symbolic of my life at the time. Broken, but existing. Shortly before the hurricane, I was informed of his new relationship and I felt like the rug was ripped out from underneath me. All of the images I had created in my mind were gone. Here's where my breakthrough began. The pull I had to this land was still there and stronger than ever. I took a solo trip to the island to assist with relief efforts. I spent minimal time with my son's family and more time on my own literally picking up the rubble, mentally and physically. With every moment of cleanup, things became more clear. It's easy to recognize clean up in the physical world, but mental cleanup can be some of the hardest work we ever do. It became clear to me why I was doing the things I was doing. Did I really love him? Or was I was in love with protecting the image? This wasn't me. I didn't like the way I was being treated and I would never experience true happiness if this pattern continued. The work went on.

I came to terms with many of my decisions and remained aware of the fact that, as a mother, I was willing to do whatever it took to protect my children. I was fearful that my son would experience the same pain I did growing up in a fatherless home. I had to protect him from things I had experienced. It was a powerful realization when I discovered I was projecting my fears onto my son. Those weren't his fears. I knew I had more work to do regarding the pain that I still carried from my childhood.

Embracing who I am became the foundation for what I was about to do next. I was Heather Beebe. A strong mother of three and truly unstoppable. I opened my coaching practice and started to share some of the tools I had learned for building self-awareness, or the lack thereof! But was I done with Puerto Rico? Was all of that just a waste of time? My heart was telling me differently. I could still love this place. The island had given me so much and there was no reason why it couldn't remain a part of my life.

Under the umbrella of my coaching practice Unstoppable You, I took all of this and created an experience for women to witness their own transformations. My retreat is a direct response to hurricane Maria and allows me to give back. I shop local as much as possible and educate participants about the history of the island. I help to bridge the gap of understanding about the relationship between Puerto Rico and the United States while providing a life changing curriculum that I personally know works. Thus far, I've spent over $40,000 in local economies in Puerto Rico and will continue to host this retreat into the unforeseen future.

Although I don't recommend it, getting pregnant on vacation was one of the greatest things that has ever happened to me. It pushed me down into the dirt of my life so hard, I had no choice but to face it. It pushed me to accept myself and face my judgments in the mirror. To grow and then accept that I am so badass, I could do this alone. To be proud of anything I go through in life. Sometimes I experience grief, sure. Random events or memories can trigger it. But I could be angry with this man or I could choose to be thankful. To accept that this gift wasn't possible without him. I don't know why we were pulled towards each other on a handful of occasions or why he didn't show up when he had the chance. It's none of my business to try and understand that. The reality is that we created one of the most amazing little people together. My son is my greatest teacher. There's no doubt that he is meant to be here. And now with this story, I continue to push forward without overlooking my own self and heart. I strive to change lives all over the world and make an impact on an island that gave me so much. I finish this story with gratitude. For him. For his family. For my son. And forever may they know that. This chapter in my life is not stopping me and it truly never did.

ABOUT HEATHER BEEBE

Creating Unstoppable You in her notebook for several years, Heather has always been an entrepreneur at heart. She holds her certification as a Personal Trainer from the Personal Training Institute of America and also received her training and certification as an Integrative Holistic Coach through the Legacy Training Institute.

Heather holds a B.A. in Interdisciplinary Studies with a triple concentration in History, Technology, and Globalization. She now blends her educational background with personal growth work tools to help people embrace who they really are and achieve whatever it is they've been yearning for. She breaks down patterns in human behavior and gets to the root causes of the vicious cycles we find ourselves in. Once we become self aware, anything is possible. Changing lives is what she feels she was born to do and claims that it's a powerful experience showing people that being "you" is enough.

Heather enjoys traveling, hiking, the beach, writing, and volunteerism. She can often be found giving back to her community and beyond in any way she can and has even been referred to as a humanitarian advocate. She resides in Utica, New York with her fiancé, Shawn and their blended family of six children, Rae, Lilliana, Alysa, Karina, Mateo, and Norah.

To learn more about Heather, please visit
www.UnstoppableYouCoach.com

There you will find information about her retreats in Puerto Rico, social media pages, contact information, and the release of her upcoming online courses; Unstoppable Academy.

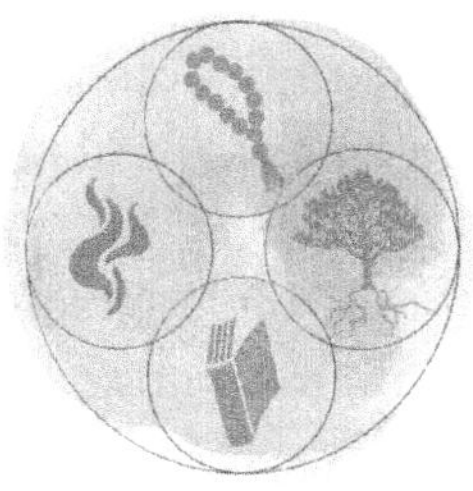

LIGHT THAT SHINES BRIGHT

Tracey Watts Cirino

Have you ever felt unworthy of love and didn't know what you had done wrong or how to fix it? I know I have and at the time I didn't know there was any other way you could feel or be.

Hello, my name is Tracey Watts Cirino. I am a business success coach that inspires and empowers salon owners and hairstylists to grow and scale their businesses without all the stress and overwhelm. So they can have the confidence they need to earn more money, and improve their quality of life while creating a bigger impact in the world. I do this by using my Beyond Common Success Method and Framework, which we discuss often on my podcast Beyond Common Business Secrets and in my books and courses called Beyond Common 12 Essentials for Success in Life and in the Workplace. I love to help creative service business owners like hairstylists, salon owners, yoga studios, photographers, coaches, physical therapists, fitness pros, and the like get focused so that they can grow and scale their businesses.

When I was a little girl, I remember always feeling safe. Our family home was filled with lots of joy and laughter. My parents were both hilarious and a lot of fun! My mom and dad would do the silliest things to entertain us. Sometimes my parents were so funny that my sister and I laughed until pink milk came shooting out of our noses.

Do you remember that pink Nesquik powder? For some reason, we loved that stuff. You know the good old days before we knew sugar and red dye # whatever were so bad for us. Don't you just love that we could live with the idea that ignorance is bliss back then, especially when eating?

Anyway, I can't remember the exact moment that I felt a shift of energy in our family unit, but I was somewhere around 5 years old. I remember things changed rapidly. By the time I was seven, my parents were divorced and I was living in my third home with a whole new family. We went from our family of four to living with my grandfather and one of my grandmothers, which were my mom's dad and stepmother. Then we finally ended up living with my mom, her new husband, and his 3 children to create our very own version of the Brady bunch during the week and my dad's new apartment on the weekends. I had made the decision that I wanted to take care of my little sister. She was younger than me by a year and a half and if I could have created an invisible force field shield of energy around her the way they do in superhero movies, I would have. I wanted to protect her from all of this family pain in any way I could. I took it upon myself to be the family mediator and help everyone communicate more effectively. I know, who did I think I was at just 5 years old? No one gave me that role or appointed me to this new position. I just did it. I'm not sure if it's because I knew early on that I was pretty good at communicating and I could mediate to help my parents when they weren't getting along and having a disagreement or if there was another reason behind it, but I just stepped in into this new role as if I owned it and it was mine.

Looking back, I realize I spent my days internalizing the pain I felt over my parents' divorce. I lost the feeling of safety and security that was associated with our four-person family. I held that pain inside and thought that I was somehow to blame and that I was a bad girl unworthy of love. I thought I wasn't loved by God or anyone for that matter and that maybe I was just really bad and not good at all.

I was actually one of the really lucky Children of Divorce because my parents are all really amazing people. They were trying to do the very best they could with the cards they were given. I ended up having three wonderful parents, because my mom re-married her childhood sweetheart after she and my dad got divorced. I was blessed as far as divorced families go.

I had a mom and two great dads. So, by those standards, I couldn't complain. It›s not their fault, it was just how I personally internalized my own version of my childhood trauma. I think you naturally blame yourself when you're a child of divorce. You always see it that way even when your parents tell you it›s not your fault, either that or maybe you block out what they say like wha wha wha.

I honestly don't remember if my parents ever told me that it wasn't my fault. The truth is I did blame myself and I didn't tell them how I felt. I don't even know if I knew enough back then to form the words. It is strange how, looking back, you realize these things. I've never been the type of person to not speak my mind or tell people how I feel, but back then I was not equipped with the skills necessary to do so. I just tried to protect my sister as best I could and I shoved my feelings of unworthiness and shame down deep, as far as they would fit.

Around the time I was 12 years old, I had these disgusting waxy red bumps that flacked off my scalp. I felt ugly and truly unlovable. I wanted to make myself invisible instead of dealing with the daily trash talk from the Mean Girls, which most of us dealt with at that age. Since I had internalized all of my childhood pain, I had developed the feelings of blame, shame, and unworthiness. These emotions kept growing inside of me until finally. like all stress in life. it came to a head. It erupted like a volcano of pain all over my hair and scalp. It had to come out in some way.

Our pain and stress will always reveal itself unless we learn to confront it If we don't work through it. The hurt will always come out in some way even if we are unconscious of it. As a child, you don't have the knowledge or the tools to handle all of that heavy trauma and stress. You don't actually know how to deal with the heavy stuff in a healthy way. As a child, you actually don't even know what it's called or that it's even happening. As I suffered in silence, I got to the point where I couldn't take the pain anymore and I wanted to remove it. So, I locked myself in my bedroom with a garbage can and a tiny little lice comb and I sat down and scraped every single waxy scab off of my head along with 75% of my beautiful hair. In my efforts to remove my pain, and what I believed was the true source of my suffering, I also removed my beautiful hair as well as what I linked to my own personal beauty. Of course, I did not know this at the time.

Going through all of the pain and suffering on the inside, as well as what was showing physically on the outside, is what lead me to find my path of healing. It took years and once I truly got better, I wanted to help everyone and anybody that had suffered with feelings of trauma, unworthiness, or what we now call imposter syndrome. If I could keep just one person from suffering the way I did then I knew it would make a difference in someone's life.

Helping people look and feel their best has never been about a beauty salon or the superficial side of Beauty to me. For me, it was always about aligning my True Heart and Soul Purpose to serve others from the greatest place of goodness. You learn throughout life That you cannot stay the same. When you go through something it changes you. Everything changes in some way, no matter if we accept this as absolute truth or not. The healthy way to go through the process of change is to deal with your problems and find a way to learn and grow from it. Any way you can find to process what has happened to you and learn from it is always going to be healthier than shoving things down and not dealing with them. Having psoriasis and scraping my own scalp nearly bald at 12 years old actually started me out on my journey of learning how to find my voice and speak my mind. When you hold that much pain and suffering inside of you it will always find a way to come out one way or another.

When I was young, I didn't have the skillset to help myself or to help others. I was drowning in so much pain and I didn't even know I was drowning. I am sure, looking back, that my sister, stepsisters, and stepbrother were going through something really heavy and painful too, but we were young and not equipped with the life skills necessary to handle life's heavy stuff. I would like to think I would have been able to not only help myself, but to help them too. At the time I just honestly thought that's how life was. Like this is your life, welcome to it. It may suck and make you feel like the worst version of yourself but it's your life so deal with it. I definitely remember feeling like a victim and that the world was out to get me.

My grandparents were always saying to me and the rest of us that, "children are to be seen and not heard." This was something they said all the time. They actually thought it was funny. They had lots and lots of grandchildren and they wanted us all to be quiet and stop talking. This is actually hilarious in retrospect when you surround yourself with that many grandchildren and expect them to be quiet. It is really just laughable. I remember overhearing them talking to my mother when we moved in with them right after my parents got divorced. They were talking to my mother about keeping us quiet. I knew at that moment that my perfect little life bubble was over and it was no longer acceptable to laugh, cheer, yell and scream with joy and allow the pink milk to shoot out of our noses. If I wanted to fit into this family and not make trouble for my mother I had to change. The message was clear, stop being loud and stop being too much for everyone around you. I played this mantra on a repeat loop in my mind for as long as I could remember. Stop being yourself! No one cares what you have to say, You are too much!

I learned very young that I needed to be quiet, dim my light, put my head down and not be fully myself so everyone else could feel comfortable. It was no one's fault, it's just the way I processed the words people spoke to me when I was young. Being told you are too much can make you have feelings and beliefs of unworthiness and the kind of shame that you want to hide under and use as a blanket of shame all your own. I carried this shame blanket with me everywhere and it continued to grow. Not to blame anyone else, that's the mantle that I wore like armor. This was my struggle and perspective of my life situation, which I internalized. I tried to bury my feelings deep down inside while I was hiding under my shame blanket. I dimmed my light to make everyone else feel comfortable because that's what I thought life was like for me and for everyone. Who knew that psoriasis and the pain I felt from scraping my scalp nearly bald would be a defining moment in my life that would put me on the path to realizing that I do have a voice that it is worthy of greatness? I discovered that I can shine bright and help even more people when I'm at my best and shining the brightest. I do have something to say, and it can help someone else find their way. Even if I am so loud it burst someone's eardrums, not that I would want that to happen to anyone but, you get the point that I am trying to make right? If I'm doing it with love and heart it's worthy of sharing. My main personal, life mission has always been to help people see the best in themselves no matter what. If I can help you see the best even in challenging situations, even in the moments when you may feel as ugly as a hairless cat and totally unlovable the way I did, then all of that past pain was worth it for me.

Throughout my evolving beauty career it didn't matter if I was doing hair, teaching hair or fixing a crazy color correction that had gone wrong, training my team or training another salon team, coaching a bunch of business owners and business coaches, or interviewing people on the Beyond Common Business Secrets Podcast. I have always set out to help people look and feel their best so that they could live their best life. So, they could look in the mirror with absolute and total confidence every day and say, "I got this and I can do it!" My passionate pursuit of wanting to help women look and feel their best led me to use my strategic problem-solving brain to create a systematic method that they could use whether I was with them or not.

I created these success systems and strategies in the hair world to help stylists become more successful at earning more money to grow and scale their business behind the chair.

Then in the coaching world as I trained more business owners, leaders and coaches and in the business world as I coached and trained more business owners on how to set up the Beyond Common Success Essential systems in their life and business. Once I really mapped out and created the Beyond Common Success Essentials that we have all actually been using to be successful I wrote a book about them called Beyond Common 12 Essentials for Success in Life and in the Workplace to help everyone achieve success on their own terms. Then, so we could help even more people, I created an online course about how to apply the Beyond Common Success Essentials into everyday life. If I can help just one more person feel positive and find the confidence within to love themselves, flaws and all, then it is worth it for me to share my story no matter how painful it is for me to bring up and remember those dark days when I didn't know where to turn and I was a scared little girl, so lost and so afraid.

If I can find the courage and strength to develop the confidence to find my voice and develop a success mindset then it is truly available to anyone willing to do the work. This work puts you on the path to discovering the light that shines bright inside you even if everything else in your life has led you to believe you must dim your light or that you're unworthy in some way. Now is your time to quiet the noise and shine bright because you and the world deserve to see your light. I would love the opportunity to work with you on discovering your WOW so you can shine bright and map out your Beyond Common Success Journey.

Share your story with me Instagram @TraceyWattsCirino or at www.TraceyWattsCirino.com and join the conversation with me on all social media @TraceyWattsCirino.

Thank you so much for sharing this moment in time with me and reading my story. I hope it helps you in some way find your confidence to shine bright like the diamond you are.

ABOUT TRACEY WATTS CIRINO

Tracey Watts Cirino is an entrepreneur, coach, writer, author, podcast host, thought leader, and unshakable optimist dedicated to helping you get out of your own way so you can become the person you most want to be. She is the creator and founder of Beyond Common Coaching & Training Company and the Beyond Common Business Secrets Podcast. As an all-in, no BS, passionate female business coach and leader Tracey loves to inspire and empower women to have the confidence to look and feel their best while making more money & improving their overall quality of life so that they can make a bigger impact in the world with her proven Success Essentials Method that delivers results. Like working smarter and more strategic to have more profitability, by setting up the essential training systems you will get back 10 hours or more per week.

Tracey's dedication to teamwork and guest experience has created numerous award-winning companies. Now she uses that experience and focus to help grow and develop her clients at Beyond Common Coaching and Training Company where they help creative service business owners, leaders, and their teams get the focus they need to grow and scale their business and live the life of their dreams. Tracey is a Cleveland native and one of the most sought-after business success coaches in North America. On any given day, when she isn't working with business owner clients, writing, recording a podcast, or running a leadership training class you can find her on a hike, doing yoga, or cooking with her kids and her husband with their dog, Rocky, right at their heels.

To Connect with Tracey:

www.TraceyWattsCirino.com

www.beyondcommonbusinesssecrets.com/BCSE

Tracey@TraceyWattsCirino.com

www.facebook.com/TraceyWattsCirino

www.instagram.com/traceywattscirino/

www.youtube.com/channel/UCSqLGOUTW6xB5vSypUc8dGQ

www.linkedin.com/in/traceywattscirino/

www.tiktok.com/@traceywattscirino

www.pinterest.com/beyondcommonwithtracey/

www.pinterest.com/TraceyWattsCirino/

www.clubhouse.com/@traceycirino

podcasts.apple.com/us/podcast/beyond-common-business-secrets/

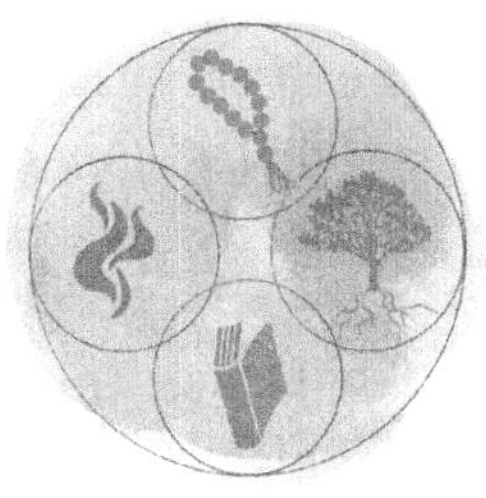

STAND IN THE WAVES

Brooke A. Conaway

"A dream is a wish your heart makes—no matter how your heart is grieving, if you keep on believing, the dream that you wish will come true."

~Cinderella

I was the girl who believed in that statement with all of my being. I wanted the Cinderella Fairytale more than anything. I wanted it all and when I met my future husband, I thought I found it. It felt like I met the man of my dreams, my Prince Charming, an aspiring dentist who was going to be in the military after dental school. I was swept away in a whirlwind of love bombing with compliments and admiration for me. I had never met anyone like him before and never thought anyone with his background would fall for me, a simple girl who believed in fairytales.

Soon the compliments ended, and the judgements began. I was fun loving and confident, but I had some insecurities, and those insecurities were used against me as I was reminded how I wasn't the one who carried three letters behind my name. Years continued like this. I would be given breadcrumbs, morsels of goodness and strung along with consistent inconsistency which kept me in a perpetual state of confusion, but at the same time hopeful that if I was just "perfect" or "better," supported his career, followed his dreams that things would go back to the way they used to be.

We had a rich man's family, one girl, one boy and in July of 2017, my son was just shy of his 1st birthday when I found some news about my marriage. I had a decision to make, do I stay, or do I go? I felt lost and didn't know where to even begin. I went to Google and searched for something as simple as the word divorce. I stumbled upon a Podcast with that exact title, "Should I stay, or should I go?" It was a sign. I dove into Kate Anthony's Divorce Survival Guide Podcasts, followed her workshops and joined her support group. There was a whole world of women out there with the same fears and anxieties as I had. I chose to do the work and I wanted to save my marriage. I could not picture my son not ever knowing what it would be like to have his mom and dad in the same household. I grew up in a home where my parents had been happily married for over 40 years. It wasn't perfect, but they loved each other, worked through life's problems and those tough values were instilled in me. My parents were a great example. I had to make my marriage work. I had to see it succeed, I couldn't let my fairytale fail.

My husband and I had been in couple's therapy on and off since the beginning of our marriage, but this time I wanted to try individual therapy and that was the key to true growth and healing for me. I was honestly hopeful that this would finally work, and I walked into my new therapist's office and profoundly stated to her, "save my marriage." Our individual work went on for about a year until a shift happened for me and my belief system started to become altered. There was not much change in my husband with his individual work, only accusations against my therapist as being biased. I was given tools to educate myself on personalities on relationships and family dynamics. Two pivotal moments that helped me make my decision were when I read the book, *The Gaslight Effect* by Dr. Robin Stern and I chose to embrace the theory that raising children in two happy homes and seeing their mother even if it was half of the time in a healthy loving relationship was better than giving them one home filled with fears and anxiety. That was an extremely hard pill to swallow and a theory that completely contradicted everything I had ever known. However, I asked myself what example was I teaching my children? I needed to break that generational stigma for me, my children and generations to come. I never wanted my daughter to feel as trapped or scared or unloved or worthless as I felt. I never wanted my son as a man to feel that he could have a part in a woman ever feeling that way. I never wanted either of my children to think that it was ok or acceptable to have any of those feelings in a relationship.

I'll never forget the moment I sat on the front step of my lakeside house, the home I had always wanted in a great neighborhood, yet on the inside I felt completely alone. I knew I had to leave and I vowed to myself that I would not be silenced by my fears any longer and tell my story, if I could give just one woman hope in the face of such despair it would all be worth it. I sat there as the PTO President, coach, volunteer, and Pinterest stay-at-home mom, who also worked in our dental practice, with her own small crafting and design business on the side. I did it all. I was a doctor's wife and married to "my Prince." From the outside looking in we had everything. No one enters into marriage thinking it is going to end. I never saw myself as a single mom with two kids and I never saw myself having to move again, especially after having seven moves in less than ten years with the military. Yet there I was on the step of what was to be my forever home knowing I had to leave.

What gave me that power inside? As a teenager I had to go through some tough experiences that most do not and I hope never will. I had to learn at a young age about redemption, it was a spark that was ignited in me that may have been dulled at times, but never able to be put out. I stood for my family and now I had to stand in the waves for my children and the life I knew I deserved. I had to show them that you can find the shift and the power within yourself to take that scary leap of faith into the darkness of the unknown to come out stronger on the other side of the storm. Because the fear of the unknown was the scariest part. I had to trust myself, trust my gut, trust the signs from my spirit guides and know that I would be protected.

I no longer wanted to cry on the kitchen floor taking video diaries of the aftermath of arguments, I no longer wanted to lock myself in closets or bedrooms to get away and I no longer wanted to run to my car when I had nowhere else to go. At one of my lowest moments, I was seven months pregnant with my daughter, a long way from family and home, and I didn't know where to go. I put the dog in the car and I ran. I ran until I got to a Walmart parking lot where I cried uncontrollably to my unborn baby, apologizing to her because I knew she could feel her mother's pain, stress and fears. I thought the worst was going to be over when I filed for divorce and I never imagined how bad it really could get, how much my children would see, or how much of a financial burden I would be faced with. Nothing could prepare me, but I did it, I survived. At times I felt like I was drowning, but I stood in the waves for my children.

During the separation, from 2019 and through Covid 2020, we shared our marital home at separate times to keep the kids from shuffling back and forth until the divorce was finalized. We only had access to the house during our parental time with the children. However, we lived behind closed doors in an awful situation and one I'm ashamed to have lived through with my children. We were on constant video phone recordings during interactions, we kept our bedroom doors locked when we were away, and separate food was labeled to the point that lines were drawn on the of milk containers. One day we only had a small frying pan to cook with and my daughter asked how we were going to eat our spaghetti, I told her I'd boil batches with what we had. We went from a traditional family home with two parents to a lost sense of safety and security. So, for a year and a half the three of us were all packed into one room and I slept on the bottom bunk of my daughter's bed to try and help them sleep at night.

What did I do to prepare myself? I continued along my educational journey with support groups, my therapist, books and I turned to music, exercise, a women's boot camp, family and friends. I was going through the most important battle of my life. Divorce doesn't have to be a battle and I didn't want it to be, but it was my reality. I needed a release, an outlet from the stress to lower the fight or flight cortisol that consumed my body. Almost every morning I would walk in the neighborhood I was leaving and the first song on my playlist was Rachel Patten's, "Fight song," followed by Lizzo's "Good as Hell." It's all about balance, right? I had constant struggles of whether or not I was doing the right thing for my family, but one morning while volunteering at my daughter's kindergarten during their walk-a-thon, her friends and the kids I had coached marched proudly around the halls flexing their little muscles to the "Fight song" on repeat. It was another sign. Their innocent faces gave me the strength to stay grounded in the waves and be that example that moms can do tough things.

Along with the emotional preparation, I needed to be ok with not being ok. I needed to use my voice to ask for help. The more I opened up to the people around me of the silent battle I was fighting, I felt less alone and realized others were children of divorce or had stories of their own. When I was in the thick of things, family, friends, friends of friends, neighbors and people I had met for the first time all showed up in droves. It was a surreal experience while going through it. I often thought, was this my reality? Was it that bad that people dropped everything for me and my two children? I had an amazing amount of support through this entire process and I'm forever grateful for the people who shared their personal experiences with me, the friendships that were made and the abundance of love and compassion that was shown in support of my decision and their help in getting me out of the scariest position I had ever been faced with in my life.

During the separation process I had to find income. I didn't control the finances and I had no idea where I was going to get the money to leave. I hadn't had a real nine-to-five in eight years because I stayed home to raise my babies. I reached out to everyone I knew, consulted with friends, and applied online for anything. A teaching opportunity at a private school presented itself. I could start work part time and then move into a better full-time position where I would gain experience and then I could pursue a stable career. I loved the job because I felt like a mom to my students and it reminded me of my volunteer experience. However, being away from my own children and working put a strain on my daughter. One day she asked me when I was going to be a "normal mommy" again. The wind was taken from me with that one innocent statement. She said she wanted to know when I was going to be home again with them, like I was before. It was one of those moments where I felt like I failed as a mother. I wasn't there for my children the way I always had been before, but I had no other choice. This was our new normal and I had to start teaching my children that families are designed differently and can be built in many ways. I found myself having to give a lot, and I mean a lot, of hard and difficult conversations to explain to my children the process of divorce. I ordered books for them and two copies of the same parenting book for their father so that we could be on the same page. I wrote a note inside and left it by his locked bedroom door only to find it discarded back to me. Divorce conversations with my children were the worst and by far the hardest part of the process. They still are and I honestly have not stopped having to give them. One's life never prepares you for those tasks, but all you can do is your best when you are faced with every difficult situation.

I felt like I was on the right career path to my goals, but then another job opportunity presented itself. I didn't see myself making this change, but I made it because it felt like another sign. I know my uncle who had passed saw how much I was struggling, and he helped make this position available with a company he had played a key role in to help keep me moving forward on the right path. If I hadn't made the move my financial security would have been altered when Covid hit and I would have lost my private teaching position. There was an angel watching over me and one of those moments that I had to trust the process.

I had a goal, to provide a safe and stable home environment for my children. I had to continuously put myself through some big waves and scary situations where I didn't know how it was going to work out. I had to take new paths, stay graceful and make decisions on my own, trusting that my internal guide would protect me and point me in the right direction, sending me signs along the way. I'm okay with where I'm at. I can't have it all at one time. The success has come in the small steps along the way. Every decision carries the weight of three lives and I'm carrying that weight by myself. There is only so much one person can take at one time. Everything comes in seasons and at certain moments I needed to pause and just breathe and that's okay. I needed to remind myself that it was okay for me to take that pause, take that breath, and tell myself I did a good job, I made it happen. My goal wasn't to come out of divorce and be a millionaire, my goal was to get out and give my kids a safe and secure home. I wanted to show them that another way is possible and that even a regular softball and soccer mom can do hard things and that hard things aren't suffering.

In the summer of 2020, my divorce wasn't final, but I needed to continue to prepare for my children and find us a home. Litigation was still alive and active; the divorce papers weren't signed, and we hadn't been seen before a judge. Yet, the perfect house presented itself after months of looking and I took a leap of faith and made an offer over asking price. The emotional waves were coming in hard and strong; I had no money and no guarantee of how things were going to end. I sat on the beach in a panic writing a letter of plea to the sellers to accept my offer and give my children and I that new beginning in their home. Then the rain showers came, but the skies parted, and rainbows appeared over the ocean as I was given another sign and the news that the perfect little house with the white front porch was mine. Rainbows are a sign from my mom-mom, whose name my daughter shares. She has sent them at significant times after she was born, like during her surgery when she was just 49 days old, her 1st birthday and at other times of despair when I was struggling or needed guidance and reassurance from above. I could feel the stress melting from my shoulders as I sat in my beach chair, smelling the salt air with the waves just a sound in the distance. I was surrounded by my family and friends at our happy place and I was grateful to have found the strength to stand in waves and shine in the darkness. I knew at that moment I was embarking on my new beginning and I was home.

Today, I wake up with a purpose. I sit with integrity. I trust in the light. And, most importantly, I now trust in myself. Above all I am grateful. Grateful for my beautiful children who received all the best from me, grateful for the life lessons in my marriage, grateful for the opportunities to grow and grateful for the person I get to be today, and I am looking forward to the next chapter. I am still that simple girl who believes in Cinderella, only this time I am a single mom who's weathered a great storm and I learned if I want my dreams to come true, I'm doing it on my own and we'll leave Prince Charming for the movies.

ABOUT BROOKE A. CONAWAY

Brooke's main mission has been to focus on being the best mom to her two young children. Her family devotion and love of the ocean, namely the Jersey shore, Exit 6 to be exact, is where she has spent her summers to rejuvenate her motivation to keep her and her family physically and emotionally healthy while riding through the waves of a difficult divorce. Brooke has a business degree in Hospitality Management from Stockton University where she then went on to work in corporate America prior to starting her family. Like a lot of women, she set her goals aside to support her husband's career and accompanied him in his military travels. She dove into her family, volunteered and coached as a stay-at-home mom and her children, along with her dog Cola, have brought her the greatest of life's joys. During her time at home, she created her own online crafting and design business, Old Blue Home Decor, but that too was put to the side after her son had a difficult first year of life in and out of Children's Hospital of Philadelphia. Her separation shortly began after then and she hasn't picked up a glue gun to create for her clients since. Her love of volunteering and crafting would revive who she was before this trying time in her life and she will get back to it one day after the waves have settled. Now she finds empowerment from family and friends to focus on self-motivation and self-healing. Through it all, she remained true to herself and knew that positivity and keeping life fun would be essential in preventing hard times from changing from who she is. In her growth, Brooke has come to recognize that it's important for her to help other women find their strength to #StandInTheWaves and she hopes that her story will resonate with others to remember to fight their fears and Shine through the darkness.

Scan this QR code to connect with Brooke on her platforms

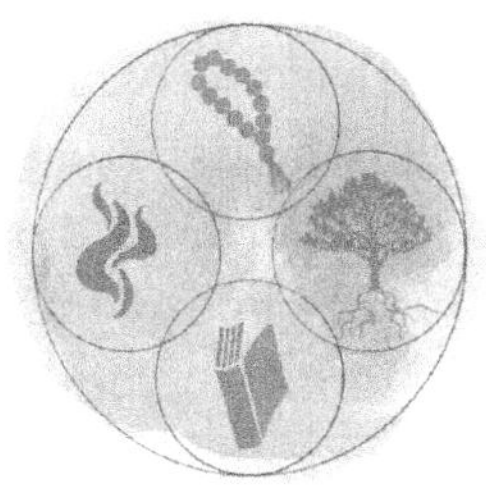

CHOOSING GRACE

Sarah Grafton

When I was seven my dad left us. I sat at the bottom of the stairs while he and my mom argued. He walked down with his brown weathered suitcase in one hand and his car keys in the other. I could see he was angry. I remember looking up at him, crying, begging him to stay. In anger all he said was it was my mother's fault and he walked out the garage door. That moment has never left me.

Thirty years later and I couldn't tell you what they argued about that night or even how many days he was gone, but in the pit of my stomach I still get this deep sense of fear when I think about it. At seven you don't understand the intricacies of an adult relationship, that the threat of leaving can be used as a tool or even that sometimes people say things they don't mean. I thought he was leaving our family behind. I thought he was leaving me behind. He came back a few days later, but I was left with this fear that someone I loved could leave me.

In the moment that my father walked out the door I learned that family units are capable of breaking. Prior to that day, I thought my family was like every fairytale story I had ever read. My parents met, fell in love, had three children and were living their happily ever after. We had everything we could have wanted. We had dinners together around the table, dancing in the kitchen, our parents cheering on the sidelines during our soccer games, church on Sundays and even good-night kisses from both mom and dad each night. It's funny to think of the picture-perfect family we all develop in our minds as children. No one tells us the stories of strength or brokenness you enter a marriage with. No one tells their kids that the foundation they built their love on could use some mending.

Something changed in me the day my dad left. I never wanted anyone to feel what I felt. I felt alone, I felt scared, I felt helpless and worst of all I felt like I was not enough to keep him from leaving. I never wanted to feel that way again. In fact, I never wanted anyone to feel that way. From that day forward I was always going to be more than enough. I was going to build others around me up to make sure they were enough too.

When you are young you don't learn that validation comes from within. You learn that value comes from achievements, from those little blue ribbons, the trophies, the gold stars or the high marks on a report card. So, it was simple really, I was going to earn love, I was going to achieve. I was going to win every award, get every A, and raise all the trophies, because if I did no one would want to leave me. Or so I thought.

So, I did just that. I became an overachiever in every sense of the word for the next twenty years. You name it, the dean's list, homecoming queen, Varsity letters, scholarships, I brought them all home. When I look back on my childhood, I am grateful for so many blessings, but it was exhausting for a child to always feel like she had to succeed to be loved.

Listen, fifty percent of marriages end in divorce. Every child of those marriages is affected differently. My parents loved me unconditionally. They were good humans who loved their children, but when their marriage didn't work, my seven-year-old self-assumed their three children should be enough to save it.

We weren't. What I didn't realize at seven was having two happy healthy homes with parents who loved me was better than my parents staying in an unhealthy marriage.

Here is where my story is a little different. If you're lucky, and old enough to comprehend what is happening between your parents, you can choose to let it affect you negatively or positively. I chose the latter. I let the hard times make me stronger. I tried to see the positive in them being apart. I was still sad and angry, but I was choosing a positive outlook. I began to appreciate the small things like rides to basketball in the car with my dad on weeknights. I loved to help people. I began to serve others and help lift others through hard times.

The divorce roller coaster ride didn't stop there for me. The next few years were a little awkward. I took on some untraditional roles. I became my mother's best friend. She confided in me, cried on my shoulder, and I stepped up around the house to get things done. As the oldest, I felt like it was my responsibility to take care of my brothers when we had weekends back and forth, whether they liked it or not. I was a mother figure, especially to my baby brother who was only seven when my parents divorced. I developed this sense of empathy for everyone around me. Over the years, I never stopped achieving at school or in sports. Maybe subconsciously I hoped that would fix things. Imagine trying to piece your grandmother's china plate together with scotch tape. I was using the wrong binder, it was helpful, but it was not solving the issues and it was not going to last. What I now know as grace was ultimately what pieced my family back together.

Over the next five years my parents both dated and raised the three of us as single parents. Their time apart helped them both grow into the individuals they were destined to be. A huge part of that transformation was each of them spending more time in their faith and really developing a personal relationship with God. My mom became this independent, strong, and beautiful woman who finally realized she was capable of great things. She also began to appreciate what my father brought to the relationship. The time apart from my mother allowed my father to see all that my mother brought to his life and our family. My father changed his preconceived notions of the way relationships should be and he grew to respect my mom as his partner.

Here is what they don't tell you in therapy. Why would they? There would be less to talk about. Don't get me wrong, I am a strong proponent of therapy, but when you've been hurt by someone one way you can truly heal and move forward is by practicing grace. I am convinced it will never be by understanding. You will not wake up one day and suddenly rationalize the reason your ex-partner hurt you and the pain will go away. I don't have any friends who suddenly thought, "now I understand why they cheated on me or why they left me?" Do you? You must choose grace. My father and mother decided to give each other grace for the mistakes they made in the past and for their differences moving forward. Five years after my parents divorced, they remarried.

At the time I didn't understand why they divorced in the first place, so at seventeen it was even harder to comprehend how life was bringing them back together.

This time things were different, and everyone could see that. They were partners. Their foundation was strong. They were partners when it came to parenting, in decision making, in big ways and small. If my mom washed, my dad dried. They met in the middle and to this day they have an incredibly healthy relationship. They love each other for who they are not who they hope the other will become. They just celebrated twenty years and have only grown more in love with every passing year. They are a good example to their children, grandchildren and others. They show that with a little elbow grease and a whole lot of grace marriage can be a beautiful thing. I learned a lot from my parents' divorce. I think being a child of divorce you learn through experience what to do and what not to do as a parent going through a divorce.

Fast-forward to exactly ten years after their divorce, at the age of twenty-two when I got married. I met Ben my Senior year of college. He was everything I wasn't, in the best ways. He was calm, cool and careless. He was laid-back and most importantly he had no fear of the future. He was four years into his college experience and had no plans to finish anytime soon. He was the typical guy you find working at a Surf Shop and that he did, right on the beach. He surfed and partied through college. He was just happy and didn't let the weight of the world or other's opinions affect his life. As you now know, I on the other hand, was almost never laid back or relaxed. I was busy achieving, earning everyone's love, and never very far from my planner, which was marked up with highlighter and post-it notes. My life was all planned out. My life revolved around this question, How was I going to:

- Build My Family Business
- Run for Office
- Write a NY Times Best Seller
- Get Married
- Start the Perfect Family
- Accomplish all my goals and dreams
- All before I turned forty?

I was still chasing after the next accomplishment. Ben and I met right before my graduation, and he embodied the opposite of everything I feared. He was an escape from the pressure of the constant chase of achievement and all my responsibilities. For the first time in my life, I was spontaneous, and by that, I mean I did the most spontaneous thing one could do. We dated 6 months and then we eloped. Go big or go home, right?

Ben and I just fell into the married life. We worked, we bought a house, we had a dog, we had two boys of our own all in three years. We let the world tell us what marriage was meant to be like. We didn't put up any boundaries to protect our family. We were busy, so busy that we didn't really notice that there was no relationship between the two of us. In fact, if we took a closer look, we would probably have found out earlier that we were very different in almost every way. Ultimately, we were co-parenting. It was my worst nightmare. I was in an unhappy marriage.

To his credit it couldn't have been a very fun lifestyle for a surfer. He was landlocked. He was living with a planner, a goal setter, a woman who had big dreams. Everything he thought was a fun idea I didn't want to do because in my mind we had responsibilities. I was trying to raise the perfect family. I had pulled together this idea of perfect from what I saw on television and what I read in books. I was wound so tight because I didn't want to fail.

We were so young, and we didn't have the skill set or knowledge needed make a marriage work. Personally I'll admit that I was quick to give up because I stubbornly expected love to be like the fairytales I was raised on. I expected butterflies, dancing in the rain, maybe an impromptu musical number. I think there may be a whole generation of people who think love just falls into place like the fairytales we were raised on. Who were we kidding? I was far from the damsel in distress. The next few months were a whirlwind of avoidance, regrets, hope and fear. We decided to divorce.

Having lived through a divorce as a child I knew everything I did and didn't want to do when it came to my children. We decided the most important decision we were going to make in the process of the divorce and after wasn't for ourselves, it was for our children. We were choosing to get the divorce and we were responsible for our choices, not our children. They deserved two parents who loved them, gave them happy homes and who loved and supported each other. We were both capable of not being selfish when it came to our children. Yes, ultimately, getting a divorce was a decision made for us, but we were going to put our children's mental, physical and emotional health first in the process. I agree with so many of you who think you must put yourself first when it comes to divorce, but I think you are naïve if you don't realize how much all your choices affect your children and family during the process.

Looking back, putting the boys first was the best decision we ever made. That decision ultimately led to grace. We gave each other grace. When we disagreed, we gave grace. When we were frustrated, we gave grace. When we were lost, we gave grace. We both knew that by giving grace to each other we ultimately were giving the gift of love and childhood to our children. We showed grace in little ways like making it a priority to always verbally support each other in front of the boys. We never put the other down or talked poorly about their choices. We lifted the other up. If I couldn't fix one of their toys, I would say things like, "I bet Daddy can fix it, he can fix anything!" I wanted them to see their Daddy through the eyes of a child. I wanted them to build a good relationship with their father. I knew how important that relationship was for them in so many ways. He did the same for me. He always tried to be positive. We talked positively about who the other chose to date as well and ultimately bring into the family.

My family grew up in the church and the best way I know to describe the action of Grace comes from my faith. The idea of God's Grace is that we as humans wake up each day and we make mistakes, we sin. It doesn't matter how big or little you Sin; in God's eyes all sins are equal. They are all marks on your slate that day. As a child I imagined each night, when I said my prayers and went to sleep, that God chose to forgive me. He wiped the slate clean and when I woke up the next morning, I was made new. Our sins from the past day were gone. Your slate is clean. Beautiful, flawless and clean.

"But if it is by grace, it is no longer on the basis of works; otherwise, grace would no longer be grace."

—Romans 11:6

I have spent the last eleven years practicing grace with others. My ex and I are very different people. The way we raise our boys is different, but we choose to give each other grace rather than understanding sometimes. I choose who I give grace to, and ultimately the price of grace has many times been my understanding or my control of a situation. In the long run, by showing grace, I recognize the positive impact it has had on my family, my relationship with my ex and my children. It has been worth it ten-fold.

My ex-husband and I are both in very happy relationships now and we continue to co-parent our children together with grace. I would be willing to bet that we both practice grace in our new marriages as well. We have been divorced almost ten years now and we have seen blessing on blessing because of the way we handled our divorce. My husband Jason loves me for who I am and what I bring to the table, not for what I have achieved.

Through practicing grace, I have been able to ultimately give my dad grace for walking through that door. More importantly, I realized that it was never my dad who I needed to be giving grace to. I needed to give myself grace. I was enough. I was Grace-FULL.

When I look back on my childhood, you know what I remember? I remember that I had everything I ever wanted, dinners together around the table, dancing in the kitchen, my parents cheering on the sidelines during my soccer games, church on Sundays and even good-night kisses from mom or dad each night. There may have been a few bumps along the way but I learned from them, they strengthened me and I became a better person for them.

I learned a lot as a child going through the process of divorce and as an adult going through a divorce with children. I decided that if I could help one family or one child of a divorce with my story that I needed to share it. The Grace-FULL way of navigating divorce was successful for me and I know with practice it can help others navigating their own divorce.

In 2020, during the pandemic, I started a group called the Fellowship of Women Leaders. This group is for all women who consider themselves a leader in any capacity of their life, whether it is in their career, at home, in their family, at church, etc. This group's mission is to create a safe space for women to build their foundation, strengthen their leadership skills and learn from one another.

For more of my story, how you can be GraceFULL in your divorce, or to learn more about the Fellowship of Women Leaders be sure to visit my website www.SarahGrafton.com. Follow me on Instagram @SarahGrafton

ABOUT SARAH GRAFTON

Sarah Grafton is a servant leader who believes her purpose in life is to help others. She is a #1 International best-selling author, speaker, entrepreneur, philanthropist, and community organizer. Sarah launched her career at Grafton Wealth Management where she and her family team have a heart for the local community and serving those in need. Over the last decade she has worked together with the community to raise millions of dollars for non-profit organizations. She has received many accolades for her work including being named Woman of the Year by Orlando Magazine, Orlando Business Journals 40 under 40 recipient at 29 years old and awarded the United States Service Award by both President Barak Obama and President Donald Trump.

Sarah's passion for helping others improve their lives through a positive outlook and more specifically by practicing grace has become her mission in all aspects of her life. She has been able to help many families navigate divorce and co-parenting successfully through sharing her own personal experiences as not only a child of divorce but a divorcee herself.

To learn more about Sarah and the GraceFULL divorce method please visit her website at www.SarahGrafton.com, where you can find her books, blog and inspirational products. Follow her on Instagram at @SarahGrafton.

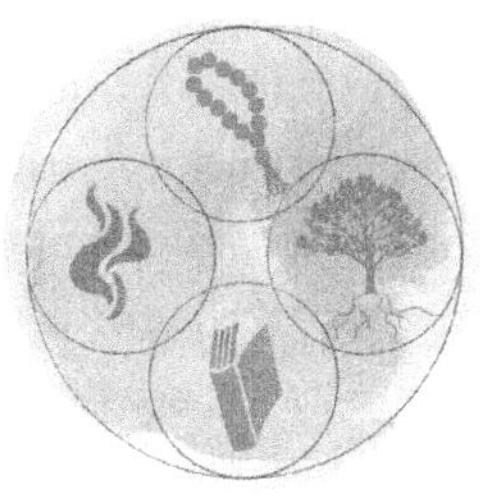

THE OTHER SIDE

Susan E. Grubb, LPC

This story is one of strength and risk taking. It's a story of healing, of reaching a place where I could process some incredibly challenging events in my life. Even though there is still a portion of my life that I would like to heal, I have dedicated this portion of my life to helping other people through the healing process. I took what happened to me and made it my life's purpose to help others. I believe that it is possible to heal from trauma and get to the other side.

My story really begins in the 1990s. Since childhood, I have dealt with some mild depression and undiagnosed Attention Deficit Disorder, but it became more significant in the late 1990s. I grew up in State College, Pennsylvania and moved to Southcentral Pennsylvania in 1984. In 1987, I married a man that I met through a coworker. We settled in Elizabethtown, Pennsylvania and had two children, a daughter in 1988 and a son in 1992. At various points along the way, we realized that we were not the right fit for each other and we decided to part ways in 1995. We were managing the best we could after the divorce, but unfortunately when it came to custody and parenting issues, there were intense challenges.

I was going through the pain of a failed marriage and trying to manage the dismantling of our family unit as we knew it. It was during this painful period of my life that my mother became an amazing confidant and support system for me. She was a strong, independent woman. She was an adventurous risk taker. When she was in her 40s, she left her teaching career and obtained an MBA. On September 27, 1997, my mother drowned, along with a family friend, when she and my father went on vacation to Marco Island, Florida. I will never forget the shock and horror of receiving the phone call that my mother was dead. I was 37 and my mother was 60. I never expected to lose her so young. Here I was, already grieving the loss of my family unit and now I had to deal with the unexpected loss of a parent. My father was dealing with his own loss and his own grief. This meant that he was unable to support me while going through his own journey. I felt that I was on my own.

I felt myself sinking low in my depression. My resilience to deal with contentious custody and parenting issues was low. I found myself wishing that I was dead and felt overwhelmed. During this time, my relationship with my daughter struggled. I take 100 percent of the responsibility for that because I feel I wasn't the mother that she needed. Instead, she saw my anger regarding the custody and divorce issues. Eventually, our mother-daughter relationship came to an end. I am not proud of it, but I bowed to defeat and stopped fighting for her after more than five years of struggle. At the time, I thought that I was doing the best thing for her, but I never stopped loving her.

I was struggling to survive. I was able to work and care for my son, but I felt like I was going through the motions. I tried therapy several times but left because I didn't feel heard. I didn't know if I wanted to go on with life. My son became my lifeline, however. I knew that killing myself would do irreparable harm to him and perhaps to my daughter too. I also didn't want my father and my brother or sister to have to deal with another loss, especially one that would be by my own hand. My Christian faith was also a factor in my deciding to stick around and hope that things would get better. I reached a point where I really doubted that I would ever be happy again and I felt that I was simply putting in the time. It was an excruciating number of years, which culminated when my father died on December 13, 2007.

I did grieve when my father died. This also opened up my emotions allowing me to truly grieve the death of my mother. For years, I had remained somewhat numb to her death, feeling perhaps that if I gave myself permission to truly grieve, I would fall apart. I remember going to the beach with my son for Easter after my father's death and sitting on a beach alone at sunrise. I released a flood of tears for both my father and my mother. The tears flowed not only for the loss, but also for my daughter and for myself.

My father's death represented a pivotal awakening for me and how I was living, or not living, life. At the age of 47, I was the oldest member of my family now. I knew that I needed to find a way to be happy, process my grief, and go through the forgiveness process regarding my relationship with my daughter and the custody issues. I also needed to forgive myself. I realized that I was harboring a lot of anger and resentment and that it was a significant contributor to my own depression. I also didn't want to be a burden to my son, who by now was entering high school. I had a choice to make, I could either go along with my anger and depression and just exist or I could face the painful and challenging task of facing myself and perhaps begin to find some happiness in life.

I began to see a therapist who walked me through this process. I had been in therapy before, but either I didn't make a connection with my therapist or I wasn't willing to be honest with myself. I also felt that therapists didn't really understand what I had experienced with my daughter. This was a lonely situation, in that I didn't know anyone else who had experienced the same thing. My therapist conveyed that he understood my pain and viewed me as a valuable person. Research has shown that one of the most significant healing factors in therapy is not necessarily the theoretical approach to therapy, but the relationship between the therapist and the client. It was not an easy process, and there were times that I left his office in tears and didn't want to go back. That is okay and is actually normal for therapy. Not only did he help me process the events of the past 12 years, but he also helped me to process some shame from my childhood. He was the one who noticed that I had undiagnosed ADD. This shed a lot of light on my childhood behaviors, such as being disorganized, not performing to my potential, and being verbally impulsive and interrupting people. I had spent much of my life feeling that I was not good enough and that I was flawed. In short, I felt a sense of shame. Receiving this diagnosis helped me to understand that my character was not flawed and there were reasons behind my perceived shortcomings. It was not an excuse and it didn't absolve me of responsibility for myself, but it helped me to rewrite my narrative on who I was and allowed me to release the shame.

To backtrack, about six years before I began my therapy journey, I had started to think about becoming a mental health therapist. This was born partly out of my frustration at finding a therapist who I felt heard and understood me. For various reasons, I didn't pursue it. My son was in elementary school and needed me home in the evenings and I didn't want to work full time, go to school, and be a parent. I was also still locked in my own pain. As I began to see healing in my therapy process, I began to revisit the idea of becoming a therapist. From my own therapy process, I learned that I could use parts of my journey as strengths in my life and my calling was renewed to help people. I felt a sense of hope and optimism about my future, something that I could not have said prior to starting the therapy process in 2008.

Another motivation was the fact that, in two years, my son would be graduating from high school and leaving for college. As

I mentioned earlier, he was my reason for living during the worst of my times. When he left for college, I would be on my own and have a significant adjustment. I didn't want him to worry about how I would do when he left. I wanted to give him the gift of embarking on his adult journey unencumbered by worry about his mother. After some prayer and consultation with various people, I made the decision in 2009 to leave my 20-plus year journalism career and start graduate school. My son was still a junior in high school at the time. I had timed it so that I would graduate and begin my new career as he was leaving for college. I was 48.

I took an intense course load and achieved my Master's degree in professional counseling from Liberty University in August 2011, the same week that my son left for college. I graduated with highest distinction with a 4.0 GPA, quite a change from the less than stellar performance in my earlier years of school. I continued my growth during this time by remaining in therapy and doing some deep introspection as I completed my course work. After graduating at the age of 50, I worked as a mobile therapist and behavioral specialist consultant in the community and schools with children. In 2015, I began working as an outpatient therapist with a large counseling agency. During this time, I became licensed and felt a sense of fulfillment. I was finally doing the work I envisioned when I went back to school in 2009. I worked with that agency for 5 ½ years and gained a lot of valuable experience. I continued to grow as a person, too.

In the summer of 2020, I made the decision to leave my agency and open a private practice close to home. I named my practice Hope's Journey Counseling Services, LLC. The name was intentional to reflect that I believe there is hope no matter what has happened to a person. I also believe that healing is a journey and one that I, as a therapist, am honored and privileged to join in. I feel fulfilled because I have the opportunity to do for others what someone did for me.

I also feel that I have turned out to be an inspiration and positive role model for my son. He is very vocal about the positive impact my healing journey has had on him and on his motivation and determination to work hard to achieve one's goals.

These are my son's words: "As strong as my mother was during her healing process, there is only so much one can do to hide their pain. Her resilience and determination to overcome her grief and not let it consume her has been very inspiring to watch. I have learned a lot from watching her go through her journey, but the most important takeaway is that you just have to keep moving. No matter how difficult it may seem, no matter how much you don't want to, as long as you keep pushing forward, you will eventually get to the other side, and you will be a stronger person because of it. This is a lesson that I have applied to my own life countless times (both personally and professionally), and, so far, it has never let me down."

If I look back to who I was before the events and traumas leading up to my own journey of healing, I am happier with who I am now. No, I would not have gone through the traumas and losses by choice. But I also believe that, had I not experienced them, I would not have been willing to eventually go to the deepest parts of myself and learn to love myself. I certainly would not have been in the position to open my own therapy practice at age 60 and feel a sense of mastery over my professional and personal life had it not been for my own journey through adverse life experiences. I have learned that I am a strong person who is resilient and a survivor. I feel a sense of optimism about my future. I sincerely desire to help others achieve this same sense of hope and healing.

ABOUT SUSAN E. GRUBB, LPC

Susan E. Grubb, LPC is a licensed professional counselor in Elizabethtown, Pennsylvania who has used her own story of strength and healing to help other people heal from their own hurts and traumas. She is the owner of Hope's Journey Counseling Services, LLC, and has a decade of experience helping people journey through life's difficulties. She is particularly passionate about helping women of all ages work through anxiety, depression, trauma, grief, parenting, and life transition issues. Susan helps clients identify beliefs that are keeping them stuck and to develop thought patterns and behaviors to move toward a happier and more fulfilling life. Underlying her therapeutic work is a person-centered approach, where she recognizes that the relationship between the therapist and client is key. She views herself and clients as partners as they develop the path toward healing and fuller functioning.

Susan graduated with high distinction from Liberty University in 2011 with a Master of Arts degree in professional counseling. Prior to that, she worked as a newspaper reporter for more than 20 years. In her free time, she enjoys spending time with family and keeping up with an assortment of household pets.

More information about Susan can be found at:
www.hopesjourneycounselingservices.com

Susan can be reached by emailing her at:
susangrubb@hopesjourneycounselingservices.com

Her business Facebook page is:
www.facebook.com/hopesjourneycounselingservicesllc/

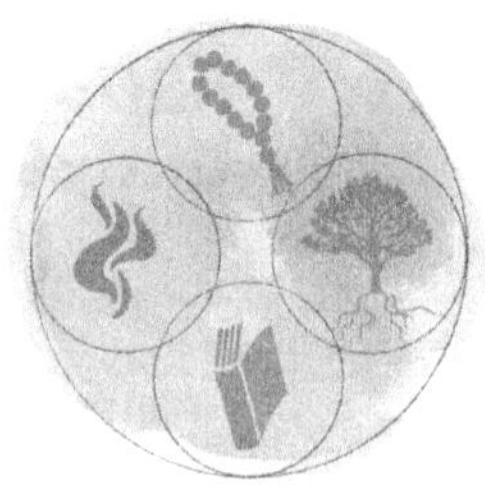

BECOMING MY OWN HERO

Gaby Juergens

That morning it all seemed so routine, but unbeknownst to me, it would end up being a morning that I would replay repeatedly in my mind over a 78 hour period. James had been acting differently, I had credited his recent behavior with problems at work involving a malpractice case against his firm. Of course, I would later learn that work wasn't the issue.

That morning, I made breakfast for my husband and watched him eat it as I drank my coffee. He had the news on, which he seemed intent on listening to rather than indulge in small talk. When he was done, I picked up his breakfast plates, took them to the sink, and walked with him to the front door as I always did.

Funny, the things that are indelibly carved into your mind during certain events in your life. They say everyone remembers where they were, maybe even what they wore, when they heard the news of the towers in NYC. I can still see in my mind's eye exactly what he was wearing that morning. He wore black slacks and a crisp, white dress shirt that I'd ironed that morning like I had always done. It was October and fall coolness was breezing through the door.

"I'll pick you up at the airport and then we'll go pick up the dogs at the boarder." He told me, his eyes holding mine intently. "Have a great trip."

I remember I nodded, and he leaned forward to give me a light brush of a kiss. He pulled back and his eyes held mine for just a moment. I smiled and said, "drive safe, I'll text you when I get in."

He nodded and then I watched him climb into his big SUV, the family car, the one we had used to drive our only son to college. I watched it pull away and I waved from the door.

He didn't.

That was the last time I would see my husband for 19 months. The next time would be in divorce court two weeks after returning from fighting stage 3 breast cancer.

My neighbor drove me to the airport that day. I boarded the flight to Dallas, blind to what was going on back home. What was going on back home was that the minute I had driven away, my husband had circled back to the house. He had not gone to work. He'd waited for me to leave, entered the house and divested it of his things, clothing, chipped coffee mug, our family papers, our life contained in plastic file containers. They would be gone. Along with him. How did I know that he came back to the house that morning, that he had looked me in the eye and had known what he planned to do? Because a neighbor saw him return and thought it odd that he was home and placing things in his car trunk.

Funny, how you don't see the Mack truck heading towards your life until your right under it, a semblance of roadkill, but you aren't dead. Not yet, you just feel dead. First you must go through the gauntlet of trauma that accompanies what is the disrobing of a life you thought you could count on. My husband was everything and he would never harm a hair on my head. This I believed with all my heart.

I came home from Dallas to a helter-skelter of empty hangers all over the floor. Gone were the foot lockers of college days kept in the closet, I found the rug pushed up against the bedroom wall. It was chaos. That was the moment when I fainted for the first time in my life. While coming to, I heard a wailing cry and realized it was coming from me.

At that time, I had been married for 26 years to the love of my life. He was the only speed dial on my phone, my best friend, the one person I would have gone in front of a firing squad for, professing that he would never hurt me. We had our ups and downs; how else do you grow? But we were a team and I believed him to be a man of honor and one that would always take the harder right than the easier left. I married my Hero.

And me, well, I gave all appearances of a strong and confident woman, speaking in front of groups, presenting my amazing family and I would have gone to the mattresses if anyone were to harm them. My family made me stronger, he made me stronger and now my world was forever changed, and that strength wasn't there, because I had been strong for them and not for myself.

I look back now, five years later, and I often say to friends, "you wouldn't recognize that girl from the one that sits in front of you. That girl was a frightened bird kicked out of the nest she had so carefully tended. The girl in front of you was forged by fire."

What would unfold as the days progressed from that horrible reveal, would trigger what my doctors would later describe as a PTSD like situation that would release massive amounts of Cortisol into my body. The first few weeks I remained in the house we'd rented. I was scared, embarrassed, alone, and had no explanation from my husband as to why he had done what he did, other than an almost rote statement of, "We are getting a divorce," offered when he deigned to answer the phone. The man on the end of the phone was no one I recognized. He was cold and I felt the fait accompli of his actions. This was a planned exodus, long before that farewell at the door that fateful morning.

Fast forward to what I would learn as the months waned on. Infidelity, I will never really know when it started and how a man, who railed his whole life against that very act in others and the breaking of marriage vows, had taken that step and lost his moral compass. I wasn't eating and the weight was just falling off me. Persistent vomiting became something that had me rushing in the night to the bathroom and by this point it was bile. Sleep was something I would only remember as pre-abandonment, which is how I came to view my life at that point.

Friends rallied and drove to my side to see me through those first days and weeks. One said to me at first sight, "I now know what that phrase, a broken woman, looks like."

I was broken, but this nightmare wasn't over, it was just beginning. It became a snowball that seemed to continue to roll down the hillside like a landslide until it reached the next discovery. I found out that I had stage 3 breast cancer and it was aggressive. Even my personal doctor didn't doubt that the shock and stress of what I had just suffered, including the end of my marriage and how it had occurred in such a stealth manner, could have been a contributing factor to the cancer. What does it say about a situation when the word cancer does not resonate as much as divorce or "I don't love you anymore?"

Cancer. That dreaded word, filled with such unknowns. That diagnoses that would soon become what would fill my world. Would I fight it? Could I beat it?

Well, in those days I told myself I would fight it. But the thin, pale face in the bathroom mirror every morning taunted me with "why?" Understandably that was my depression talking.

I spent those long months with an aggressive battle of Chemo for 15 weeks along with another six weeks of daily radiation following two surgeries, one of them a mastectomy of my left breast where the cancer had been found. There were also several emergency room visits for infections. I was rail thin by this point, my large dark eyes looked out at me in the mirror with a haunted look I had to shake off in order to dress and smile and face a Chemo bay-again. I can still remember one morning seeing myself in the bathroom mirror, with my hair gone, all the milestones of a cancer fight, it was expected, but you are never really prepared. It wasn't vanity, it was just one more thing out of my control. There was never any real idea if this was going to be a fight I would win. Fear was a constant companion, like a cloak, I hated it, but it had become so familiar it somehow kept me moving forward. To this day I can remember sitting on a bench outside the hospital waiting for an Uber and staring up at the sky and marveling at what my life had become and there was always the why that plagued me. Along the way, during treatment, I learned I would only have one more year of health insurance. I was missing an all-important extra year in my married time that would have allowed me to keep all my benefits. More uncertainty in an uncertain new world.

But I would be remiss if I didn't mention that no matter how terrible the blow I experienced, all I had lost, it was replaced by an angelic man of such kindness and generosity of heart that if it weren't for him, I wouldn't be here today. I can never say thank you enough John.

The day I rang my bell the sound radiated as if heaven-sent. That door had closed, and I hoped to stay healthy.

So, I got my life back from cancer and from divorce. But this woman still wondered at how a person you shared a life with for decades, the kind where you finished each other's sentences, could change into a cold-hearted man determined to eradicate our collective history as a family from his life. So, I searched for answers and then, I found my answers.

I wasn't alone in this sliding door of horror I had just been through. I call it a sliding door because one minute you are going about your life, confident in the mutual love, looking forward to the years to come, and discussing memories of your child's experiences only you would know, and the next minute it's all gone. Who would he remember those life stories with now?

Vicki Stark and her book *Runaway Husbands* found me. And

in it, I discovered I wasn't alone. Thousands of women around the world were flotsam to this horrendous act by the one person they trusted. I'd soon join her private group where each story played out in a pattern as if each man had been given a playbook that they all followed. The stories were heartbreaking, cancer figured into many, the symptoms we went through of vomiting, shock, hair loss, and more.

What I read was my story replayed repeatedly. However, I was lucky in one respect, I didn't have children I had to hand over to the ex and the paramour. I wasn't left pregnant with a husband that was now devoid of any interest in his future offspring. I was discovering I wasn't alone in this nightmare. Vikki Stark, who had experienced her own Runaway Husband, had researched for answers and then wrote the book that saved so many of us scrambling to understand. This was no regular affair, divorce, or abandonment. This was different and its underpinnings were psychological.

I discovered a tribe of sisters I could cheer for as every day we moved closer to the end of this tunnel. The stories are so similar, but when I said that I was forged by fire, so were the rest of my fellow sisters. It didn't kill us. We fought through cancer, illness, depression, anxiety, anger, and fear of our future and how we would move forward. At 50, this wasn't what I thought my future would be, none of us did.

This book I am a part of is called *Women Who Shine. I beca*me one of those women and the light was from within. I discovered a strength I never imagined I possessed, and it showed up for me when I needed it most. I discovered I was a survivor in more ways than one. A Hero showed up and that hero was me.

When we share our stories, as difficult as it is to recall what is firmly in the past, I shared my story for those who are experiencing it right now, this was not a normal leaving and ending and there are men and women who share the same pain and story. I want you to understand what it took me two years to discover it will perhaps aid in moving you forward. So, you may feel like this chapter in your life, this bewilderment, this loss will end you, but it won't because you discover there is a stronger person that will become your hero—you.

So, all of us who have been marked by this experience should leave a path for others to understand where they're at in that moment, they too can overcome. I am still scared about the future, no lies, but I'm not that little bird cast out, that woke up in an ice-cold state that shook her very soul that morning after.

Every life has a beginning, middle and an end; sometimes the chapters get rewritten for the better.

This time I am holding the pen. You can too.

ABOUT GABY JUERGENS

Gaby Juergens is a licensed artist/designer/writer with her Homefront Girl® Brand. With a portfolio of over 10,000+ designs, Gaby's artwork has been licensed to Enesco, LLC and The Yankee Candle Company, to name a few, all with her trademark style and inspirational writing.

A cancer warrior, first battling stage 3 breast cancer in 2016-2017 and beating it. In late 2019 the cancer came calling again and Gaby has spent the better part of 2021 fighting but, that hasn't stopped her from moving forward with projects she is energized by, which include joining Philanthropist and humanitarian Mitzi Purdue in her Win This Fight campaign to stop Human Trafficking. She has spoken to women's groups on moving forward despite life's challenges and continues expanding and evolving with her brand, Homefront Girl®.

On cancer and being brave she has often been quoted, "I'm no hero, but I lived a lifetime among them." In 2020, during the Covid crisis, she put her time into hosting Homefront girl® The Podcast, interviewing Hollywood celebrities, documentarians, filmmakers, military spouses and women making a difference and telling their stories.

Follow Gaby on Instagram: @homefrontgirl
and @homefrontgirl_the_Podcast

Her website: www.Homefrontgirl.com

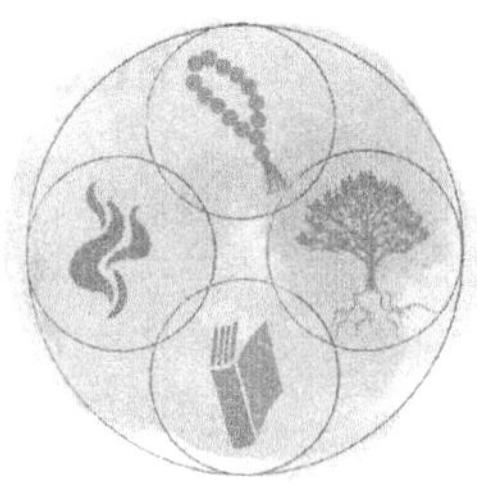

CLEARING THE PATH TO STAND UP AND SHINE

Ann Klossing

When I turned fifty, I embraced my age, not so much when I turned thirty, which I define as the messy thirties, followed by the fearful forties. Fifty and fabulous is my mantra, which will continue into the time I transition. There is something to be said to have fifty years of experience behind you. Fifty years of building blocks. Some of those blocks I built and fell from. Each time I fell, I dusted myself off and stood back up. How? Why? I don't know, but I did. It was a motion, that was all. Just stand. However, I remained in a fog every time I stood back up.

It wasn't until recently that I received a great epiphany while showering one morning. That is where all great epiphanies occur, in the shower, or sometimes on the latrine. Some people refer to epiphanies as an "Aha" moment. What sparked this great epiphany was a conversation with a new friend who is an attorney. The conversation sparked a memory when my divorce attorney fired me because I offended her with a very direct question. I thought I was quite pleasant in our conversation, direct but pleasant. She contacted me the following morning. I was fired because I stood up for my rights. Surprised, I took a step back to observe the situation. My husband begged me to hire her, a narcissistic move on his part, as this woman was the best friend of the attorney he hired, a woman whom I had consulted with on another matter, but never procured. Trumped by my husband, I was unable to retain the woman he hired. Skeptical of the "bestie" situation with the attorneys, I pushed feelings aside. This should work, wrong. With the sucker punch of being fired, I sought out a well-known, hardened attorney. He would gladly take the case, only to contact me two days later informing me he was over booked. I was silently devastated, frozen, unable to utter a word. He began to speak, informing me his partner agreed to take my case. The frozen devastation melted away. The Universe was working for me while I sat oblivious to its power, unaware and uneducated to the Laws of the Universe.

While recalling this memory, this story, the epiphany struck me. As I continued to replay the memory, I received the "Aha" moment that shot through my very core. As the water streamed over my body, memories washed through me, one after the other. Each memory contained the same theme. I reacted to the event, gave my power away, and collapsed. In time, I would stand back up while repeating the same reaction to each significant life event.

The suds of the shampoo ran down my face. The water cleansed away all of "it" revealing an ear-to-ear smile as the epiphany came to light. I damn near ran out of the house screaming, "I know what my agreement with God is!" After all, it was December, snowy, twenty degrees, and slightly windy in southwestern Wisconsin. I was so freaking happy to realize my agreement with God is to stand up for myself and SHINE!

Each life event made perfect sense. The memories streamed through my head like a deck of cards. As I dealt each card, the memory displayed on the gaming table. One by one each card lay before me: abuse by my grandfather, miscarriage, post-partum depression, major clinical depression, affair, divorce, narcissistic relationship, more clinical depression, loss of my father, second divorce, attachment, dark night of the soul. My deck was full. It was a complete deck of lack. Somehow, some way, I mustered up the courage to stand up to each event, face it, forgive it, and release it.

The water continued streaming over the top of my head. I remained smiling. Why? My card deck revealed lack, a losing hand. That display of cards was the old deck with a dealer who didn't understand the Laws of the Universe. As I continued rejoicing in my revelation, I grabbed a new deck of cards. I began to deal. The cards displayed before me: love of my life, happy family, lessons with a Reiki Master, more classes in self-development, discovering my purpose, discovering my gift from God, author, angels, God, and me. Yes, that one card with my face on it. I found myself. When I found myself, I found God, my truth, my true authentic self. I am smiling because I know I will continue to stand up. The difference is, back then I stood up and dusted off. Now I am standing up, speaking my truth, being my truth and shining!

What is an agreement with God? Agreements are one of the Laws of the Universe, The Law of Agreements. Before you were born, you had a meeting with your clan. Your clan is your soul family. You and your soul family lay out a preliminary grid for the lifetime you desire to be born into. You chose your parents, your siblings, your purpose and many numerous agreements. There is great planning that goes into each lifetime. Once the grid has been designed, your soul presents the grid to God. Both God and your soul review this grand plan, make changes and finalize the grid. God pats you on the back, gives you a hug and tells you to live joyously. Off you go to enter the Earth plane as this innocent baby, ready to breathe in life and live within the basic parameters of the grid.

Agreements may not make sense to a human. When I first learned of agreements during a meeting with a respected medium,

I was confused and irritated by what I was hearing. "What do you mean I agreed to be abused by my grandfather," I asked. Preposterous, appalling, outrageous, I thought to myself. Frankly, I was pissed. Thankfully, the medium knew I was not upset with her, just the news. The first half of my life, I spent with my fist in the air, or buried in the abyss of depression. Who was this person to tell me I agreed to be abused? Bullsh*t! My deceased grandfather came through in a second reading. Resistance surged through my veins. Who is my grandfather to come through this reading to give me advise! He abused me when I was four. I wanted nothing to do with him. How dare he come through and give me advise. I wanted to remain the victim, call him a bastard and any other descriptive flare I could think of.

Once I settled down, the practitioner explained how agreements work. In heaven there are no disagreements, no judgements, only love. The agreement is made in love, pure love. Some agreements are set in place to create a shift within the human during a particular lifetime and may not be pleasant experiences. My agreement with God was to stand up for myself, a reoccurring theme in each event in my life. My agreement with my grandfather remained the same, to stand up for myself. In this example, someone must be the victim, and someone must be the perpetrator. He chose the more difficult role, the role of perpetrator. I had to trade places with my grandfather to act as if I was the abuser. When I imagined myself as the abuser, I felt icky, dirty, guilty. It did not feel good at all. Being the victim was a much easier role to play. The act of abuse is unforgiveable. It is not the act that is important. It is the transpired reaction and the lessons learned by the event that are most important. I am not referring to the physical results as in the act of abuse. I am referring to soul growth. Although this event occurred when I was extremely young, the shift within me did not take place until I was fifty-one. Why did it take so long? I held onto "it." I held onto the memory, the event, and the role of victimhood.

What I experienced was synchronistic events in my life, similar in nature, that formed the reaction of victimhood created from other agreements with various people in my life. It was the compilation of many events I had stacked on top of one another to create the abyss of despair. Behind the despair, lie the agreement to stand up. Each person in my life played a role in an agreement while the soul of the other was rooting for me to shift. This act is what we as humans fail to see because we are in the world of the physical, the world of the ego. We judge, we accuse, we hurt, we blame, we become victims to our own thoughts and believe the lies we tell the self. And the soul of the other participant begs you to shift.

God provided me with a deck of cards to create memories from. I chose, no fault of my own or anyone else, to paint my cards with unpleasant events. I kept my hand hidden, guarded. In time, I didn't play at all. The cards sat there. Until one day I decided to play, turn the cards to show the hand. With each memory, I had to forgive the person I held the agreement with. I had to do the work of forgiveness and release the layers of remorse, guilt, victimization, regret, grief and despair. Feeling better was the goal, however I remained unsettled, nervous until I discovered I had to forgive myself, to learn self-care, self-love and how to think.

Depression was no longer a way of life for me. Being miserable no longer felt normal or comfortable. I was changing, unfolding and at times unraveling. I was shifting, awakening to my true authentic self. Sometimes the process was unsettling. There was a moment where I thought I was going crazy, losing my mind. With each shift, I stood in front of the mirror looking at myself for the first time. "Who are you? Who am I? Why are you here? What is my purpose? God, why do I feel this way?" I began journaling in my mid-forties. I wrote letter after letter to God, the angels and everyone I needed to forgive. Then I began to automatic write where the pen was answering back to the questions I had placed on paper. Soon I was conversing with my deceased father, my grandmothers, my grandfathers, the angels and God. At times, the answers came in the form of questions. I had homework and I would complete it. The assignments caused me to go deeper within myself. I became obsessed with finding out what was wrong with me. "What is wrong with me" became a mantra I had engraved in my brain. I would soon discover there was nothing wrong with me. Everything was right with me, just the way I am, perceived flaws and all. I set ridiculous expectation on myself with proficiency in the art of self-sabotage. Learning to undo this habit, required journaling, releasing and self-love. I became a fan of Louise Hay, Wayne Dyer and Abraham-Hicks. I began to study Louise Hay and immersed myself into *Ask and It is Given* by Esther and Jerry Hicks. I was self-taught by using the tools each author provided. I began to evolve, awaken. I began to observe the courage within me.

Deep within me I felt the urge to write. An idea gnawing at my gut while limiting beliefs held me back. I found myself staring at my computer screen, one click away from enrolling in the Hay House Writer's workshop. One large cleansing breath. Click. I was officially enrolled. Four months later I stood up in the O'Hare terminal shaking, waiting to board the flight to Las Vegas. There was no turning back, no looking back.

I came home supercharged, committed to writing thirty minutes every day prior to work. This meant getting myself up at 4:30 a.m. through the winter months. I worked at a full-service agricultural center where spring is all work, no self-care and normal hours don't return until July. I had little energy to devote to the book. After the spring season, I treated myself to a reiki-massage session where the practitioner's guides announced to consider quitting my job. My eyes flew wide open. "What? Her guides cannot be serious!" She looked back at me in surprise as we laughed. The seed was planted. I wasn't happy with my job. It was a job and that was all. Six months later, I stood up, walked in the office and resigned. There was no turning back. I am an author. I took two months off to complete the manuscript and another year to find my courage and a publisher. I am an author!

The year 2020 found me in exponential growth. I studied the Law of Attraction and began changing my thought process. I needed a job. I walked into the local bank to cash a check and waltzed out with a part time job. The Law was working. I was loving it.

Once again, I found myself sitting in front of the computer, one click away from committing to an online training course. One large cleansing breath, click, enrolled. The next four months were supercharged. I was challenged in every way possible. Prior to July 1, 2020, social media was the devil to me. Now I found myself in the heart of Facebook, thriving, completing live videos, and posting daily guidance from the Universe. Fear, fear, face the fear! Confronting each fear, I found myself standing and shining. "Who am I" quickly shifted into "I am enough!" I discovered my purpose, taking my gift of automatic writing to a new level, channel clearing. I was challenged to offer ten free readings on my personal Facebook page. All ten sessions booked in less than two days. With each reading, I discovered accuracy, confidence and joy.

My purpose is using my humor and enthusiasm to intuitively and spiritually assist those in a chronic state of negative being to expose any block that prevents the individual from seeing the magic within themselves. My purpose is a mouthful. Channel clearing is a process to expose the block within an individual. With approval from the client to speak with their soul, I begin each session by writing a letter to God requesting permission to speak with the soul of the client. I never know where the soul will take me. I may receive snapshots or a series of snapshots to piece together. Once I write or draw these visions out, the pen will take off. The soul knows what information to bring forward. Some readings derive from the Akashic Record where a lifetime may have a fracture, a debilitating reaction created by the person in that lifetime. Fractures result from a traumatic experience where the individual was profoundly affected by the event. The feelings derived by the reaction were brought forward to the present-day life. The event cannot be changed nor can the outcome. Only the reaction to the repair may be rewritten by the soul. It is here the journey begins. The fracture is identified and brought forth to the surface to be viewed by the individual in the present-day life. I minister the ceremonial repair between the past life and the present-day life as guided by the soul.

Not all readings bring forth the Akashic Record. Some blocks are present day blocks prohibiting someone from moving forward. The block could involve the loss of a loved one, a traumatic event, or a limited belief they hold themselves captive in. There are two common occurrences in my readings. One is the support from the angels and the second is homework. There is always homework. Homework may involve, journaling or writing assignments, eating specific foods, getting out in nature, self-care, or perhaps doing something fun.

Most readings are quite emotional for the individual. The block within stopped the flow of feeling energy. With release, comes tears, a process to purge what is no longer needed or wanted. Clients often tell me they feel off for a day or two after the reading. This reaction is completely normal. This block within may have been carried around for months, years or even lifetimes. The block, now removed, creates an enormous release followed by a shift to a new energy. This is your body reacting to the change in environment. It takes time for the mind and body to adjust. Self-love and self-care are the main ingredients to healing following a reading.

Channel clearing is my gift from God. It is here where I truly shine, where I feel my true, authentic self. I do not know where this journey is taking me. Once again, I find myself dealing the deck of cards, this time with excitement, a renewed energy as I become one with my soul on this journey called life. Each card within the deck will be different, a new chance to be vulnerable, a new opportunity to be CLEAR and STAND UP and SHINE.

ABOUT ANN KLOSSING

Ann Klossing is an author and an intuitive coach who tutors and performs channel clearing sessions with individuals who are willing to take 100% responsibility in transforming their lives. Through Ann's own transformation and ability to channel through automatic writing, she spiritually assists those individuals in a chronic state of negative being. By exposing the energetic block within the client, she provides a new perspective for the client to address and remove the block within. Having overcome major clinical depression herself, Ann understands the challenges of chronic negative thinking and habitual thought patterns. Ann has a passion for mindful thought to overcome depression and an understanding of the Laws of the Universe, combined, she tutors to restore the power within.

She is the author of *Finding You IS Finding God*, her personal memoir and teaching tool to overcome abuse, depression and fear, soon to be published. Ann is following her passion and calling to Stand Up and Shine.

Ann resides on a dairy farm with her life partner. She has one diamond of a daughter and cherishes the time with her family. Ann loves the country life, spending time in nature and in her gardens. She is often found roaming the farm walking her four dogs.

You can connect with Ann at her website:
annklossing.com

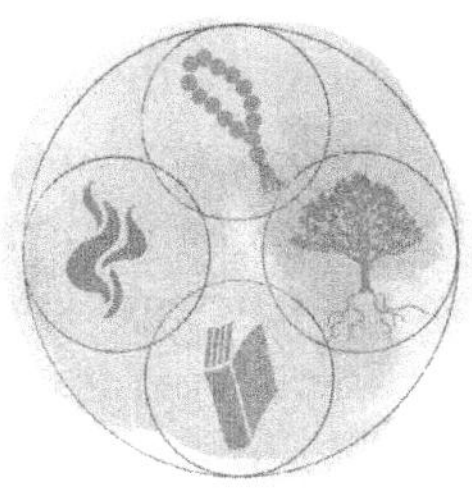

TRANSPORT TO JOY

Shari Lillico

I don't remember much about my younger years, but I know that I loved playing hide and seek, and I was enthralled with exploring and using my imagination to create my own little world and safe space. Sometimes I was so busy being in that wonderful world that I would lose track of time, and then when I was getting called, I thought it was all part of the game, or I just wouldn't hear them. I know now, after being a parent of a child who did the same, just how much panic I caused, but at the time I didn't realize why my parents were angry with me; I just knew I was in trouble. As I look back now, I realize this planted a belief in my subconscious that it wasn't okay to do what I loved to do or be my true self.

When my twin and I started school, a whole new world opened up. It wasn't just my sisters and me anymore. I had friends, and in particular, one good friend. It was great. I would go to her place then she would come to mine, and we had so much fun together playing and being silly. So my identity started to shift to one of my own instead of always being a part of two. Don't get me wrong, my twin and I got along well together, but as we got older and life changed, that dynamic also changed.

When I was seven, my family moved to a tiny community. The school we went to had two classrooms, each with three grades in them. My grade had two boys and one girl, besides my sister and myself. Shelly became fast friends with the girl, as she was always the more outgoing one. I was more reserved and quiet and for the first time, I felt like I didn't really belong. I tried, oh did I try. I tagged along with my sister or attempted to play with the other kids. Still, more often than not, I was on either the swings or the monkey bars, not playing with anyone in particular, but more by myself. I also never thought of myself as very creative or a great student. By working hard and putting a lot of pressure on myself I got decent grades, but I still didn't value myself or feel like I was anything special. I was just there; nothing really and that theme continued into high school.

When Shelly and I started junior high, Shelly integrated quickly and got in with the in-crowd. As for me, as most of you know, when you are quiet and unassuming, you get labeled a misfit or unpopular, whichever you want to call it. That's where I landed. Once again, I felt like I didn't belong, and the truth was, even though I said I didn't, that is all I wanted; to be seen and be accepted as me. The complicated thing is when you don't believe in yourself or show up as your authentic self, others don't see you. No matter how much you may want them to. So you see, that belief that was planted so many years ago continued to follow me.

Getting married and having a family was one of my long-standing goals, as I always loved kids and wanted some of my own. Once I was lucky enough to have found it, I poured my heart and soul into being the best mom and wife I could be. Even though I had many demands on my time when the girls were small, working full-time shift work, looking after the house, preparing meals, and tending to the farm, I loved playing and reading to them. Bedtime stories and even daytime stories were daily occurrences and something that none of us wanted to miss. I also loved buying them new books, but what I loved even more was when I found one they liked so much that they wanted it read over and over again. In my eyes, that was the mark of a good book.

Early into our family life, I was introduced to Homeopathic medicine and aromatherapy as an alternative to Western medicine for the care of the girls. This was something so utterly new to me, and I found it so intriguing and incredible that I began to use it when I could. Then, a little later on, I learned about a lady who taught reflexology. I signed up. I don't even remember why, but I knew I was where I was supposed to be once I got there. I could feel energy! How wonderful and weird is that! After I became a Certified Reflexologist I discovered other healing modalities, and I enjoyed them just as much as reflexology. This is where I belonged, but I didn't really feel I deserved it, so I couldn't to figure out how to do it profitably. So, I let my dreams of starting my own healing business go. Now was not the time to put me first, so I focused entirely on being a mom, a wife, a homemaker, and a good employee of my good-paying job, to help support our family and save for the future. This was my priority.

Well, I did the best that I could, but when I was in my thirties anxiety, depression, and worry became a constant companion. As well as night sweats, which suggested my hormone levels were out of balance. Even though I had achieved my goal of having a family, I also knew that I wasn't really happy either. I blamed it on working in a job I didn't like and found to be very stressful. I didn't realize then that my night sweats were caused by anxiety, which also causes hormone imbalances. I just thought I had health problems, but honestly, it was my body's way of letting me know that I couldn't continue the way I was. As it happens, I ended up hitting bottom when I was on my way to work early in the morning on icy roads. I lost control and hit the ditch. I was so overcome with worry and self-recrimination that it led to a minor break. I knew something had to change. There was no way I could continue to work in a job I dreaded going to every day. As it turns out, the universe had my back and provided me with a temporary position that I loved. However, the anxiety, depression, and night sweats continued. When the five years were up and the position came to an end, I had to choose to either go back to my original job or leave altogether. The dread I felt when I thought about going back was all-consuming. I knew that I just couldn't do it if I wanted to maintain my health.

After a year of staying home, I was ready to get back out into the workforce and contribute to society and our financial well-being. I eventually found a job I enjoyed but, deep down past the surface, I still wasn't happy and anxiety and worry plagued me. I continued to wake up in the middle of the night, my heart pounding, drenched with sweat and not being able to go back to sleep, all because my mind was racing and I couldn't calm it. It was a vicious cycle. As I know now, my body was still showing me that I wasn't in alignment with myself so I could finally get to the point of saying enough is enough; it is time for me, and I need to break through this.

Well, that time finally came when both girls left to go to school and be on their own. That's when I found myself with an empty nest. It wasn't so much of the emptiness that bothered me or the fact that it was just my husband and me, but it was a question of; what do I focus on now?

I started to look inside. What do I need to do for myself? What do I need to change? The answer was clear. I wanted to get into shape. So I started to exercise. This was the first big thing I did for myself in many years. I began to take care of myself more and because of it, I became more aware of my body, which opened me up to new realizations and new things. I finally started to be more true to myself and as that was happening, I became more open to beliefs that talked about how the universe will send us signs and lead us to where we are meant to be.

Around this time, a friend that I hadn't seen for years started to show up in my life again and again, and I finally got it. It was like a slap to the forehead. It was clear that I was supposed to reach out to her! So, I did, and once again it started sending me back to the world that I had delved briefly into so many years ago.

She was very into the metaphysical and self-improvement. Being around her started me down the path to self-realization and so much more. As I began to learn, I fell into a trap that many spiritual people fall into. I waited for a sign or a feeling for my next step. It worked so well to get me back on this path again, so why wouldn't I wait? I waited and waited and nothing came, so I would take a small step, and I moved forward a tiny bit. Then I waited again, but nothing would come. So I would take another small action. I did this repeatedly, and yes, I was learning as I was going but, I was getting frustrated. I still had that empty feeling, you know the one that says there was something more, but I couldn't figure out what it was, and waiting for signs just wasn't doing it for me. Finally, I took the plunge and signed up for the foundations class of Eden Energy Medicine. Wow, that started a whole new journey, and opportunities and paths opened up. You see, when I began to take action, I started to build up the confidence that it was safe and necessary to finally show the world the real me and that I was ready to move forward.

I began to delve deeper into the metaphysical, crystals, angels, guides, and dragons. Yes, even dragons, and I absolutely fell in love with them! Well, it all ultimately brought me to belief work, Theta Healing, Shamanism, and becoming a Certified Eden Energy Medicine Practitioner. Which finally allowed me to overcome my anxiety, depression, and hormone imbalances by using all the different energy tools I learned.

Along with all of that, self-realization, improvement, care, and love, as well as goals, didn't just become a priority but a necessity. After all those years of feeling like nothing, I was finally embracing who I was and what I wanted. This led me to realize that it was time to go after my dreams and no longer ignore them. As I started to look at my goals, there were a few that stood out. Like so many years ago, I wanted my own healing/coaching business, to become a speaker, travel the world and learn about different cultures. Then there was one deeply buried dream; to become an author of a children's book because what lights me up is to make children happy, just like how reading to my girls made them happy. I dreamed of being able to transport children to a joyful, fun place and show them that it's okay to be themselves and to go after what they want, no matter what others say and do.

I am blessed to say this dream is becoming a reality later this year and it is time for your dreams to blossom as well. So I encourage you to stop waiting and take that step. It is time to let your true self shine through. You are worth it.

ABOUT SHARI LILLICO

After so many years of feeling like she didn't belong and hiding who she truly was, Shari has finally found her voice and is going after her dreams. The dream of bringing joy to young children through publishing a children's book is becoming a reality. Her first children's book, which features a lovable and persistent little red dragon, will be published and available to acquire later this year.

Shari is also realizing another dream by continuing to develop her business designed to help women who have lost sight of who they are and what they want after years of putting others first. She helps them step into the joy and excitement of living as their true selves, allowing them to embrace their power to go after their dreams. Using all her training as a Certified Eden Energy Medicine Practitioner, a belief work practitioner, shamanism, along with her own Divinely downloaded healing modality and her life experiences, Shari works with her clients one-on-one using techniques that rely on energetic responses, mindset, meditation, and self-help techniques and tools.

To find out more about Shari, how to work with her, or to check out her children's book

Visit: www. sharilillico.com
Email: shari.lillico@gmail.com

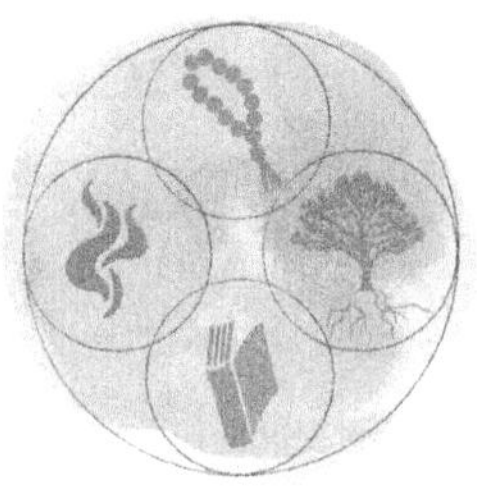

I WAS NEVER ALONE

Christina Macro

My mom was a stunning, stoic, strong, independent woman who was never rattled. Ever. Not when her oldest child was shot. Not when her youngest son died at only 35. Not when her own husband had affairs. Not even when her husband shot himself in their marital bed while she stood in the kitchen washing her beloved little dogs, just feet from the scene of his suicide. Not when her brother died tragically. Not when her beloved father died unexpectedly. Not when her mother died. Not ever. As a child, whenever I went to my mother for comfort from the bullying, the teenage tragedies, or just feeling sad and wanting a comforting word—my mother always gave me the same sweet answer in her quiet and cool tone, "What are you going to do, Christina?". It was this answer time and again. As a teen, this answer annoyed me to no end—I just wanted her to get mad with me! As an adult, I realized just how much it taught me to focus on what was actually within my control. I found myself asking this question many times throughout the course of weeks, months, and years of my life. For every disappointment, for every misfortune, for every heart break, and for every complete failure, I would find myself uttering these words to myself. They somehow grounded me full center to face forward and get myself out of the dredges of victim mindset and into solutions.

"What are you going to do, Christina? *What are you going to do*?"

I remember so vividly the night I learned that my husband was having an affair with my best friend, also our maid of honor. I raced home from my office and picked up the phone to call him. He had already left and was staying at a mutual friend's home at this point, but had agreed to one last counseling session scheduled for the next day. He answered. And I ripped into him at decibels that only woodland animals could hear. I screamed. I screamed so loud that the neighbor across the street called to be sure I was ok—she could hear me through my kitchen walls, through my sealed windows and doors, and across the street into her own kitchen. At the end of my tirade, I breathed for only a moment to ask him why? "Why did you do this to me? Why would you choose my best friend? Why would you hurt me like this? WHY?" I never got an answer. With all the arrogance in the world he just responded with a profound condescending hatred, "You're crazy, everyone knows you're nuts and you can't prove a thing!".

He never returned home after this conversation and never showed up for our final counseling.

At that moment I recall telling myself that I had two choices, I could let this situation destroy me and could cry in the corner like a schoolgirl or I could let this situation define me. Defining meant finding inner strength to carry on with respect and dignity. I chose respect and dignity. More than that, I chose self-respect. I chose the high road. But I also chose intense bravery to ensure that my son and I were protected financially, emotionally, mentally, and physically. I had so much to lose. And losing was not in the cards. I also knew that I had to go about it covertly, mission impossible style. I had to find the courage and strength to focus. To get right out of victim mindset and stay true to myself. And true to what I valued—honesty and integrity.

In the following weeks, I laid low. I read a book about divorce with a spouse that cheats. I learned about the shame and guilt of the cheater, but also this anger that is projected onto the victim, while the victim drowns in the sadness, hurt, and the devastation of rejection. Armed with this information and new found knowledge of the human condition as a result of this dynamic, I learned to craft my skills in manipulation for the greater good of my well-being.

From that moment on, every conversation with my soon-to-be ex was riddled with language designed to foster his guilt. I morphed into a mental architect; I used victim mentality to anchor his behaviors and decisions in his shame, guilt, and their betrayal. Our conversations consisted mostly of me crying and pleading for mercy. He couldn't stand to see my cry. It was my greatest defense.

From the very beginning, Sean made it very clear that he wanted out FAST. He knew that the state would grant a divorce in six months since we had no children together. He wanted to move on with his life and his new relationship. Every time we spoke, I would lace the conversation with words like "If we do it this way" (aka my way), you'll get a faster divorce if not, we can do it "this other way" (aka his way) and each hire an attorney, spend a year fighting over it all, and then go in front of a judge for final decisions on belongings." I reminded him during every conversation that the house was solely in my name and so were all of our personal belongings—the cars, the truck, the jet-skis, the bank accounts. You know, a "don't forget, all this may not go in your favor since nothing is actually in your name" type of thing. Kind of a subliminal dialogue whenever it felt appropriate to inject into the conversation. Not to mention that I purchased and maintained my home before we were married and without his financial help or support. My son's college fund was a culmination of a lifetime of my blood, sweat, and tears as a result of working 2-3 jobs for years. All sacrifices that Sean was never a part of; cars, personal possessions, and a bank account that he had no rights to whatsoever. It was keen and cunning and deliberate. I had to keep my message consistent and my voice clear. I also had to keep a level head. I could not risk losing anything to a cheating bastard. I had to allow him to remain angry at me while I cried like a defenseless child. Keeping a cool head meant that he could never figure out that I was manipulating him all along.

This guilt and manipulation kept him agreeing one-by-one to terms that would benefit me. Like laying arsenic laced bread crumbs to a hungry bear. I truly believed that he should get exactly what he deserved, NOTHING. I also knew that the state could rule otherwise.

I played my cards close to the vest. I told no one, other than five hand selected confidants who were thoughtfully and carefully chosen for their trustworthiness. They knew exactly what I was doing behind the scenes—closing bank accounts, talking to a well-respected attorney, hiring a PI to keep tabs on them both, and learning what my rights were.

I learned that the state sees all assets as marital assets for at least the percentage of time the assets existed during the marriage. He would have been allocated a percentage of the proceeds based on the amount of time that we were married as compared to the amount of time that the asset was owned. That meant that he quite possibly could have been awarded 50% of the net proceeds. However, there were other considerations and it turns out he might actually, and most likely, have been owed as little as 10% of the net proceeds. The good news was that I would not be forced to sell my home since he was not on the title or the deed. Ultimately, it came down to protecting my financial position.

I also learned that extra marital affairs are a criminal offense in the state of VA. This is why I hired a PI after he left. I needed some compelling proof that they were having an affair. Photos, phone calls, emails. Anything that would offer up a guilty verdict for a criminal trial.

I also learned that he was responsible for any of the financial losses or debts of the marriage, including his truck that I had just bought him, which was upside down. It also included several credit-cards and some other debt that he racked up while he was galivanting around town with his new girlfriend.

I sat with an attorney and we scoured the list and devised a plan. Ten percent of the net proceeds from the home equaled approximately $17,800. From there, we started with deductions. The losses were significant, which meant that I really owed him about $1,450. But I had also sent a check to his mother as a loan the week before our trip to the lake house (shady as hell, after I looked back) and that meant that he actually owed me a little over $1,000 when all was said and done. Remember, that this is based on a 10% payout. That was my assumption and I had to sell it. And it had to be believable. One hundred percent believable.

I gathered the information that the PI had collected. I also researched all of the laws pertaining to affairs and a criminal offense. All the while, my confidants were helping me to sort through and keep me posted on their behaviors. I needed to be sure that they knew nothing and the only message from any and all communications was that of pure grief. I needed them both to think that I spent my days in a corner in the fetal position crying, completely unable to cope.

After I researched and laid out my master plan, I asked the attorney to draft up the legal documents outlining what Sean had verbally agreed to, with a big blank space for the division of assets. Sean thought we would be discussing the financial payout when we met to review the separation agreement. However, during our weeks of regular conversations leading up to our final meeting, I had not committed to anything financially.

We set a time and date to meet at my office. One of my confidants was someone in my office. One of the Notary Public's agreed to be there while we were in the conference room. My confidant agreed to sit in the office right next to the conference room. I feared for my life with this man and I wanted to be sure someone was watching his every move while he sat with me. I knew that he would get angry at my proposal.

The stage was set.

It was a cool fall day—the sun was shining and the air was crisp. It was a little over a month after learning that my idyllic life had descended into a shocking tailspin. I sat in the glass enclosed, goldfish bowl-style conference room in my real estate office. I had to remain calm and cool. I was nervous and my insides were rattled. I put on my best suit and placed a mini recorder in my pocket, my briefcase stuffed with every possible supporting document to ensure that this ended on my terms. If Sean did not agree with what I was about to lay out it would mean a year of attorney's appointments, court dates, and the possibility of enormous financial losses. It had to go exactly as planned. I rehearsed the script. I remained calm.

In walked Sean. My heart palpitated. My tummy flipped and flopped.

We each took a seat at the small round table. I turned on the recorder and I began to speak slowly, calmly, and deliberately.

I started with the spreadsheet. I laid out the numbers on the house. When he saw the $17,800 his eyes lit up. As I went down the list and started to deduct the debts, his demeanor slowly shifted to disappointment. I remember saying, "Basically, you owe me money".

The silence was ear-piercing.

After he looked at the documents and what I had prepared. He said," I think I'll need an attorney."

I said, "Great! Let's do that. Just to let you know, if you want to go that route then we can. I'll be filing criminal charges against you both for adultery, it's a criminal offense in VA." He laughed and said, "You can't prove anything."

With the coolest demeanor possible I retorted, "Yes, certainly proving that she sucked your cock would require something that I don't have. However, proving that you spent time with her in photos, phone calls, and other circumstantial evidence certainly doesn't weigh in your favor in front of a criminal court room. I'm not sure how you feel about a criminal offense, but you may want to ask your new girlfriend how she feels about it. Because I'll be filing criminal charges against both of you."

Sean looked at me like he's never looked at me before. Suddenly, I was the woman who stood up to him. The woman who had put up with his abuse and drama for five years. The woman who, not once, felt strong enough to give it right back. The woman on a mission. I could see it in his eyes. Internally he was afraid, but on the outside, he laughed in his typical condescending way.

What happened next was an act of every angel ever to grace a room when I needed it.

Sean said, "I'm not signing that. I'll see you in court."

With all the strength I could find within me and from the core of my internal strength I stood up, I reached out to shake his hand as if closing the largest real estate deal of my career and said "Perfect. I'll see you in court."

He got up. He grabbed the door handle and opened the door to leave. Just as he was about to go, he turned around and said, "If I sign this today, we'll be divorced in six months and I'll never hear from you again?"

I said, "Yes. That is correct. And I won't file criminal charges. You'll be divorced on March 24, 2004."

He sat back down. I gave him a pen and motioned for the Notary who had been watching Sean's every move from across the office.

I sat and watched as he signed the agreement in triplicate in beautiful blue ink in front of a Notary.

It was done. I protected myself emotionally, financially,

physically, and mentally. My soul was releasing every fear ever laid within me. My heart was calm. I was sad, but also elated.

When my husband was done signing, I gave him a copy and he walked out for the final time. The click of the door latch is the final sound that ended our life together. Click. My relationship with my husband was now a culmination of events over our five years together summarized in the sound of the click of a door latch closing behind him. The sound resonated through my entire being . . . click. Gone. Just like that.

I sat there alone. I felt tired, relieved, angry, and emotional. I cried. I cried that hard, reaching for air crying that is dizzying. The hard crying that lets it all go. The crying meant to heal. The crying meant to release.

In the moments after he walked out that door, I quickly flooded my mental headspace with this range of emotions from euphoria to resentment. Up until that very split second and snapshot of a moment in time, the depth of anger served a greater purpose than I was even aware. It swelled into my being and transformed me into a woman with a cause. I became my very own advocate. Emotionally, I could hardly recognize myself. When it became clear that no one was able or willing to advocate for me, I had to do it myself. Blissfully unaware of the enormity of what I had just accomplished—he signed our separation agreement in triplicate as it was presented without a single edit other than a spelling correction. The anger shifted to relief while bitter, seething resentment spilled from my gut due to the reality of what my life had become. It was a tattered shamble of a mess from the loss of what was supposed to be my road to joy, stripped from me by a best friend and a husband. About to turn 40, my son was about to graduate high school and head to college, and all the plans we made as a married couple slashed from my internal vision board. On top of all of that, relations with my family and friends were strained at best. I felt completely alone. Stranded on the proverbial island with no one searching for me. I was lost and a lost cause. My weight had ratcheted back up over 200 pounds. My immediate future became a life reel filled with a probable future of pain and loneliness. I mean, after all, Sean made it clear that I was "old, fat, and ugly" as he exited our marriage.

I kept telling myself to breathe. And to let go.

I didn't want to talk about it anymore. I wanted to rise above it. I knew no one could help me. Except for me.

I stopped breathing between the salty tears searing my soul. Internally, I screamed at him and called him every name in the book. In both English and Italian. I bathed in the shock through the silence surrounding me. I was drowning in the sorrow and betrayal that I felt. Then, out of nowhere, penetrating the silence, the words rang so loudly in my head as clear as if my mother were standing right next to me, "What are you going to do, Christina? *What are you going to do?*"

My mother's words, through her soothing voice, in all of her strength and stoicism, shifted my footing. I was NOT going to be a victim any longer in this ongoing saga of this book called "fuck my life." I had to turn a page. I had to re-write my story and this chapter was just yearning to be written.

That evening, I sat in my bedroom in my then home in Falls Church and heard my mom's voice asking me, "What are you going to do, Christina?" Like a broken record on repeat the words played on in my head.

I knew that this trauma was something too substantial for me to process and heal on my own. I knew that it was layers deep. Years of stuff. You know, the stuff we carry, or at least the stuff that I carried going back to the day my father stood in the kitchen of our home on Cape Cod and informed his beloved and adored children that he would be leaving that day. The abandonment. The resentment. This decision would change everything, mostly the life my father left behind for my poor mother to sort and pick up on her own. I knew that there were layers upon layers that had to be peeled away to get to the core of where it started for me.

Why I was never able to have a loving relationship with anyone. Not a man. Not my mother. Not my brothers. Not girlfriends. Not my bosses. Not my colleagues. I was always this strong and independent soul with this iron clad guard surrounding my heart and soul. No one could penetrate my walls, which also meant that no one could hurt me. Yet, here I was living a life of hurt over and over and over and over again in every relationship.

So, I stumbled upon and immediately read *Fearless Loving* by Rhonda Britton and I learned about self-sabotage and deep-rooted fears. This led me to a therapist and life coach. I needed help. I was desperate to share my side of the story. I had spent the entire divorce process declining to tell anyone what they did to me. Our mutual friends only knew his version and I flat out refused to air dirty laundry as he had done. The stories he told were an unhinged and mostly a deranged version of reality. All of them.

At that point, I gained clarity. And through clarity, three things became particularly important to me. First and foremost, I needed to sort through it all. I spoke quietly to myself, "Christina, figure this shit out." Then I said it out loud. "Get your act together and figure this shit out." I knew that I needed to look deep within myself to decipher my contributions to my life failings. But look, let's not get this twisted here. I did NOTHING to condone a decision as hurtful as my husband having an affair with my best friend. That said, I also had to accept and come face-to-face with my part in all of this. There is a balance between loving myself, accepting my contribution, and forgiving myself along the pathway of this cruel journey.

My next decision required me to find the right support system and new friends. I could not remain friends with our mutual friends and all the people that did weekends at the lake, ski trips, and life adventures with me and my ex. I needed to find friends that knew me as Christina and not as Sean's wife, but this girl named Christina. I needed a tribe. I needed to remove myself from anything that would trigger my anger and sadness while healing. Lastly, I needed to heal the relationship with my family, mostly my mom. She was the first person I called after I mustered the courage and bravery needed to extend an olive branch and to say that I was deeply and truly sorry.

It was one of the most heartfelt, raw, and memorable conversations of my lifetime. "I did it mom . . . he signed everything and it's done. And mom, I have done NOTHING that I am ashamed of." My mother, as sweet and kind as can be, soothed my soul even further by saying, "Christina, I never thought you would do anything to be ashamed of. It's not the kind of girl I raised and it's not the woman you are. And I'm proud of you for being strong and standing up to the abuse and that bully. And, by the way, I've booked a flight to Antigua and you're coming." The joy was overwhelming. While I was with Sean, I sent my mother a scathing letter filled with my own anger and bitterness about who she was. During our reunion call, she told me how sad that letter made her. We both cried and it was the start of the most amazing relationship of my life.

When these three decisions became important to me, my focus shifted to healing and love. I got to learn what my contribution to my own life failings where. I am a personification of all of my decisions and where I was emotionally, mentally, financially, physically, and spiritually the day Sean signed.

I let go and I let it be.

I spent two years in therapy continually working on the layers, peeling them like a big tear inducing sweet Vidalia onion. My mom and I traveled twice a year to her favorite Caribbean Island. My broker called me and basically demanded that I go to Italy to earn a highly regarded real estate designation that was being taught in Rome. I was terrified to fly, but I got a passport and did it. This is when I met my beautiful friend Brandon, which led to friendships with Fany and Alexana, as well as countless other women who loved me for me, who are my tribe.

My son graduated high school and was achieving high marks in college. He visited as often as he could.

I sold my marital home and found an amazing Penthouse condo that was a dream for me with incredible views and enormous space. I designed and decorated it like a pro and always had guests over. I rediscovered my love of cooking and baking. I had parties all the time. I was literally living the life of a rock star.

My career took off. I was a Top Producer in my local real estate market and living the dream. Travel, a beautiful home, and amazing friends. My own mother, who I resented for not being the mother I wanted, and I grew closer than any relationship I had ever experienced. She died knowing how much I loved her. I learned so much about her and the complexities of her life. My younger brother was present in my world and he was a joy. I was working with a Grammy artist, meeting Miss USA contestants, and people wanted me in their world. I was invited to all the red-carpet events. I was spending time with some of the most influential people in the DC area. I was brimming with joy, and by brimming, I mean overflowing. I was bursting at the seams.

I lost the marital weight gain and looked better than I had ever looked and I felt better than I had ever felt. I was at the gym two hours a day. I was outside running with my little Mac the Jack Russell for two hours every morning. I had envisioned an amazing life and kept that vision clear. Nothing would stop me from rising above the fray in order to transform into this person so filled with love that the energy resonated for hundreds of miles. It was the lifestyle that I dreamed of.

It took me two years of focusing on being a better person. It took two years of meeting amazing people who loved me. It took two years of nonstop affirmations to truly believe that I did nothing to cause this betrayal. I had to let go of blaming myself for what they did. This was no easy task. It also took two years to realize that walls are ok and anger serves a valuable purpose in healing. Being guarded made me kind. The wall held all the love inside, a love within myself that was reserved for the love that I deserved.

Ultimately, I knew that I had to accept my part in my life failings while releasing the habit of blaming myself for their decision to betray me. It was an extreme in receiving from both ends of my psyche. When I succeeded, the layers fell off like the dry pine-needles of a Christmas Tree starving for water far too long. These layers were suddenly replaced with layers of understanding and I began seeing life from a kaleidoscope rather than a toilet paper tube.

There is something purely magical about packing an overnight bag and going home. I loved to go home to visit my mom. There's this solace that allows me to be me, without apologies. My mother knew me better than anyone and loved me more than she ever could express. On a summer visit home, sleeping in my childhood bed in my childhood bedroom, I awoke to the fresh salt air. I inhaled so deeply and I breathed it all in. I held it in as if I were breathing two years of love and a life changed immensely. I exhaled, and when I did I blurted out, "I forgive you both." Then I wished them the best. "I forgive you both and wish you the best." And I meant it. From the depths of my soul, I meant it. I finally got the answer to my mom's sweet response to everything. She taught me so much in those seven words, "What are you going to do, Christina?" And it became very clear to me that through those few words, I was able to experience relationships like I had never experienced before. I learned that I was not, in fact, a failure at relationships. I was a failure at accepting and loving myself.

What are you going to do, Christina? My answer was clear and simple, I chose to love me. And that changes everything, for everyone.

ABOUT CHRISTINA MACRO

Christina was born and raised on the shores of Cape Cod, MA to her police officer dad and hair stylist single mom. She is the only girl in a family of four kids from immigrant roots of Italian and Portuguese heritage. Christina has always been fascinated by human interaction and how we deal with foibles along the way. Christina has spent her life working hard in several successful careers spanning hotels, IT, and real estate, but has always maintained a love for all things creative like singing, modeling, writing, and creating. She's quirky, but fun. A series of unfortunate life events led her down a path of self-discovery; so, she decided it was time to start sharing her stories. Between her childhood, her teen years, being a parent as a young single mom, failed relationships, and general heartache, she has found ways to find her inner voice and share her stories which are moving and pure but with a sense of humor that only she can convey. Christina's purpose in life is to use her passion, courage, intelligence, kindness, and authenticity to inspire others to their most self-aware, trusting, and finest version of themselves.

Contact Christina Macro The Brainy Broker™ at:

(703) 597-3497

hi@thebrainybroker.com

@thebrainybroker: LinkedIn, FB, Twitter, and Instagram

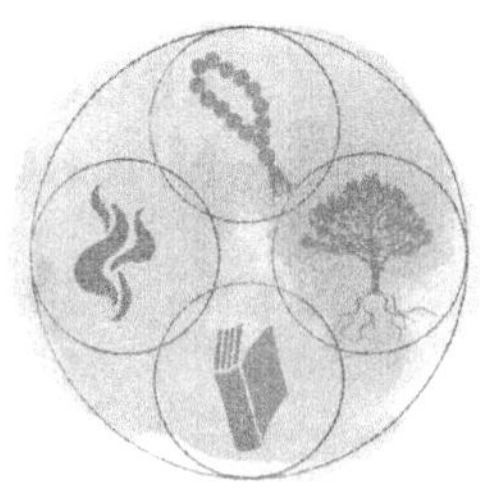

TRUST IS A MUST!

Lori Parks

Trust is a Must!
I have a plan. Do you trust me?

~God

At the age of 9, I had a Soul-level knowing, born of crystal clear Heart-Whispers, that I had been blessed with a gift. My joy, and life's purpose, would be found in inspiring others through writing. I was a Poet.

I discovered this in Grade four, when we were asked to write a Halloween poem. From the second my pencil hit the paper, I was in a state of pure bliss. The words came to me and flowed through me, effortlessly. I wrote all weekend, even hiding under my covers at night with a flash-light, so as not to bother my sister. I couldn't articulate the feeling of knowing I had found my true calling, but now as I reflect back, I can.

I felt vibrant, aligned, and complete. I had found my voice, my confidence, my truth. There was no doubt, or question, just belief. Writing lit me up inside; I couldn't not do it! I trusted 100% in God's plan for me, and would receive validation in Grade six, that I was on my true path, through winning my first writing award. What a beautiful gift, to know at that early age what my soul's purpose was. The problem came as I grew older. The Heart-Whispers would grow fainter, muffled by outside voices, a label, and most tragically, my giving power and truth to limiting beliefs, silencing my inner guidance. I would forget to Trust!

I always did well in school, but in High School I began to struggle. I had to read things over and over, and write endless pages of notes, in an attempt to absorb the information. Whereas my friends would study a few hours for a test; I had to study for days. I knew something wasn't right, but I kept my struggles to myself. Building frustrations resulted in my losing interest in my academics. I had to work so hard to accomplish what others could do so easily. I was in a constant state of anxiety, unable to demonstrate the skills required of me. I would sit in the back of my classes, secretly working on my poetry. I did graduate, but it was no easy feat.

As a pre-requisite for College, I had to do testing. I remember staring at the pages, crying. It was like trying to make sense of an unknown foreign language. I can still hear the Guidance Counselor, upon reviewing my results, "You have a Spatial-Visual Learning Disability. You have a hindered ability to perceive, analyze, and absorb information taken in through the eyes. Expect to struggle with this for the rest of your life. College would be very difficult for you."

This was both a blessing and a curse. I remember the sense of relief; I wasn't stupid. There was a legitimate reason for my challenges. I could now put a name to the invisible obstacle that was wreaking havoc in my life. The tragedy was when I unnecessarily, and cruelly, labeled myself as less-than or inadequate. I stopped viewing myself as a whole person; my disability became my identity. I wish I had understood then, as I do now, that my disability was just one component, one facet of me. I had so many strengths. The Heart-Whispers, telling me that I had a gift, were replaced with doubt. I wasn't intelligent enough for greatness. I was destined for a life of mediocrity. I no longer trusted God's plan for my life; it had all been a cruel lie.

I would allow the label, learning-disabled, to stick to me like glue, boxing and trapping me into a category. I believed I was incapable of achieving anything of real value. Feeling incapable would lead to procrastination. Procrastination would keep me from taking steps towards my dreams. "As a man speaks—so he becomes!" I would learn the truth in Self-Fulfilling Prophecy. I would allow five words from a stranger, "You have a learning disability," to dictate the trajectory of the next four decades of my life. I would forget to trust!

Poor self-concept would lead me down a long and winding road to nowhere. I would numb my pain and frustration with alcohol and seek validation from men. I just wanted someone to tell me I was of value. The quality of men I chose clearly reflected my lack of self-respect and love for myself. I wasn't deserving of real love, the beautiful kind. I was lucky that anyone would have me.

I would give birth to my son and daughter in my twenties and would raise them as a single-mother. Shame from bringing them into my less-than perfect world, coupled with the struggle of providing for them financially, would lead to further feelings of inadequacy and crippling guilt. They deserved so much more than I could give them. Their happiness was all that mattered to me. I, on the other hand, didn't deserve happiness. I deserved to be punished for the poor choices I had made, those that would result in their feeling pain and being raised without a father.

I would meet my partner of 23 years, Frank, and we became a blended family with five children. Wanting to contribute to our finances, but still believing that I wasn't capable of purposeful work, I settled for exhausting, strenuous labor. I cleaned hotel rooms and waitressed. I even served as a line-cook. I had decided that not trying at all for a meaningful career was less painful than trying and being met with failure. The Heart-Whispers were ever-present. I've learned that your truth never goes away, even when you desperately try to ignore it. I often heard God's gentle nudging, "Lori, there's an easier road. Why do you refuse to trust my plan for you, the one you once believed in with all your heart? Things don't have to be this hard."

In an attempt to appease the relentless whispers, and because I was truly missing what fed my soul, I began entering song writing contests. I would win countless awards; even placing 2nd in the world with one entry, which was further validation that writing was my soul's purpose. I continued to regard it as just a hobby. I wasn't meant for greatness. These wins were just a stroke of luck.

Around 2005, I began to notice debilitating pain throughout my body, accompanied by constant fatigue. I would continue to work, but would collapse at the end of the day. After numerous tests, I was diagnosed with Fibromyalgia; a chronic pain condition with no cure. In trying to explain this condition to others, I ask them to remember the last time they had a horrible flu; this is what I feel like every second of every day. I always feel like I've been awake for a week and no amount of sleep will catch me up. This became, and remains, one of my greatest challenges.

I could no longer work outside the home and deep depression set in. I felt useless. I can't be sure what caused this condition, but after reading, *You Can Heal Your Life*, by Louise Hay, I have an educated guess. For years I had been consumed by guilt. Guilt for being less-than, for not being able to give my children the life they deserved, for them being raised without a father, for being a disappointment to everyone in my life, including myself. It's believed that pain is an indication of guilt. Guilt always seeks punishment, and punishment creates pain. I had been punishing myself for years, carrying a cross I didn't need to bare, simply for having a learning disability, for making mistakes; for not being perfect.

Once again, I could hear the voice of God, "Lori, now that you've been slowed down with this pain condition, will you set foot on your true path? You have all the time in the world now to focus on your writing. Will you trust my plan for you? Are you done punishing yourself yet?" I wasn't meant for greatness. Why did he keep messing with me? I would spend my days helping my husband with our family business, grateful to have something to focus on to distract me from the pain, but I longed for purpose.

The years from 2015-2017 would leave me on my knees. Our son would battle Cancer. We would lose our daughter to MS, and I would lose my brother in a tragic passing. I was so knocked about by life that I felt like a rock in a tumbler. The repetitive impact of heart-break and loss, was tossing and turning, cutting and breaking me, as I rolled around in darkness. I was trapped in pain, praying for someone, or something, to reach in and pull me from the grip of grief. I was decimated, shattered. The coming months would be spent simply trying to put one foot in front of the other, moving forward with what felt like half a heart.

One morning, in the spring of 2019, a year and a half after my brother's passing, as my eyes opened, I did as I always did; I prayed. I prayed that my heart would be a little less broken and that the pain of Fibromyalgia would be miraculously gone. It had become more of a ritual of begging and pleading. I was merely in survival mode. It was winter in my soul.

The pain was still there. Hot tears stung my face. I could feel myself at a crossroads. I couldn't live one more day this way. I had hit a breaking point. I didn't care if I was here anymore, and it scared the hell out of me. In a sudden, and long overdue, moment of compassion and grace for myself, as I reflected on everything I'd been through, I felt a wave of strength and determination wash over me. I sat straight up and yelled, "I'm not going down like this! I haven't pushed through all these trials to end up wasting away in this bed. I'm only 58 years old. I have dreams!"

I knew I had eyes on me, those of my children and grandchildren. They were carefully watching to see what we do in the face of great adversity. Do we give up, or dig deep and pull from our strength? My giving up would be giving them permission to give up too. I wouldn't be responsible for that. I fell to my knees and prayed.

"God-please help me. What do I do?" This was my moment of Surrender. I didn't have the answers, and for the first time in a long time, I put my trust in God. The reply was instant and crystal clear. "Lori-turn back to your writing. You've had the answer all along. If you had just trusted the Heart-Whispers, you could have saved yourself a world of hurt." I smiled and laughed, imagining God laughing, not at me, but with me. Of course it would take my greatest joy to pull me out of my greatest sorrow. It took me hitting rock bottom, but I was ready to trust.

My eyes were drawn to the old writing trunk that sat beside my bed. It was filled with dusty old poems, my neglected heart-songs. On the top of the pile was a poem I had written for my grandson, called *The Power of One.* I had written it for him during a time when he was struggling to believe in himself. He was questioning whether one person, especially a child, had the ability or power to make a difference in this world. I wanted him to trust his Heart-Whispers. I wanted him to trust that he could be, and do, anything he desired. As I read the words, I was hit with the irony of how important it was to me that he believed in himself and his dreams, yet I failed to believe in mine. It was time to walk the talk.

When you bravely set foot on your true path, when you trust, miraculous things begin to happen. People with similar purpose begin to find their way to you automagically. The Universe rises up to meet you by bringing you the exact people, circumstances, and messages that your soul is ready for at the right time. I was ready to step into my greatness and synchronicity was abounding.

I began searching Amazon for Inspirational Children's books, taking note of publishers to send my manuscript to. I came across a fellow Canadian, Children's Book Author; Miriam Laundry, whose intention was to also inspire children to believe in themselves. I began following her on Facebook, hoping to learn from her journey as a writer. One day, while browsing her page, I saw that she was seeking children's books to publish. She would choose, and guide, six aspiring authors through the journey of becoming a published author. My heart skipped a beat. This was it! The opportunity I had been dreaming of. With trembling fingers, I sent my manuscript off. In the fall of 2019, I received a life-changing email; she loved *The Power of One* and wanted to publish it.

It's most surreal, the exact moment when you realize your life-long dream is coming true. I remember a huge exhale and a beautiful release, as I felt the weight of everything I'd been through fall off my shoulders. I ran downstairs sobbing to tell my husband and I called everyone in my family to share the news. I wept as I signed the contract.

The Power of One was released in the fall of 2020. My greatest joy is in knowing that through living my passion and purpose, I am now inspiring children to do the same. Through trusting and putting action to my Heart-Whispers, I have risen from the darkness, shining as my authentic self. I am grateful for my struggles, as without them, I wouldn't have found my strength; the strength to set foot on my true path.

It was a long and winding road that led me to finally living as my authentic self. I know now that sometimes the detour is the path. There were powerful lessons learned at every turn and the obstacles along the way were working for my greater good. They were little re-direct signs from God, trying to lead me to my true calling. If not for my Fibromyalgia, I'm certain I wouldn't have turned back to my writing. I would be working at some unfulfilling job, yearning for purpose.

What are your Heart-Whispers telling you? Listen! Allow yourself to reconnect with the truth of who you are. Find what lights you up inside, what you love to do, what you CAN'T NOT

DO. Do that and TRUST, and if you can find a way to help others in the process you will have struck gold!

Let your Heart-Whispers be your compass. They will never lead you off course.

Here's to all your dreams coming true! Love and Light

—Lori

ABOUT LORI PARKS

Lori lives in Ontario, Canada with her husband, Frank, and their beloved Golden Retrievers, Comet and Nevaeh. She considers her greatest blessings to be her children and grandchildren, whose love and support inspired her to put action to her Heart-Whispers and share her writing with the world.

Lori is overjoyed, and grateful, that her life-long dream of becoming a published author has come to fruition with the release of her inspirational children's book, *The Power of One*.

Her intention for this book is to help children understand, at the earliest age possible, the incredible personal power they possess, as well as their ability to make a beautiful difference in this world through sharing acts of kindness.

Lori believes all children come into this world with wings, blessed with unlimited potential, and the ability to soar. She is honored to know that through her writing, she is encouraging children to FLY!

Lori's other passion, a love of animals, has called her to donate proceeds from her book to her local Humane Society.

***The Power of One* hardcover can be purchased at**
loriparksauthor.com

The paperback and kindle editions can be purchased on Amazon.

FB and IG: @loriparksauthor
Email: authorloriparks@yahoo.com

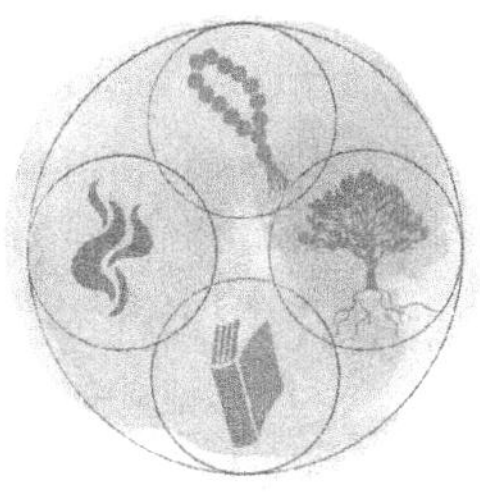

BELLY OF THE WHALE

Dr. Lisa Patierne

We are all born with a song in our heart, which is our life's purpose. When we are singing that song or living our life's purpose, we are in a state of joy, peace, and wellness. I knew from the first time I dashed through the doors of a school as a kindergartner that I wanted to teach. Every day after school, I would go home and play school in my make-shift classroom. It was located on our front porch and despite the brutal heat of the summer and the frigid cold of the winter, I would faithfully go out and instruct my students. Sometimes those students were my dolls and stuffed animals. Other days when I got really lucky, I got to teach my best friend since second grade, as well as my younger brother. I had a chalkboard, art supplies, and so many books. To this day, my brother claims that I ruined him for school because he knew all he needed to know by the time he got to kindergarten and the classes he had to take were never as fun and exciting as mine.

As the years passed, I worked really hard to get good grades in school. My parents relentlessly pushed me beyond my limits because they knew I would be the first one in my family to go to college. My senior year finally came around and I was all set to go to college to fulfill my dream of becoming a teacher when my plans were suddenly dismantled. My parents got divorced and I was crushed. I felt like my whole world came crashing down. Through that devastation, I quickly learned about the need for a Plan B. I was hired at the New York State Senate as a word processor, made a lot of great friends, and was exposed to the kind of learning that college could not compete with. However, that calling to teach was still yanking at my heart and so I began taking night classes. I married the love of my life, my high school sweetheart, and we bought a house. Life was great, but yet, I still felt something missing and I still longed to teach. My best friend came over one night and brought me a Precious Moments figurine that played, "I'd Like to Teach the World to Sing." She said, "I didn't sit in your classroom all those years on that scorching hot porch for you not to do what you love doing. You can make this happen."

I was so inspired by her words and thoughtfulness that I immediately took action. My very supportive husband and I worked two jobs and I went to school full time. I diligently focused on reaching my goal of becoming a teacher while having a beautiful baby along the way. Finally, my dream came to fruition and I was a teacher! I loved, loved, loved, what I did. I was planning for the next school year a week after the last one ended. My colleague and I took students on amazing trips and created lessons that took students on magical adventures. We did projects, taught to the academic as well as the emotional needs of each child, and most importantly we built up their self-esteem. I never felt like I was working because I was doing what I loved and loved what I did!

As I entered my ninth year of teaching, I was recruited into administration. I never thought I would leave the classroom, but the superintendent and principal both felt that I was a leader and compelled me to complete the educational administration program. From the moment I took my first class, I was hooked.

I was hired in a very prominent suburban school district as the assistant principal of the high school and was given autonomy to make the job my own. I worked collaboratively to create amazing programs that supported students. I was privileged to work with our most needy population of students who I liked to call our "at-promise" youth. I read a story in *Chicken Soup for the Soul* about kids, who like birds, may have a broken wing. Once they are nurtured and healed, they can fly as high or even higher than anyone else. I made it my mission to heal every broken wing and encourage them to fly higher than they ever imagined possible. I made a difference every day, I was still teaching the world to sing, and I felt so fulfilled!

I have always been a Jack Canfield fan from the time I read the first *Chicken Soup for the Soul* book. I used the stories in every speech I delivered and in my work with students. I also studied *The Key to the Law of Attraction* and *The Success Principles* and I have always lived my life following those teachings. I would come up with a goal, visualize it, use my affirmations, and the right people and opportunities always emerged to bring my dreams to fruition.

One of my goals was to earn a Doctorate Degree in Educational Leadership. That was a break-through goal. Me, Lisa Patierne, earning a Doctorate? Again the right people and opportunities showed up and not only did I get my degree, but I did my research and wrote my dissertation on active school shooters. When I got into education, I never imagined I would be training with Homeland Security, attending bomb training school, and learning to become an Incident Commander. However, in light of all that had been happening around the country regarding school safety, this was a perfect topic to research in my quest to make schools safe for all students, faculty, and staff. I brought all of my knowledge and expertise into my school district and together with our police department, we became a model school for safety and we were recruited to host workshops and seminars for other school districts.

I loved my job. I was on top of the world, but I felt that it was time to move on to a principal's position. I applied for a few openings and I was offered a job in a neighboring school. It took about three weeks for them to get back to me and during a conversation with the superintendent I had a nagging feeling in my gut that I should decline the position. Ralph Waldo Emerson's words about listening to that inner voice were dancing in my head. Emerson noted the importance of listening to, acknowledging, and following our inner voice regardless of the other voices that may be pulling us elsewhere. I still had time to run as fast as I could as my resignation had not been accepted from my former job. I ignored the feedback and I accepted the position. Within the first month I was confident about one thing; I had made a mistake. Through hard work and perseverance, I have always been very successful in both my personal and professional life. I have been an accomplished educator, student advocate, and leader for 25 years. I always received glowing reviews, I made a difference for many students and adults, and I worked diligently to earn my Doctorate Degree.

The two years that I spent in that position were the two worst years in my educational career. No matter what I did, it was not right. I was beat down and emotionally shattered over and over again. Although I tried to remain positive, getting up and going to work with a smile on, no matter how awful I felt, I knew I was way off course. I had welts in my mouth, I was sick all the time, my whole body ached, and I lost the light that had always shined so brightly from within me. I worked so hard to act as if I was ok at work, that when I got home, I had nothing left. My family and friends were so worried about me. I became withdrawn and had no ambition to do anything outside of school. No matter how hard I worked, I felt like a hamster on a wheel going nowhere fast.

One day, I went to a service for my cousin and the pastor

began speaking about Jonah and the Whale. Jonah was not on the path to fulfilling his purpose and he was being sent signs, feedback if you will. He chose to ignore those signs and continued down the path of his own design until he was thrown overboard and swallowed by a whale where he spent three terrifying days. The whale eventually brought him to the land where he was supposed to be and where he was meant to deliver his message and fulfill his destiny. After telling the story, the pastor said, "If you are in a dark place where you are feeling sick, unhappy, unmotivated, and not living the life you were meant to live, that is feedback you are receiving. You need to listen to that feedback and GET OUT of the BELLY of the WHALE!"

Every attending member of my family, those who didn't know how to help me or who I had become, turned to me and said, "Get out of the belly of the whale!" Wow! I was like Jonah. I was ignoring the blatant feedback I had been receiving that I was off course and I got swallowed by the whale. That was an eye opener to me, but at the same time, getting out of the belly of the whale is easier said than done right? Every time I thought about quitting, the *other* holy trinity, fear, roadblocks, and considerations would swoop in. I have held some form of a job since I was twelve years old and to just resign without having another job lined up, well that was scary and difficult to do. Questions and doubts would flood my brain. "What if I don't get another job?" "What are people going to think, I'm resigning after a year and a half?" "Who would want to hire me if I couldn't make it here?" I am a firm believer in synchronicity and I believe that story was a message for me to take inspired action and get my light back. One of the ways I've been successful in my life and in my career has been to **take action—face my fears and do it anyway!** That is exactly what I did.

That next week, after another emotional beat down, I resigned, effective at the end of the year. It was difficult to go there and fulfill my obligation, but I forged ahead, putting my students at the forefront. I remained positive walking into that building every day. My mother would call me every morning before I left and say, "You look in that mirror before you walk out that door and tell yourself, I like me! I am a worthwhile person!" I actually hung a mirror in my vestibule and as I walked out of the house I would look into that mirror and repeat those valuable words. Day after day I continued to find the good in students, faculty, and staff and walk those halls with my head up and a smile on my face. I continued to heal broken wings and lead with poise, even though my situation got more challenging each day.

I knew in my heart that I would land a position where I was living my life on purpose. I set my goals, I wrote them down, I believed it would happen, and I meditated every morning. I said my affirmations every day and I prayed constantly. I applied for job after job and I was a finalist for many of them. I picked up the phone, which is not always easy to do, and I asked everyone I knew to assist me. Superintendents from my previous districts and my network of administrative contacts and friends who knew I was a great leader and a person that got caught up in a bad situation, were all reaching out to support and help me. Despite the unwavering support, I was struggling not to get frustrated when I finished as a finalist for almost every position I applied for. I would have to endure the stress of preparing for each interview, go through the grueling process of the interview, and anxiously await the call, only to be told no. Each process took weeks and this went on for months.

That did not stop me. I surged forward and my mantra became, "Some will, some won't, so what, someone's waiting," and when I heard the word no, I would say, "Next!" I re-read my Canfield books, I listened to positive videos, and I knew the right job would show up. After nine interviews, and nine rejections, the exact job that I visualized, wrote about, prayed for, and affirmed every day manifested for me. Fortunately for me, on the tenth try, the whale safely delivered me to the shores of a new school district where I have been privileged to work with the kindest, most caring, and compassionate team of leaders, who have the same beliefs and values as I do. In the four years that I've been there many of my hopes and dreams have come to fruition. As I went back to my goals from 2010, one goal was to be a successful principal in a kind and caring school and the other one was to be a highly successful motivational speaker and author who brings love, light, and hope to the World.

My new superintendent asked us to dream big and think outside the box as we worked to help every child be successful. An opportunity presented itself to me. It was a chance to submit a proposal for attendance at the Success Principles-Train the Trainer Live Event with Jack Canfield. Although I had only been in my position for less than a year, I decided to put a proposal together. I petitioned the district to pay for my attendance at the training, noting how I could bring this important work back to my students, teachers, school district and community. Although they loved the idea, they couldn't afford to send me to California and pay for the live training. They offered an alternative, which was the on-line program. I accepted, but in my heart, I knew that I would be attending Train the Trainer Live. I visualized being there, I kept in contact with Jack Canfield's Office, and, most importantly, I believed I was going. In fact, I cancelled a trip to Italy with my friends because I knew I would be in California in September of 2018.

In March, a lovely woman, whom I was working with on poverty, trauma, and school safety, came into my office and we began to talk. I told her about the Success Principles' training and she loved it. She said, "Lisa, I can give you some money to go if you come back and teach it to the teachers in my region." She offered to fund a huge portion of the training, but I was still short. Knowing the importance of asking for what you want, I called the Canfield office and asked if there was any wiggle room. Jody Schwartz, the wonderful woman that I was working with, said she would ask and get back to me. Twenty minutes later, she called me back and said, "All I had to do was tell them you did your dissertation on active school shooters and in light of all that is going on in the country, they said, 'Get her here!'" As the saying goes, "The rest is history."

I am so happy and grateful that, like Jonah, the whale safely delivered me to the land where I am supposed to be so that I can share my message, fulfill my purpose, and continue teaching the world to sing. Since I got out of the belly of the whale my life has changed for the better in so many ways. I have been afforded numerous opportunities to share my knowledge and build success skills in students, teachers, faculty, staff, and the community at large. Further, I am now a highly successful author and speaker changing lives, as I help people, teams, and organizations realize their passion and purpose and assist them in reaching every goal they set. In addition to having the honor to co-write this amazing book *Women Who Shine*, I am co-authoring *RESPONSIVE Leadership* with Lieutenant Colonel (Ret) John Nawoichyk, Associate Athletic Director at the United States Military Academy at West Point. Our book is designed to help individuals, teams, and organizations discover how to build confidence, increase resilience, live with passion and purpose, and accomplish every goal you set, no matter who you are or where you came from. I am also training hundreds of police officers using the concepts of RESPONSIVE Leadership, in order to build resilience, strengthen leadership, and understand and minimize the effects of trauma on police officers, their families, and the communities they serve, which will ultimately create bridges of peace, hope, trust, and success for all. I am so happy and grateful that I've been afforded the opportunity to bring love, light, and hope to the World in so many ways.

By listening to the feedback, both internal and external, I believe and gratefully declare that I am where I am supposed to be. I have never felt this exuberant and alive and I look forward to many more years of teaching the World to sing. My wish for all of you is that you find the song that has been placed in your heart and sing it loudly. In the words that changed my life, "If you are in a place where you are feeling sick, unhappy, unmotivated, and not living the life you were meant to live, that is feedback you are receiving. You need to listen to that feedback and GET OUT of the BELLY of the WHALE!"

ABOUT DR. LISA PATIERNE

Dr. Lisa Patierne is a dynamic motivational speaker, author, success trainer, and coach, drawing upon her 28 years as an educator, leader, and high school principal. She has combined her experience, training, and research to deliver unforgettable experiential keynote presentations and workshops that assist organizations, teams, and individuals in reaching their greatest potential.

Lisa holds her doctorate in Educational Leadership from Sage College of Albany, a formal certification in both the Success Principles®, and is a Barrett Values Centre Consultant. She is currently working on certification in Regenerating Images in Memory (RIM) ®

Lisa is currently co-authoring another book entitled *RESPONSIVE Leadership* with Lieutenant Colonel (US Army Retired) John Nawoichyk (Associate Athletic Director, United States Military Academy at West Point), which is designed to help individuals, teams, and organizations discover how to build confidence, increase resilience, live with passion and purpose, and accomplish every goal they set, no matter who they are or where they came from.

As the educational consultant for the State of New York Police Juvenile Officers Association, Lisa has provided training to hundreds of police officers using the concepts of RESPONSIVE Leadership, in order to build resilience, strengthen leadership, and understand and minimize the effects of trauma on police officers, their families, and the communities they serve, which will ultimately create bridges of peace, hope, trust, and success for all.

She is so happy and grateful that she has been afforded the opportunity to bring love, light, and hope to the World in so many ways.

Lisa can be reached at
RisingtoGreatness19@gmail.com

Facebook: Lisa Patierne
Website: www.LisaPatierne.com

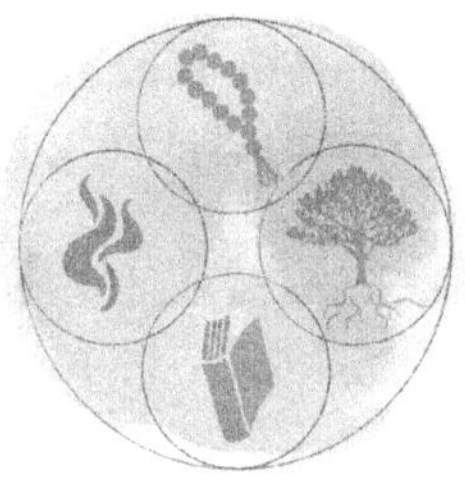

FINDING MY INNER SHINE

Maria Ramos

I am a mom, a wife, a professional planner, a travel agent, a backstage mom, an Ironwife sherpa, a volunteer, and a servant leader. Others' shining moments are my success. Although, long ago, I did take center stage once.

I practically grew up on stage. I started dance lessons in grade school and I loved the dance floor. I excelled in tap, loved jazz dance, and loathed ballet. Eventually, my teachers said, "it's time you take some ballet classes or else you won't improve in jazz and tap." So, I took ballet classes reluctantly. We started competing and we thought we were big time dancers. The competition team took the stage at recital and everyone looked up to us. We were a small group of maybe 10-15 girls. The stage was where everybody knew my name. I shared my joy of performing each year at recital. I enjoyed the accolades from friends and family each performance.

I went to a small, private, Quaker school where the arts had a strong presence in the curriculum. I played the flute. I loved being part of the ensemble and performing in our concerts. Creating music with my peers was a thrill for me. I loved performing in plays. I was never a lead role, always an extra. I did land a few dancer roles, and that was where I belonged. That was my place, that's where I shined. I wasn't all just about the performing arts. I also dabbled in other activities, like yearbook and prom committee. Yes, my love for planning events started in high school. I recall when we traveled into Philadelphia to take a tour of the room where we would eventually have our prom. I remember we searched for deejays and photographers while planning the décor and theme, We've Got Tonight. I enjoyed it, party planning was fun. Little did I know how this would be a steppingstone for my career.

Growing up in suburban South Jersey, born to immigrants from the Philippines, my dad was a hard-working physician, and my mom paused her career in the medical field to raise my sister and me. She's a jack of all trades. She volunteered for the women's auxiliary and worked side careers as a florist, real estate agent, and banker. With nine and a half years between my sister and me, I grew up for the most part like an only child. My sister moved away to college when I was eight years old. Therefore, all the attention at home was on me and I was lucky to do almost anything I set my mind to. However, going to college for performing arts was out of the question. I needed to pursue a real career and I was okay with that. Was my life on stage coming to an end? Had I taken my final curtain call?

I moved north to Rhode Island to go to a small liberal arts school for college. It was a five-and-a-half-hour drive from home, close enough to drive home in a day, but too far just to come home for the weekend. I enjoyed my independence. I was growing and learning how to become an adult. I didn't abandon the performing arts completely. My freshman year, I decided to try out for the dance team. I thought it would be a great way to meet new friends, stay fit, and do something I loved. What I didn't expect to gain out of the experience happened before I even made the team.

Tryouts and auditions can be nerve-wracking. The thought

of someone judging you for how you look and for every move you make for 90 seconds can be overwhelming. I consider myself lucky, because I tend to flourish in these moments. One of my first friends in college was also trying out for the team. She was struggling with the combination we were given for the audition. I took her under my wing and worked with her. I wanted her to succeed. I needed her to succeed because I wanted us to be on the team together. I wanted her to make the team more than making it myself! Making it through the audition process, I remember being so proud of her! Honestly, I don't remember how I did. I do, however, remember watching her and almost willing her to nail the routine. She did! When the team roster came out, we were so excited that we made the team together, but honestly, the high of seeing her progress through the whole process and make the team was success for me. It was a new high and it was only the beginning.

Dance team was a great outlet for me. It fulfilled my need to perform, but wasn't a burden to my schedule or my main priority. I had flexibility to join other activities if I wanted, unlike when I was in high school. It was the perfect first-semester activity to engage in on campus, while doing something that felt like home to me. However, I wanted more.

College is full of opportunities and I was ready to fill my schedule and become as active as I could. When friends introduced me to a co-ed business fraternity that they were looking to bring on campus, I was intrigued. I had declared a business major early on, so I was interested about what a co-ed fraternity had to offer; or more so, how I could contribute to bringing the organization on campus. Having been immersed into college life, it almost felt natural for me to step in as an active player and see my friends' goal to bring a new organization to campus come to life. What would I to bring to the table, though? I was a freshman, just skimming the waters and finding out what my intended major was all about. The process of chartering a new chapter on campus was quite the undertaking. The application, the recommendations and participation from faculty, the recruitment of members, the pledging and initiation were intense. However, there was a key element that needed expertise of unique individuals that I fit perfectly. A banquet needed to be planned for the initiation. I eagerly volunteered to serve on the committee and I knew this was my place in the new chapter of the fraternity. It was a rush for me to help plan the final celebration of hard work and dedication for our chapter. Also, became a brother of the International Fraternity of Delta Sigma Pi.

Fraternity life was at the forefront of my college career. I encouraged and motivated my peers to hold offices and to lead our chapter. I continued to help plan fraternity events. I found my groove in the process; creating plans, agendas and outlines were fun for me. I held leadership positions, but nothing was more satisfying than supporting and helping others succeed. After graduation, I wanted to stay involved with the fraternity as I felt I had a real calling. Why was my urge to stay involved so intense?

I decided to pursue a master's degree and further my education in tourism and event management. My passion for events was evolving and wanted to immerse myself in the industry. I moved to Washington, DC and was fortunate enough to have my sister take me in until I got settled. Moving from a small Rhode Island town to the nation's capital was quite the adjustment. Luckily, I had my fraternity network to rely on. I went to an alumni meet-up with other brothers in the area. In one chance meet-up, I fulfilled my urge to stay involved in fraternity life. It was natural. I volunteered to help charter a new chapter, just as I had done at my alma mater. My fraternity brothers were quickly my new friends, helping me find roommates and establish myself in the area. I became the go-to gal for planning our alumni events and gatherings. Pursuing an advanced degree in tourism and events made me the expert amongst my brothers.

I was making friends in high places, within the fraternity

that is. Not long after installing a new chapter together, one of our alumni brothers shared that he was looking to run for a leadership role on our national board. He already held a position that he was appointed to as a collegiate, but this was a new and exciting journey that he was about to endure. I found myself in an integral role in his campaign, and during his tenure, as his planning gopher; a campaign manager of sorts. We were planning small group retreats with other leaders, writing speeches, and creating plans for his term. He was in the spotlight, but I got to be in the background and help him eventually win his election. A few years later, I was able to do it again when he ran for the highest office of our fraternity, Grand President. I was able to embrace the joy I got from using my skills to help him succeed in the fraternity. He and his wife also allowed me to help them with their wedding. I was their day-of coordinator. I helped plan a few friends' weddings and took on the role of day-of coordinator for others, so I felt completely at ease and honored to be a part of their day. Social events were becoming a small part of my portfolio. Event planning was my thing. It's what fueled me, gave me an adrenaline rush. It's what made me feel like I was on top of the world.

While balancing my fraternity life and an internship, I was able to complete my degree. Early in my career as an up-and-coming independent event professional, I was saying yes to all kinds of events and projects. I was commissioned by a medical alumni association to plan an annual meeting. Hosting a meeting may sound mundane to some, but when you envision an experience for your guests to appreciate, the fruition of it all is so satisfying. This event became a pivotal milestone, not only in my career, but also in life. I was eager to gain experience and honestly, willing to take any paid gig. The meeting was a success and one of the committee members approached me about helping with her daughter's wedding. This was the wedding that changed my life, the wedding of my now sister-in-law, the wedding where I met my husband.

The story of how we met is too comical not to share. However, I must provide some background. Their family weren't strangers to me. They are friends of my parents and I knew of their now adult children for quite some time, however, we were rarely in the same circle of friends and I was still living in the metro DC area while they all lived in South Jersey and Maryland. While waiting for all the groomsmen to arrive at the church for the rehearsal, in walks a confident, casually dressed guy. I approached him and possibly quite sharply, asked where the rest of the groomsmen were. He gave me a look and a shrug, turning to his older brother asking who I was. Without a stutter, his older brother points out that I'm the wedding planner. With a puzzled look he was surprised his sister had a wedding planner. Long story short, yes, I married a groomsman from a wedding I was working.

My husband is a triathlete. Not just any triathlete, he's an Ironman. Two-time Ironman finisher. Now, he wasn't a triathlete when we met. This only became a hobby to him a few years after we had our daughter. His dedication to training and endurance is awe inspiring. We are here supporting him. An Ironman race is a very complex adventure. Not only for the triathlete, but for the support crew, or sherpas as we're affectionately called. We are Ironwife and Ironkid. While he prepares with training and acquiring the proper gear and nutrition for the race, a trustworthy support crew is essential for all the other details; the travel, accommodations, understanding the course for catching a glimpse of your athlete, and preparing for their post-race wind down meal and recuperation. They cannot do it alone. The thrill of a race for me is helping my husband prepare, insuring we have adequate accommodations, and tracking him throughout the 12-plus hour day. Watching all the athletes push their bodies to intense extremes is inspirational. However, I get a rush every time I get to start the race as part of the support crew. There are so many moving pieces to a spectator's experience at an Ironman race, it's so invigorating. It's the same awesome thrill I feel when I'm working an event, with all the pieces falling together just as it's supposed to happen. When he crosses the finish line, there's excitement, pride, relief, and joy felt by everyone. He may be up on that podium, but my daughter and I are truly shining on the sidelines with a sense of accomplishment.

As one may have guessed, I'm naturally the family planner. Not just for our nuclear family, but our extended family. From family dinners to family vacations and more weddings, when you excel at your profession, your family depends on you. I happily oblige. I'm the family planner, not only because it's my profession, but it's my passion.

My daughter followed in my footsteps, taking dance lessons at a very young age and to be honest, she really did not have a choice. I just prayed really hard every year that she would still enjoy it and return for more. And she does. If I may brag a little, she is 100 times the dancer I ever was at her young age of 11 years old. Every parent wants to see their child succeed. We insure they have all the resources we can provide to them in order to grow and flourish. As an event professional and former dancer, I take her performances and recitals very seriously. Now this is not only for her to succeed, but for all the dancers as well. I use my planning and logistic skills to insure all the performers have what they need backstage in order to perform onstage. I took this on as my own project. Most moms are not like me. The planner in me is over prepared with an arsenal of extra supplies. For every performance, I bring a supply kit, fully stocked with hair pins and safety pins, first aid and make up, glue guns and stitch kits. My motto is "No performer will be ill prepared." Now this is no fault of themselves or their parents. The culmination of my experience as a performer and a planner evolves me into this mega dance mom on steroids. I enjoy watching my daughter perform on stage. As a plus, I love being able to support all the performers and add a bit of organization to the joyous chaos of backstage life.

Throughout my career and throughout my life, the desire to help others has always been strong. I've found my place where I find joy in my career and outside of work. Volunteering and offering my skills to organizations big and small, parent-teacher associations to not-for-profit charities, has always been a satisfying draw for me. Being able to use my skillset outside of work, even with my family, gives me gratification. I'm the supporter, the #1 fan, the sherpa, the dance mom, all of it, and it's what I love. Giving people, in all dimensions of life, a way to flourish is my joy, because when I can help empower others to do their thing, the fulfillment from their success warms me to shine within.

ABOUT MARIA RAMOS

Maria Ramos is the founder of Innovative Meetings, LLC and a certified meeting professional (CMP). Prior to establishing Innovative Meetings, Maria served in the association industry in marketing and meeting planner capacities. A servant leader in her community and network, Maria has over 20 years in the meetings industry and has produced events, meetings and conventions spanning the social, medical and association industries. As an independent planner, Maria engages with colleagues throughout the events industry, collaborating on large-scale conventions and events. Known for her extensive project management experience, Maria has systematically created custom planning strategies for all of her clients. Her expertise is in creating and implementing standard operating logistical procedures and for annual events. Born and raised in Southern New Jersey, Maria resides in East Greenwich Township with her family. She is a proud wife to her triathlete husband, Ron, and mother to their 11-year-old daughter, Jacquelyn.

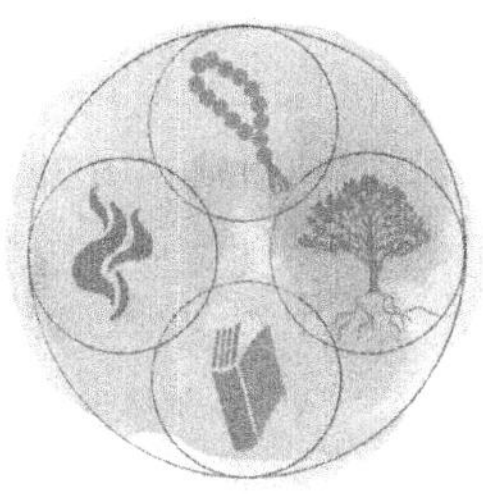

WE ARE MEDICINE

Emma Alexandra Williams

Little prayer

let ruin end here
let him find honey where there was once a slaughter
let him enter the lion's cage & find a field of lilacs
let this be the healing & if not let it be

~Danez Smith

Having only lived in Manhattan until I was 7, my memories of the City mainly revolve around playing in its glorious parks. I fondly remember my sister and I crawling into the enormous mouth of the hippopotamus that resides in Riverside Park with the smell of freshly mowed grass and the happy screams of children running through the spraying fountains. To learn that I was accepted to the school of my dreams and that I would be living in the greatest city in the world once again, a city that I had a deep desire to reconnect with, was beyond exciting. Shortly after the start of my first semester, a family friend reached out to me. It had been ages since we last spoke.

"Let's go out, I'd love to show you the City."

Excited to explore more than just its parks, I agreed. After all, I was seeing a now distant acquaintance who was my playmate when I was only 6 years old. What could go wrong? I hadn't seen him in well over a decade. When we met up, he remarked, "wow, you've really grown up." We sat down in a dimly lit restaurant on the Upper East Side. He ordered us two Mai Tais. Two Mai Tais became four, four became six, and so on.

After what felt like an almost exclusively liquid dinner, he said his roommates were smoking weed at his apartment and asked if I wanted to join. In my drunken stupor I agreed. I had smoked weed maybe once or twice before years ago, but never this intoxicated. One puff, and it was lights out.

That night, I was raped. It would take years before I would be able to accept it as such. Years of concealing the act I so staunchly would not, could not, call rape. If I took control over how I perceived the situation, then I wasn't the victim. Right?

I woke up in a daze, my head pounding, unsure of where I was, until I looked down to see blood covering my inner thighs, my bloody pad on the floor next to me, and my clothes strewn about. I hastily gathered my things and ran outside of his building, tears filling up my eyes. I called my mother at 6 am and told her what happened. Her response, although one that was indeed born out of deep concern, was nonetheless a product of rape culture: "Oh my God, Emma! Are you ok? How could you let yourself get so drunk?" This is my fault, I thought at the time. I let this happen.

Somehow, the immense shame led me back to my abuser, who I saw a handful of times thereafter. It's incredible how, almost 10 years after the fact, I am committing this part of my story to paper. This was something I couldn't, in my right mind, imagine myself doing back then. Even thinking about it in the years that followed made my entire being quiver with disgust.

Fast forward eight years to the summer of 2020. I was in a spa about to get a massage. The masseur rubbed oil between his hands and began. He started on my shoulders and upper back, slowly moved down towards my butt, each stroke broadening, covering a wider area of flesh, his fingers moved closer and closer to my anus, pressing and squeezing more intensely with each rotation. I was uneasy. His hand lifted my right hip and a sense of relief came over me, "I'm turning around." Thankfully, I thought, "the butt massage is ending." He told me not to turn over and as he did, his hand lifted my hip and gradually started moving toward my ovaries, pressing on my lower belly, all the way to the upper part of my vagina, coming closer and closer with each stroke, until he got there.

The horror.

I was paralyzed. "Is this really happening? It can't be. It is. Do something. Do something. *DO SOMETHING.*" my mind screams.

I couldn't. I couldn't speak. I couldn't move. I was petrified.

My recollection of the rape began to surface from the depths of my inner shadows, of my deep repression. My body was frozen. The rubbing intensified. I felt moist. I was humiliated. I wanted to disappear, but I couldn't.

Why couldn't I, a Barnard alumna, an outspoken feminist who spent the better part of four years studying Gender & Sexuality Studies; someone so fervent in her fight for equality, so defiant, so vocal, so opinionated, have been more assertive? How could I have let that happen? Where did my strength go? Why was I so powerless? How could my voice abandon me in my time of need?

All I could do was report him to the police. While he was arrested the same day, it took nine long months before he was finally convicted of a felony. But here's the kicker, the felony conviction was for giving massages without a license, even though there were several other women who testified against him for the same abuse. Apparently, forcible touching is only considered a misdemeanor. Yes, he received the highest form of punishment under the law as it's written today, however, who is the law really trying to protect?

The rage I felt after the incident was enough to boil my blood. In the weeks that followed, I was unable to keep down what seemed so easily suppressed. I could no longer live with this deep-rooted fury. My past trauma combined with this more recent one overflowed my stress bucket and my pain was spilling over. I began to notice how this spillage was manifesting in the way I treated myself and my most cherished relationships. What was worse is that with deeper introspection, I realized that I had been doing this for the entirety of my adult life. This had to stop. My relationships, and my sanity, were at stake.

This engendered the beginning of tremendous self-work that has led me to the healthy and empowered place that my soul resides within today.

In January of this year, my friend invited me to a spiritual retreat. Although nervous, I was excited to see what was in store for me, especially since I had gained a newfound desire to address my anger, understand it, and ultimately, vanquish it.

In early February, one of my closest friends and I traveled to where the retreat was taking place. When we arrived, we found a room full of strangers introducing themselves, conversing, and settling in. Little did I know that this weekend would change my life forever.

During the first night of the ceremony, I looked up from my hands to see all these beautiful souls sitting around the container, one next to the other on their pillows, wrapped up in blankets, forming a perfect circle. The energy was so potent it seemed infinite. The music was unlike anything I've ever dreamt of. It filled my ears, vibrating down to my feet and then back up only to emanate from the crown of my head. An ethereal voice vibrated, utterly encompassing me. I felt as though I was levitating, and yet at the same time I was grounded, my Muladhara Chakra rooted to our beloved Pachamama. The space we created through entering a most intimate of contracts with one another is sacred, and so are we.

The second night of the ceremony was hard work. The night started with terror, anguish, and anger. The divine Spirits were showing me a devastating world of angry machinery, eating, demolishing, destroying. The visual representation of rage on a treacherous, never-ending loop. I was terrified, trembling, and whimpering under my blanket. At that moment I remember my intention going into the retreat. To heal my anger.

Then it hits me.

These visions represented my anger, the profound anger from having repressed my trauma, the rape, the theft, the abuse, the shame, the confusion, and the hurt, of all of which left unaddressed gave way to the rage that resided in my heart. Once I realized this, the terrorizing world I was in began to break down slowly, melting before my eyes. With it, my fear dissipated, my trembling softened. I focused on my trauma and started to weep, grieving that which I pushed down, ignored for so, so long. I wept and wept. My tears washed away the hurt, the pain. I felt the cracks in my heart that once so easily let in insecurity, self-doubt, and self-loathing, begin to close. My heart became whole. I could see it. I could feel it. I was in a beautiful place, peaceful and warm. I began to smile, laugh even. My healing healed my sisters. The collective pain from the pillaging and theft of their own bodies began to heal through my newfound ability to comprehend, accept, and finally grieve.

Celestial energy coursed through my heart and soul. I loved myself with all that is in me. I loved and honored every single new and beautiful cell that had been born. I whispered, "I love you," and they vibrated back. I felt revitalized, vibrant, alive. I have healed my deepest wounds, the divine Spirits have licked them clean, kissed them with their soft and tender love. My anger was gone, my heart was at peace. I had compassion I didn't know a person could have. Compassion for the most hateful, angry, and violent people. There was nothing to forgive, only to help heal. When one heals, the whole heals. We are all brothers and sisters.

We all came from Pachamama and we will all return to Her one day. We are all one.

Before and after the ceremony, we all took a moment to share our intentions and insights with the group. During my post-ceremony share, I was the most vulnerable I had ever been. I sobbed as I described what had happened to me and that I had repressed it for so long. I shared how, through this experience and the inclusion of therapy, yoga, meditation, breathwork, journaling and all of the self-work I had been doing, that I'd reached a point where I could send love to my abusers. Something I couldn't begin to fathom even just a year before. I was able to send love and compassion to those hurting so much that they can do that to someone else, to inflict so much pain means that there exists that much pain within them to then inflict. I lovingly and peacefully detached from them and the pain they had caused me. I hope they heal, the way I've healed.

My share shook the room. "Aho! So powerful," said the Shaman. "We are all wounded Shamans."

After I shared, three other women in their share responded to mine. They told similar stories and my heart wept. Through their shares my healing was fortified. I love my sisters. We are so beautiful, we are so powerful, we are so strong.

Trust me when I say that there is no force more powerful than people's collective pain being healed in solidarity with one another.

The Shaman shared last, surprising us with his vulnerable and intimate contribution, as he typically only imparted wisdom onto what others shared. I was touched. The power of vulnerability! It was truly formidable, infectious, and beautiful. He thanked me afterwards for my courage. The amount of love I received from every single person in the space was insurmountable. This is my spiritual family.

Later when I described my second night of ceremony, the journey of self-realization, healing and formation of deep self-love, my mother imparted such wisdom onto my experience and my understanding of myself within it. She said that, as a response to all the toxic and violent masculinity that so many of our sisters have fallen victim to, I had adopted an unhealthy, adaptive, masculine energy as a defense mechanism to combat my unresolved experiences of trauma. To clarify, by no means am I alluding to the fact that the masculine energetic is one that is aggressive or toxic in and of itself, but rather in its unhealthy, adaptive form, it can take on a destructive role. My mother's wisdom helped me finally come to terms with why I had seen my abuser again years ago, when I was an insecure and naive 19-year-old. Although a seminal part of my pain, I needed to regain a sense of agency, to take back the power that had been stolen from me. I now know that having seen him again doesn't lessen the trauma I endured, no matter how hypocritical and shameful my perception of it was at the time.

This adaptive masculine defense mechanism explained the aggression I exhibited, towards myself, others, and even the spaces I navigated. All of which suppressed my inner, divine feminine. The gentle, soft, and supple side of me that was there all along. This understanding and release of my suppressed anger had allowed my divine feminine to heal and make Herself known. No longer cowering in the shadows of an unhealthy masculine shield. Ceremony helped strip away the disguising layers that pain, hurt, and sadness created, making room for enlightenment and self-discovery. All of which ultimately allowed me to come closer to living in alignment with my truest, most authentic self.

My divine feminine is nurturing, gentle, soft, and yet She is so strong. I felt empowered by having the strength to display the purest kind of vulnerability, all of which became a positive feedback loop; the stripping away of suppressing armor was done through embodying vulnerability, which in turn opened the doors for more healing and awakening. A truly infectious and invincible cycle of self-love. In fact, some may even call it a superpower. One all of us possess.

Doing the work, day in and day out, is accessible to us all. The deep inner work that propels us to heal our wounds and prevent our traumas from defining us, this is the work that allows us to accept them as a part of our past, making us stronger and all the wiser. We cannot control what happens to us, but we can control the hold that those events have on our lives. We are all capable of embarking on this journey towards our True North, wherever that may be, and to live in accordance with the best version of ourselves, for ourselves, and for the people whose lives we touch. Whether you have a daily meditation practice, journal every morning, or confide in a therapist who helps you work through all the trials and tribulations life throws at us, these practices can serve the same purpose of getting us to manifest the deep self-love that we should all continually strive for. While always having forgiveness in our hearts and gratitude in our spirits, remember that the work is never over, nor should it be. After all, life is a journey, not a destination.

I continue to be humbled by all the learning that is still being imparted to me, through sharing my experience with loved ones, and now with you, through practicing introspection, mindfulness, gratitude, and love. My heart is soaring, my roots are grounded. I am so excited for the beautiful journey that lies ahead.

To all my brothers and sisters out there:

You Are Medicine.
We Are Medicine.

ABOUT EMMA ALEXANDRA WILLIAMS

Emma has a BA in Human Rights & Gender Studies from Barnard College of Columbia University and is ardent about the pursuit of social justice. An avid trilingual traveler, her unique, multicultural experience has cultivated a deep passion for the understanding and unraveling of the human condition.

Experienced in communication and relationship building, Emma is an energetic, people person with a deep-rooted passion for service, integrity, and transparency. She finds vitality playing tennis, DJing, and studying the game of poker; while she finds balance in meditation, yoga, and spiritual work.

Instagram: @nodilemmas | **Email:** williams.ema@gmail.com

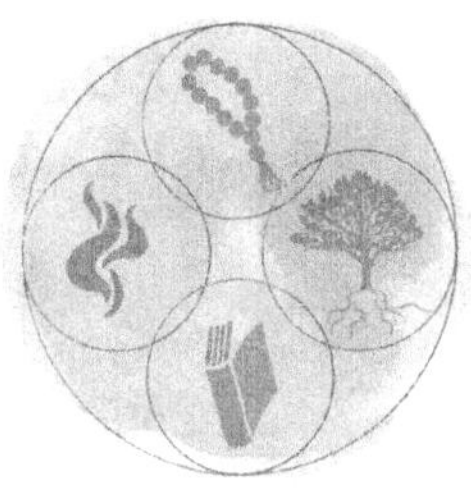

WORTHY

Kristina Williams

"Please love me. Please don't leave me. Please don't leave me by myself. Please don't leave me alone." There's a scared 5-year-old inside of me who wants to say all of that. "Please love me for who I am. Please don't think I'm too much. Please just love me." She's reaching out for a hug, eyes pleading. She just wants to know that it's going to be okay. But it's all in vain, nobody really knows she's in there. Nobody knows she's trapped in the center of my heart, alone and afraid and desperate for someone to reassure her that she's safe, that she can breathe, that everything is going to be alright. Nobody sees her because I don't let them. She's a dirty secret that I keep locked away, out of sight, out of mind for everyone but me. Sometimes people will catch a glimpse of her if they're with me enough. Sometimes she yells just loud enough for someone to hear. But we just explain that she's just acting up, seeking attention and that she's not worthy of another thought and then we patch up the hole that she tried to break through. I've managed to patch up all the windows and holes that she could possibly sneak out of or be seen through. Handy little shame band-aids worked perfectly for that.

The version of me that is trying to be what is expected of me instead of who I am makes a great captor. I've managed to hide my 5-year-old self in the sparkle-fairy costume away for over 30 years. I've spent so many years trying to shrink myself out of existence in the hope that I will one day be good enough for someone. In order to do that, the girl in the sparkly costume needed to be stopped. She needed to be hidden away because she wasn't acceptable. She is all the things I'm not supposed to be. Loud. Annoying. Needy. Chunky. Too big for this world. Too much for this world. She is a lot. Too much, really. Who would ever love her? She is imperfect. She is unlovable. She is unworthy. She is too much, damnit. I mean look at that ridiculous costume.

So, we kept her locked up and we put on the professional suit and did what was expected of us. And every time we told her to be quiet or settle down, a few pieces of the sparkle costume lost their shine. There aren't even any wings on the damn costume. We ripped those off first, obviously, she could escape much easier with those! She could let her presence be known! We couldn't have that! She wasn't going to ruin our plans of being what was expected of us, of being what other people needed and wanted her to be. Back in the cage with you, sparkle-child!

I wasn't a monster, of course. I kept her very well fed. Any time the world showed its cruelty, and she was hurt, I fed her. I ate away the emptiness, the sadness, the loneliness. All of it, just put some food on it. As I got older, I did the same thing with alcohol, with spending money, with anything I could think of just to distract her and keep her quiet. I became everything I thought the world wanted from me and just kept distracting my little sparkle-fairy hostage. I have hidden parts of myself ever since I can remember. I have always tried to hide away the parts of myself that were ugly or displeasing to others. Too tall? Make yourself smaller. Too fat? Suck in your stomach. Too loud? Quiet down. Feelings are hurt? Never let 'em see you sweat.

But while I was busy being who the world wanted me to

be and trying to make everyone happy in an effort to never feel alone, my sparkle-fairy kept taking the hits on my behalf. She kept losing the shine on her costume, of the very thing that made her special. I remember one particular day, in middle school, I was walking down the hallway to class and a couple of guys that were standing in the hall waiting for class to empty out started stomping and yelling "Earthquake" at me as I walked by. My chunky little sparkle-fairy already knew she was too much and too big, that just confirmed it. If I could have willed myself out of existence at that moment, I absolutely would have. Something that happened almost 30 years ago still makes my heart hurt when I think about it. I was absolutely humiliated, and I still tear up a bit when I relive that day in my mind. It made me want to shrink into the smallest version of myself so nobody would notice me. If I stayed quiet, and didn't make waves, nobody would single me out and make fun of me. I just never wanted to feel that feeling again. Middle School kids are a different kind of brutal, by the way. I dreaded going to school after that. It's just one of a number of stories about that. I was terrified to tell my mom and I'm not actually sure I ever did. She hated seeing me hurt and would have gone full mama bear on them. A lot of the time it happened; I just didn't tell her. I didn't want to make the situation worse by exposing the kids or being a tattler. So, I just dealt with it as much as I could. I still hate Sundays to this day because of the feeling of dread I had thinking about going to school the next day. The bullying I experienced just reinforced that all my worst fears were true. That the sparkle-fairy needed to be better hidden, because some of her too much was showing. I just needed to be more acceptable, more of something else in order to protect myself from the cruelty. I just needed to be anything but myself.

So, I continued to hide her and feed her and provide her with numbness or distraction so I could work on being the person that everyone else wanted me to be. Someone acceptable. Someone who was worthy of being a cool kid. I continued to try to change every part of myself to be more palatable to others. I couldn't totally hide who I was, though. There are parts of her that always peeked out. The kindness, the childlike wonder, the heart big enough to power 10,000 suns, that was all still there. Those have got to stay. But God forbid anyone found out that an impulsive, loud, obnoxious sparkle-fairy was behind the good stuff. Nope, she still had to stay hidden. Those other pieces of her weren't good enough. If anyone saw those pieces, they would run away screaming in the other direction. That fear of being abandoned because she wasn't good enough? That's why we kept her hidden and tried to be the acceptable, watered down, boring version of her. A shell of a person. A fallacy.

I don't know who I thought I was kidding. There were always people that saw her and wanted to help her. There were always people who wanted to pick the lock on my heart cage and help her escape. I have lied to myself for years about the fact that people couldn't see her. I didn't believe anyone who told me that they saw her and that she was fine just the way she was. They even saw the battered, bloodied parts of her. The gross, ugly scars from the cage she lived in and the cruelty of the world. It wasn't until my 30s that I even started to realize that other people were out there with their inner child just out there for everyone to see, just running amok. Free-range, just running around, not a care in the world. I was like "Umm, excuse me, what the hell is going on? You can't just let those run free like that!"

After a particularly painful breakup in my early thirties, I started going to therapy and with the help of a therapist, who I adore, I was able to start ripping off those shame band-aids on my heart to rescue my sparkle-fairy and set her free. I started looking at her and really seeing her for who she was. She wasn't some hideous secret that needed to be kept tucked away and out of view. She was a scared little girl who just wanted to feel loved for who she was and to not feel scared any more. Not to feel like one wrong move, one mistake, and it will all come crashing down around her. I'm still terrified of making mistakes and of disappointing people. It's almost crippling at times. It feels like I'm choking, like I can't breathe, when I make a mistake or do something wrong or poorly. It's one of the reasons I didn't start doing theater again until my mid to late 30s. I auditioned for the school musical in high school. It took a lot for me to do it. Like, a LOT. At the end of my audition, they told me I should have picked an easier song. I put myself out there, something that was really hard for me to do, and that one piece of feedback crushed me. It confirmed every fear I had, that I wasn't good enough, that putting myself out there was a bad idea, that I'm just going to fail. I didn't audition for theater again for another 20 years because of that one statement. TWENTY YEARS. I am so eternally grateful that I ended up putting myself out there again and auditioning for Jesus Christ Superstar with the Delaware Children's Theater when I was 35. And then again auditioning for Shrek: The Musical with the Brandywiners. I have always been blessed with amazing friends, but what I found through theater is something truly unique and it helped me start to heal my heart. Having a theater family is unlike anything else I've ever experienced.

When I was on stage, I got to become the "too much" characters. I got to be larger than life and I didn't have to shrink myself down. Hell, I literally got to play a larger-than-life fairy named Stumblina. The writer/director asked me to play the role. She mentioned she had thought of me when writing the show. Looking back now, I'm not sure I've ever been or felt more seen. I didn't just play Stumblina, I was her. A big ol' sparkle fairy who is messy, prone to breaking things accidentally, who doesn't really fit in with the rest of the fairies. One with a huge heart, who cheers on her friends, who just wants to find her people and be loved. All of that icky, messy stuff I tried to hide was visible the whole time. The people who loved me never really cared about the broken and messy parts, they just wanted to see me happy. I was the one being a jerk to my sparkle-fairy. I was ashamed of who I was, how much of me there was, how intense I always felt. I was ashamed of who I was.

And the real irony of the situation is that I was not only making myself suffer because I was hiding parts of myself, I was making people I loved suffer too. They watched me being mean to myself, being hard on myself and then extending grace and compassion to everyone else around me, and it hurt them to see me being such a jerk to someone they loved. My response now when I hear friends talking badly about themselves is "Please don't talk badly about my friend, I love them, and they are awesome." I try to run my self-talk through the filter of "Would you say this to your best friend? If the answer is no, then I damn sure shouldn't be saying it to myself." I started finding healing and comfort and self-acceptance when I realized that my anxiety and self-doubt issues needed to be handled differently. Instead of being hard on myself when I'm having a rough time or dealing with an anxious episode, I talk to the 5-year-old sparkle fairy in my heart and tell her she's safe and that she's going to be okay. It feels ridiculous to admit that, I feel silly doing it, but the thing is, it works. It calms me down when I'm nice to myself and tell myself that I'm doing the best I can. Why am I judging myself for doing something that is working? Because it's silly and a little odd? Who cares? It's working. It's healing the pain and the scars from the past. She's being seen and recognized and shown that she's worthy of love even if she makes a mistake or has a bad day or is grumpy. It wasn't until I started being vulnerable and letting people know the sparkle-fairy existed that I started seeing that I wasn't alone with this. People hide pieces of themselves all the time. Truly beautiful, unique, messy, amazing pieces of themselves because they think they're too much or they're not good enough. Because they are afraid of being rejected. But it's really something special when you see someone tell fear to sit down and shut up and then do the thing that makes them vulnerable because it's in their core and it's bigger than the fear. When you see someone show up for themselves, be their own cheerleader and kick fear in the face, it's a magical experience. I'm going to continue to choose to show up for myself day after day, because my 5-year-old sparkle-fairy wants me to be happy, and now that I've gotten to know her better, I want to make her happy too. She's worth it, I'm worth it, and so are you.

ABOUT KRISTINA WILLIAMS

Kristina is a Delaware native who, by day, works in the Workforce Solutions industry and by night explores her many creative loves. An active volunteer in the local theater community, Kristina has worked on multiple shows with the Delaware Children's Theater and the Brandywiners. When not on stage, she can be found volunteering with makeup and costuming or working on her own creative designs for Whimsical Katz, her e-commerce business for funny and clever apparel and home-goods.

Kristina is passionate about normalizing therapy and treatment for mental illness issues and helping people find access to resources for dealing with ADHD, anxiety and depression. She is also passionate about innovation and creative problem-solving, both in therapeutic and business applications. Through sharing her story, she hopes to reach others who may be struggling with finding their true voice and the confidence to shine their light into the world.

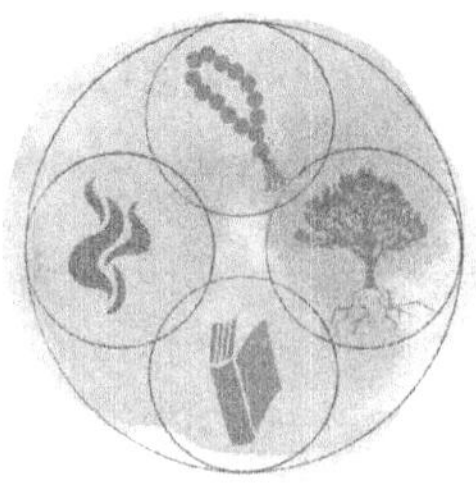

LIGHT THROUGH THE CLOUD

Peggy Wright

I grew up as an only child in a loving home with my parents and my grandmother. We lived in an upscale neighborhood where other children were few and far between. I spent most of my days playing with my dolls. But, unlike many young girls I didn't play house. I never dreamed of being married and becoming a mother. I dreamed of having a career. I pretended to own a ranch in Montana. I treated my dolls for rare diseases in my make-believe hospital. I taught school, and occasionally, I was a rock star.

My mother instilled independence in me from an early age, telling me I could be anything I wanted to be. "Just get a good education. That's something that no one can ever take away from you", she would say. Mother was a very wise woman with only a tenth grade education. She wanted so much more for me.

I graduated high school and began college, but I could only dream of working. As my interest in higher education expired, I met my first husband, Jim. We dated for over a year before we were married. He had enlisted with the navy and after only a year of marriage, we moved to North Carolina.

Jim loved children and wanted to start a family soon after

we were married, but I didn't want children, at least not so soon. We waited three years and finally decided to take the leap. We were transferred back to Memphis during my eighth month of pregnancy. I flew home to my parents' house, where we planned to live until we could find a home. Jim made it home the day before I went into labor.

JJ weighed in at 9 lbs. 13 oz. After delivery, the nurses whisked him away and I was delivered back to my room. I think this was the first time I had really felt excitement about becoming a mother. It seemed as if the entire family felt the same eagerness.

Time ticked away as we waited for JJ to make his way to my room. Now nearing the dinner hour, Jim took the family down to the cafeteria while I waited alone in my room. I could hear people laughing and talking outside the door. I heard babies crying as they were brought to their mothers. And then, silence. I called the nursery. A sweet, young nurse said, "He's a little dusky right now. We will be back in touch soon." "Dusky?" I thought.

The family re-entered the room and I told them what the nurse had said. Before they had time to digest the information, a very tall, middle eastern doctor slowly walked into the room. He asked the family members to wait outside. The doctor stepped forward and said, "I'm afraid I have very, very bad news". My mind began to race. "He's dead," I thought. The doctor asked if we understood the term Down Syndrome or Mongoloidism. I couldn't think. I couldn't even breathe. The doctor continued to state his credentials and apologize for the news he had given. I heard only a word, here and there. I remember thinking, "This can't be happening," as the doctor went on with his lengthy explanation of how and why this had happened. As my mind spun out of control, I was snapped back to reality when I heard the doctor state, "Don't worry. You don't have to take him home. You can leave him here and we will place him." That had to be the most absurd statement I had ever heard. The doctor's eyes met mine and I sat a little taller. "I carried that little boy for 9 months.

You must be out of your mind if you think I would leave him here for placement," I stated, boldly.

When the doctor left the room, the family re-entered. Jim explained to everyone about the information we had received. After a few tears and lots of encouragement, Jim walked to the elevator. My mother stood, looking down at me with tears welling up in her eyes. I told her that God had done this to punish me for all the bad I had done. She took my hand and said, "Oh honey, God doesn't work like that. He would never punish a baby for your sins. And besides, he'll probably grow out of it."

As crazy as that statement sounded, it did have some truth to it. As JJ grew and learned, he did "grow out" of discrimination, and so did I.

Safe at my parents' home, I borrowed a few books from the library. The problem was that these books were written in the 60's. The information stated that JJ would, most likely, never walk or talk, and if he did, it would be much later than normal children. I spent the entire day crying in my room. How was I to give this child what he needed?

The next day, I called every place and everyone I could for answers. I found Special Kids, an organization for children with special needs. JJ was enrolled at two months. We met with teachers, therapists and social workers each week for two years. JJ spoke before 1 year and walked at 16 months.

At 2 years, he was enrolled at Harwood, a school for developmentally delayed children who require specialized instruction and therapeutic services. He continued to flourish, there, until 6 years of age. JJ was ready for a more structured environment. He began Madonna Day School.

As the years rolled on, we moved to the county and JJ began public school in special classes. I had given birth to JJ's sister, Maggie, when JJ was 4 years old. We had a beautiful family. All seemed to be going well, but I had this nagging feeling that something was missing.

One day, while coming home from a walk with the children, I found a brochure on the front door. It spoke of a church in the area. I had grown up in church and knew that my children needed God in their lives. But I wondered if JJ would ever really understand who God is?

We visited this church and joined a few months later. We became very involved. I taught children's Sunday School and a few Wednesday night classes. I also completed nursing school during this time. Life was busy and the kids were growing fast. Then, one morning, while waiting for JJ's bus, he looked up to the sky and said, "God's in the hole." What? I glanced toward the sky and saw the sun shining through the clouds. It was mystical. I wondered if JJ would ever really understand the meaning of God in our lives. I began to pray, asking God to reveal a sign to let me know that JJ understands. But there was no thunder, no bright light, no whisper in my ear. Nothing.

When JJ was about 10 years old, he was invited to church camp. Although he had participated in summer camps before, this would be his first time with normal kids, those without disabilities. I was asked to be the counselor for the girl's cabin and the camp nurse. I accepted wholeheartedly.

I spent the first two days running back and forth throughout the camp. I would go from the girls cabin to JJ's cabin, from the clinic to breakfast, from church service, and on and on it would go until I was able to finally go to bed.

You might think I spent a lot of time checking on JJ and you would be right. This was his first time spending so much time with ordinary kids. As his mother, I worried if he would fit in. Could he understand and follow the rules? As luck would have it, taking care of everyone and everything left me dehydrated. I had to spend an entire day in my cabin. I wasn't able to walk JJ back to his cabin after the evening church service and I worried if he could even find it in the darkness, but my girls came in telling me that JJ made a new friend who helped him get back to the cabin.

The rest of the week went along without any problems. To my surprise, JJ wanted to spend time with his new friend instead of his overprotective mother.

When we had reached the last night of camp, there was a special candlelight service and a time for testimonies. A young man approached the stage and began to speak. I recognized him as JJ's new friend. He told of being on the wrong path, having engaged in alcohol and drugs. He had tried to find himself in the gay community and his parents had discovered all that he had been involved in. Apparently, it was a very ugly scene. Feeling broken, this young man attempted to end his life, but his parents found him before it was too late. They gave him an ultimatum . . . go to church camp or go to a behavioral center. He had chosen camp, but stated that he certainly did not want to be there. And if that wasn't bad enough, he had been "partnered up with the retarded kid." These words shot through me like daggers. All eyes turned to glance at me. I couldn't bear the dejected looks, so I turned my eyes to the floor. All of the heartbreak, the unacceptance, the pity came flooding back.

As his voice began to quiver, the young man continued. He revealed that he had given up and had planned to end his life when he returned home. But then he met JJ. Hearing the tenderness in his tone, I quickly looked up from my embarrassment. I'm not sure if he saw me standing there, but it felt as if he were speaking only to me. He continued the story, recounting the many trips he and JJ had made going up and down the hill to the cabin, and of the numerous reminders he had given JJ to "get dressed," "hurry up," etc. He noted that JJ never became upset. He would just pat the young man on his shoulder and say, "It's ok."

Becoming emotional, the young man spoke of the first night he accompanied JJ to their cabin. Through his tears he said, "JJ has given me something I can't even explain. I have no idea what he was saying to me, but I know that by the time we made it up the hill to our cabin, I was saved".

He had been saved. And so had I. God had answered my prayer in His own time and in an extraordinary way. JJ did know Him. He understood more than I will ever know. I had evolved from a career driven girl to a devoted mother. The pain, the loneliness, and the uncertainty had made me who I was to become.

JJ is now 33 years old. He graduated from high school with a certificate of achievement. He has been employed several times. He has also been cast in plays, participated in many different sports, and has become quite self-sufficient. His greatest attribute is his love for everyone. He radiates love to all those he meets.

I have learned there is nothing he cannot accomplish with patience and understanding. I've also learned that, just as my mother said, "I can be anything I want to be." I want to be a good mother. I have been blessed tenfold.

ABOUT PEGGY WRIGHT

Peggy Wright is a registered nurse with 21 years of experience. She has worked in hospitals, nursing homes, hospice care and home health. She has managed nursing personnel throughout much of her career. For seven years, Peggy volunteered one week each year to medical missions in Nicaragua. She now works as a home health nurse in northern Mississippi, where she dedicates her time and knowledge to patients in rural areas.

Peggy Lives in Holly Springs, MS with her husband, Jimmy, and son, JJ. Peggy's daughter, Maggie, is also an RN in Southaven, MS. Peggy and Jimmy are renovating their 71 year old home. They are anxiously awaiting custody of Jimmy's sixteen year old daughter. Peggy's family members have always encouraged her to follow her dreams. Their love and dedication have given her the tools to succeed.

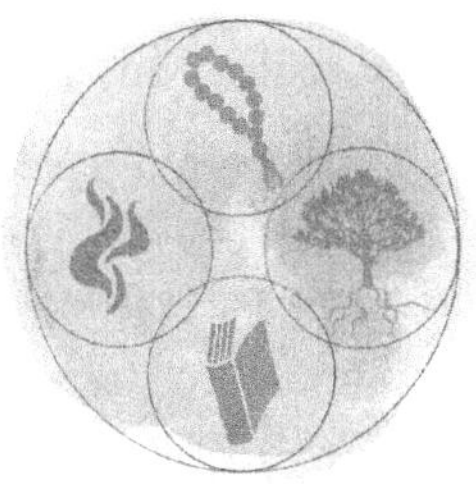

SAY YES TO YOUR DEEPEST CALLING

Dianne A. Allen

Like a lighthouse ushering sailors in from the sea, I am the beacon of light that shines so people can come into a calm and safe harbor for repair, restoration, and rest. I began to embody this way of being over the last four decades as client after client called me their lighthouse. One day, it all clicked, and the journey began.

Like many intense, intuitive introverts, life had been challenging in social settings, as well as other times. Often, I felt misunderstood or simply looked over because I was too quiet, too intense, too smart, too something. The messages of my youth were mixed, from you are the best to you will never measure up in life. Still, my gifts kept showing up and helping me along the way, even before I would have called them gifts.

I was working in the substance abuse treatment field after graduate school. My assistant at the time, Tom, and I were talking, and I mentioned that I was wondering why I was being asked to study at a local seminary. Ministry was not in my current world and seminary was never on my radar as something to pursue, so I was honestly confused by the invitation. Tom's response cut deep into my being as he said, in a matter-of-fact tone with a bit of a chuckle, "Of course they want you, Dianne. Can't you see it? Everyone comes to you for spiritual guidance and support."

His words took me back. I had never considered my name and the word spiritual would be in the same sentence yet somehow, I knew what he was reflecting back to me was true. I was speechless, which was rare. He went on to give several examples and said, "You are like a lighthouse for everyone. You shine your light, and they can see the way out of their pain and suffering." I was simply astonished.

See, I had been moving along in life and in my career as a counselor, sharing what I was now meeting head on, my intuition and spiritual gifts. I hesitantly began to open my eyes to this new way of seeing. I began to view myself through others' eyes.

During this period, I met my first spiritual mentor, David. I did not know he would have such a profound impact on my life when we met. He would share ideas and questions with me. It was clear he was acting as a mentor, and I did not know why. I struggled with some self-doubt at that time, so his behavior was nice, even if it was a bit confusing for me. As our relationship unfolded, I began to see the power of the inner light that resides in each one of us. He helped me shape how to bring my light out to shine with the highest authenticity. He would always tell me that, "God is not for wimps." This sentence has taken on some profound meanings for me over time as I have learned many lessons and walked roads that others abandoned.

David and I would go look at properties for him to purchase and he would have me walk around and tell him what I felt. He always followed what I said. Later, much later, I realized he was asking me to use my intuition and I was naive in the sense that I thought everyone had these gifts and they just were not using them. I was wrong.

David would watch Mother Teresa of Calcutta on TV and he would comment that it helped him remain grateful. As a physician, he always considered the spiritual health of his patients and would talk about meditation and being aligned on these levels. His practice, at which I was his Clinical Director, was based upon physical, emotional, and spiritual health. He was quick to prescribe meditation and attunement with nature as forms of healing. He was a physician before his time and the patients resonated with his approach and the care he offered for them. Each day, working side by side with him for years, I gained understanding and a perspective of the value of spiritual matters and the power that is within each of us. He supported my growth and exploration. We would have long talks that I fondly remember today.

The road to standing in my light has not been easy. I had to learn to protect my resources, not share too much and to trust my inner guidance. I have had to deal with dark energy and formidable foes that I never anticipated. Betrayal by many people close to me are part of the journey as well. These painful times taught me how to discern more accurately and to trust my inner knowing regardless of outer appearances. I continue to learn lessons in this area each day.

Fast forward 15 years, to a time where I was facilitating a grief recovery weekend experience. Part of the experience was to do a timeline of losses or unresolved feelings of pain. I used mine as the example for the group. As I completed the example, one of my clients ran from the room. On the next break, I found him outside and inquired about his leaving the room. He said emphatically, "Can't you see it? Darkness has been trying to stop you all along and it has been your spiritual connection, your light, that has always prevailed. You are like a human lighthouse." Again, this perspective was new to me. As I looked at what I had presented through these new eyes, I connected to the part of me that is meant to shine.

With this new and evolving perspective, I noticed I was walking a bit straighter while my mind was wrapping around the new awareness. Maybe I do have a bright inner light that is meant to shine, I thought. Maybe I am a lighthouse of sorts, I pondered.

One prominent experience that has shaped my stepping more fully into my light was the result of a betrayal and attack by a business colleague. I entered the relationship trusting and ready to serve in the highest way I was able. I learned over the next couple of years how seductive charisma can be and how it can cover deep character wounds. I was in the flow, creating programs and helping people. Then one day, I felt a significant shift, and everything changed like a bad dream. I learned later that what was happening was gas lighting. I had never heard of this and now I was living that nightmare.

Personality changes and erratic behavior became daily challenges to navigate. Nothing I did was good enough and suddenly many of my friends and co-workers were turning against me. I could feel the discord and malice, yet I could not put my finger on it exactly. I recall saying often that things are changing, and I was met with blank stares. I learned later that there was a tremendous amount of deception and manipulation happening behind the scenes. I was trusting and it never, ever occurred to me that something this wrong could be happening. Why were my friends not speaking to me? How could things be unraveling in all areas? This began one of my several dark nights of the soul.

I recall waking up in the middle of the night to my own crying and sobbing as I was saying, "I am broken. What is wrong with me?" The inner pain was excruciating, and all my support people had left my life. Now, years later, none from that time have returned. I walked this journey alone with the support and help of the Divine. I grew closer to my spiritual purpose and understanding, closer than I ever had before.

I remember praying one night that if any of my pain from the betrayal and gas lighting could be used to help another, I am open and willing to help. Within a week of that prayer, as I lifted from the depths of despair, I chose to continue to live and continue my work. Shortly after, clients began to seek me out and I was able to use my new insights to help them in new ways.

As I was healing and recalibrating from this intense and life altering experience, I had some profound spiritual experiences that were outside of my understanding at the time. I journaled the information and the visions and the dreams. I held an open mind and initially did not try to understand or explain these events. I simply sat with the experience and affirmed to myself that I was not crazy! There were moments where I wondered what was happening. This went on for about a year and I started seeing my role in life differently.

A few months after the visions and dreams settled down and I could sleep all night again, I took the risk and shared some of them with a trusted friend. To my amazement, she completely understood and helped me put perspective and meaning to these visions and dreams. Again, I was reminded of my unique intuitive gift and my inner light.

One big lesson from this time, that I still practice today, is the need to integrate all information and lessons. We can have profound experiences and be helping people in many ways, but we must still take the time to integrate and bring the pieces into a harmonious whole. Many eager people try to keep learning and growing without taking time to integrate. This creates a healing crisis. Taking time to assimilate your new lesson and growth on any level is key to a solid foundation from which to shine your light!

I am always having inspired ideas and I have had to learn that intuition and spiritual matters do not follow linear timelines. At points it was challenging for me to determine if my great idea should really be followed right away or not. I had an idea for another colleague to join forces with me on a project. She agreed then proceeded to claim the project as hers and used social media to gain interest while sharing information not meant for social media. I had to set clearer boundaries and eventually distance the project from her participation. I learned that being kind and spiritual does not mean that I am weak. Never make assumptions. Keep communicating clearly and set clear and firm boundaries. Squishiness in boundaries and communication creates discord, misunderstanding and strife. All this is unnecessary and can be avoided by being clear and not making any assumptions. Sometimes it may seem like you are being simplistic when you are clear on this level, but it pays off. I am sure I would still be associated with this person today had I been clearer and made less assumptions about her skills and motives.

Later, I attended the Genius Network Annual Event and heard the phrase, "You can't read a label from inside the jar." This was so affirming for me because I teach about the importance of multiple peer groups and the willingness to give and receive insights with others. We all have blind spots, and it is vital that we give permission to trusted others, which help shine the light for us.

I realized, during that annual event, that this is what has been happening for me throughout my life. I was naïvely doing what I knew to do, not realizing fully that my gifts were something that truly mattered beyond my little world. I had yet to see or integrate the importance and gravity of my gifts.

My profound awakening happened when I started admitting that my intuitive gift Is unique and valuable. I began to speak of this gift and how I used it in my work and personal life. When I first shared that I am an Intuitive Mentor for bright and talented creatives, I was met with support and excitement within the Genius Network community. Outside of the community and among many close friends, I was met with caution, jealousy and even some negativity. This was a turning point. Do I continue to shine my light brighter or do I dim my light?" Who was I going to listen to after all?

I remember one specific morning vividly. It was years ago when I made the strong commitment from the inside out to live my bright and vivid vision that was undeniable. My resolve was strong, and I was sure, on all levels, that following my spiritual gifts was the only way to live. The answers to my inner question were clear.

Today, the use of my inner light, my intuitive intelligence, is a focal point of my work. Through my writing, individual and group client work, speaking engagements, and my podcasts I have the honor to help open doors of awareness and inspiration for people seeking to let their heart's desire show up more fully. There have been times where I was not sure I would be alive much longer. I was not suicidal. I was simply not sure I could keep going. There were times of profound spiritual experiences that were undeniable as well.

Looking back over my life, I see how being open, receptive, and responsive to my inner curiosity has been valuable in my happiness and success. Being willing to travel the road of life while trusting the greater Universe has been a hallmark for me over these 40+ years. Remember that first spiritual mentor, David? He taught me these lessons in ways that had to incubate and develop within my psyche over time. Truly, each day, I offer gratitude for him. He took the time to show me the way without being intrusive.

The journey we all take can be tricky and challenging yet it is worth the messiness to be able to flow in the grace and peace that comes with understanding and living our unique purpose. I wish you well as you live out your unique purpose on purpose. Shine brightly.

ABOUT DIANNE A. ALLEN

Internationally known speaker, Dianne A. Allen, MA, takes her knowledge, raw experience, education, and intuition and presents life changing strategies for living on purpose with a joy-filled heart and mind. Dianne is a mentor, author, speaker, podcast host and life catalyst for bright and talented individuals. Dianne has a way of adding that needed push to help set you free as you move toward opening diverse avenues of expanding possibilities. With over four decades in the personal transformation arena, Dianne has a way of asking the deep questions and inviting you to move more into your authentic self in expression.

Dianne is committed to presenting ideas and strategies in understandable and powerful ways. As a visionary leader, Dianne takes her myriad of skills and sets the stage for exponential growth and development for her clients.

With seven published books, three live podcasts, and the Someone Gets Me community for bright and talented individuals, Dianne serves in a multitude of ways. She is a caring, compassionate communicator who uses her intuition and insights to skillfully guide you toward living your authentic life vision and personal legacy.

www.visionsapplied.com
www.msdianneallen.com
www.someonegetsme.podbean.com/
www.members.someonegetsme.com

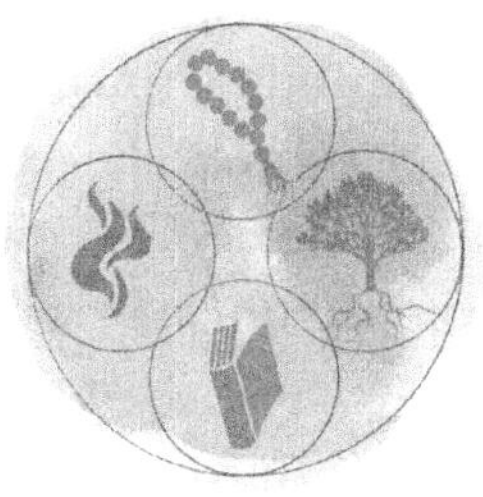

HONORING SELF AS YOU STEER YOUR CAREER

Dr. Agatha Ampaire

"Two roads diverged in a wood, and I took the one less traveled by, and that has made all the difference."

~Robert Frost

Nothing prepares anyone for the obstacles to be faced when starting one's career journey. In my case, I have had to overcome roadblocks, roundabouts, and even some wrong turns. In the end, I managed to unveil and fulfill my passions by re-directing my career and taking the road less traveled. This is my story journeying from veterinary medicine, then animal science, and finally to student affairs administration and financial services.

Growing up in Uganda, East Africa, the brightest students were always encouraged to go to university to study human medicine. That field was regarded as the most respectable and reliable career choice that was high salaried. By the end of high school, I grew less interested in human medicine and opted for veterinary medicine as an alternative. I was one of only three girls who were admitted into the Bachelor of Veterinary Medicine program that year.

I enjoyed the program, but ultimately, unlike many of my classmates, I did not feel completely ready and qualified as a veterinarian, even with the degree. One piece of advice I received was that you can only learn so much in school and would pick up the rest of it through experience. That ideology conflicted with my greatest value, which is competency. At that point, I began to doubt if I would ever achieve the proficiency I was seeking. I like to feel like I am doing what I know and know what I am doing.

Signs Along the Journey

Before finishing the veterinary medicine program, I was required to complete a capstone project during the last year. While most of my classmates were growing micro-organisms in the laboratory or doing some sort of animal-related work, I diverged and chose to do a survey and interview the veterinarians in the field about the adequacy and relevancy of their veterinary training. This shows that even early on, I was more intrigued by working with people.

For my first job, I worked at a small animal clinic where there were experienced technicians, but they needed to have a veterinarian oversee their work. I felt inclined to mostly sign the paperwork and let them do the work that they were already doing. To me this was an indication that I was not really excited about this field, otherwise, I would have been more involved and hands-on.

For my second job, I worked with a non-governmental organization where we trained students who had dropped out of secondary school, teaching them how to farm. The students raised pigs and chickens as part of their training. In addition to teaching the students, I was the veterinarian on staff who treated any sick animals. I found that I preferred to teach instead of working with the animals.

In hopes to shift into the more social aspects of the profession, I eagerly applied and was accepted into a livestock development master's program. This was a perfect opportunity to steer my career in a more people-oriented direction. Soon after starting this venture, my spouse also got admitted into a Ph.D. program. However, his program happened to be across the globe in Iowa, USA. A difficult decision had to be made between my program and his program.

Coming to America and Returning to School

We moved to the USA with a young family; the kids were ten months and just under two years old. To support my family, I became a stay-at-home mom and even had another baby. This was wonderful for a few years but soon got old. While I was growing up, my mother had always worked outside the home, and I as an educated woman, fully expected to seek employment outside the home.

I began looking for ways to make use of my degree and discovered that I could not work with my F2 non-immigrant visa. The easiest way around this roadblock was to get admitted to a school so that I could change to an F1 student visa. I also needed to obtain a graduate assistantship before I would be able to afford my master's degree. My attempt to enroll in the more people-oriented Agricultural Education program at Iowa State University was unsuccessful because I was unable to find a major advisor who had the funding to take on a new student. Luckily, I was accepted into the animal science program, likely due to my background in veterinary medicine. Switching lanes to animal science was the only available option and I was resolved to make it work.

My academic advisor was a renowned geneticist who was also involved in international development work. I was his first animal science student and had a blank slate to design a study on anything I wanted for my thesis research project. I fell back to the one thing I felt entirely proficient at and would without a doubt enjoy, which was conducting surveys. I interviewed people like I had done previously for my undergraduate degree, only this time it was farmers in Uganda. I was interested to find out how our Sustainable Rural Livelihoods project was working out for them and how it could be improved. From that study, three peer-reviewed journal articles were published. I was very proud of the thesis research work and altogether enjoyed the program. Looking back now, I realize it was because I was within my areas of personal strength, working on a people-oriented project.

However, at the end of my master's degree, I did not feel like I was an animal scientist because I had not done any animal or laboratory experiments. I needed to decide between diving deeper into animal science or switching to a more social field, such as sociology, which I had been considering. I had taken a sociology class and earned a graduate minor in women's studies during the master's program. Before concluding with either choice, I made some inquiries and found that graduate assistantships were scarce in the non-science fields. An applicant needed to have a strong background in the field of study to be a competitive candidate. The apparent choice was to keep moving forward with animal science and, with the background I had, it was an easy door to open.

I started a Ph.D. program in poultry nutrition at the University of Nebraska - Lincoln, where my spouse was doing his post-doctoral work. I completed two research studies on eggshell quality but had not started on my dissertation research yet when my spouse got hired at South Dakota State University for a tenure track position. He commuted back from South Dakota to Nebraska over the weekends or every other weekend, for me to continue with the Ph.D. program. I was taking classes, doing research, and balancing three kids' activities. My children were unhappy with the situation, and I was stressed out and frazzled. The breaking point was when one of my kids was involved in a car accident while walking home from elementary school with friends. I had to find someone to look after the other two kids while I escorted the ambulance to the hospital. Finally realizing that the arrangement in place was not going to work, I decided to transfer to South Dakota State University and start the Ph.D. program over, this time in swine nutrition, as there was no poultry nutrition option.

Connecting Head to Heart

It was during my Ph.D. and post-doctoral research in animal science, that I felt certain that I was not on the right path. I was doing important work and was on track to becoming a faculty member or researcher, but I did not feel inspired by it. Reflecting on my route so far, I could not help but notice that I was most passionate when I was working on projects with a social aspect. My internal compass, value system, and image of what success looked like, did not match the trajectory I had been on for years.

As I interacted with my fellow graduate students and professors, I asked them how they ended up in the animal science field. Most of them had known this was the right field for them from taking a class, but that had not happened for me despite being in the field for so long! I took several personality and career assessments, and the results confirmed that I needed to be in a more social career. I struggled to accept this, although I already knew the truth deep down. I was suffering from the sunk cost fallacy, believing that I should continue with animal science because I had invested so many years of my life in the field. I felt as though my identity was tied to being a scientist.

Nevertheless, I began investigating alternate academic careers, which was a lonely and intimidating process. No one I knew had done it before. When most people finish their Ph.D., they teach or do research. After several years of this, they might eventually end up in administrative positions. I decided I was going to bypass the usual faculty and research stop and go straight to administration.

Back to the Drawing Board

I knew that I loved being around and talking to people. I was energized and excited after my Toastmasters meetings. My Focus 2 Career Assessment had shown that I was highly social and enterprising. I concluded that to be happy in a career, it had to be a highly social one. My Clifton Strengths Assessment revealed my top two strengths to be Learner and Intellection. This explained why I had spent so many years in school and why I highly valued feeling competent. I figured that I probably needed to stay in a higher education learning environment.

Coincidentally, around this time a position for a professional academic advisor was created in the animal science department. It seemed that talking to and working with students all day would be a great fit for me. I visited with some of the university administrators and shadowed academic advisors to be sure that this was the path I wanted to embark on.

A mentor suggested that I enroll in the counseling and human development program offered at the university. I initially resisted the idea because I thought that, with all my years of education, I should be able to cross over to the new field without returning to school. Eventually, I decided to enroll in the student affairs administration program, which I thoroughly enjoyed. I wanted to go through the program as fast as possible and completed the two-year program in one. It was the most fulfilling year of my entire educational journey. I knew that I was finally on the right path. Like my animal science peers, I had taken a class and known that this was it!

The Journey Continues

I went into the student affairs program thinking that I wanted to become an academic advisor but quickly found that there were many other functional areas that captured my interest. I felt like a kid in a candy store! I did short internships in about five different functional areas, but I still could not decide on which of the student affairs areas I wanted to work in, so I decided that I would go with whichever functional area I got a job offer in. My first job happened to be in the career office. I enjoyed helping students tell their stories and articulate their experiences to a potential employer. As someone who had changed careers and done that deep reflection, I found working with students who were not sure of their major, and alumni who would like to change their careers, deeply meaningful. The cherry on top is that my kids, who are now teenagers, say that I am happier and much more fun to be around!

Having done the psychological work needed to change careers, and defined who I am and what I want, I now easily spot opportunities that are in alignment. I recently discovered that I could utilize the same skill set required for student affairs work, in the financial services space. There is continuous learning and satisfaction in helping families secure their finances and create generational wealth. I am excited about my new venture in financial services; it complements my work in career services.

Through this journey and life experience, I have learned so much about myself, about staying true to myself and honoring who I am. My diverse background and extensive education have allowed me to become competent in many areas, they make the fabric of who I am and how I see the world. If given the opportunity to start over and take the turn to Student Affairs or Financial services in the beginning, I would firmly decline. I have learned that it is not about taking the straightforward path or making the least number of errors in the process. The only thing that matters is continually taking the courageous steps that in the end honor the role you were placed on this earth to fulfill.

Dear reader, thanks for going on this winding journey with me. If you do not settle but continually seek what is right for you, following your internal guidance, you will find your true north. Shine on!

ABOUT DR. AGATHA AMPAIRE

Agatha was born and raised in Uganda, East Africa, where she obtained a bachelor's degree in Veterinary Medicine. She moved to the USA in 2005 and has since obtained a Master's in Animal Science (International development), a Ph. D in Animal Science (swine nutrition), and a Master's in Counseling in Human Resource Development (M.Ed. Administration of Student Affairs). She is a career and financial educator and is also a certified life and professional coach. She is a wife and mother of three teenagers; her oldest just graduated high school and is headed to college this Fall.

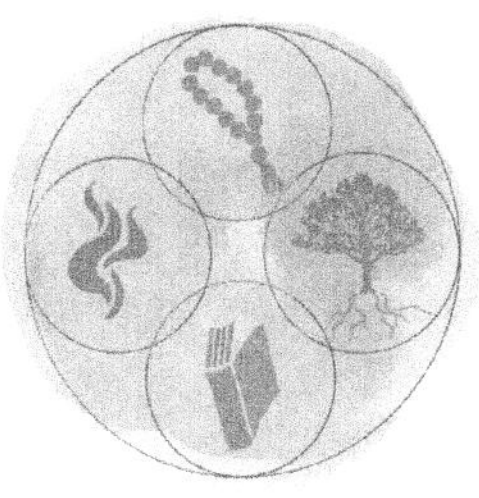

TRIUMPHANTLY RISEN

Anita Lucia La Pierre

The making of a WARRIOR WOMAN happened in February of 1960, the day I was born as the 4th child of a 21-year-old young mother. When a Catholic Nun nurse brought me into my mother's maternity room to bond, she said to my mother, "What a beautiful baby, what is her name?"

My mother quickly and sternly replied back, "She doesn't have a name, I am putting her up for adoption."

After a long encouraging and loving conversation together, my mother decided to keep me and, on that day, I became Anita Lucia La Pierre after Sister Anita, the Nun's name, who through GODS TIMELY DIVINE INTERVENTION was placed in that room at the perfect time with me and my mother.

Now at 61 years old, I have often questioned her decision to keep me.

Was it the right choice?

Would my life have been easier and safer?

Would I have been loved and protected more?

I ask myself these questions as I am possibly a child of rape. I have been told and reminded by my mother, that as she was rushing to get on a city bus in Providence, Rhode Island she was pulled away and dragged into a dirty guttered alley with a pillowcase over her head and viciously violated and raped. Nine months later I was born. No police report, no DNA test. The rapist was never found! This is where I got the childhood nickname "GUTTERCHILD," as very often I was sadly referred as. I was constantly told I was Ugly, and Unwanted, a Mistake that caused bad memories.

Since then, through the many ups, downs and curve balls of life, I have come to refer those and many past TRAUMAS as MY LIFE GIFTS! I have fought hard. I have fought the good fight and SURVIVED THEM ALL!

I became the warrior woman I always had inside of me, BRAVE, STRONG, AND COURAGEOUS, but sadly I did not realize this until I was broken inside physically, mentally and emotionally by people I trusted, loved, and allowed to betray and mentally destroy me!

I was born armed with the love and protection of GOD. I describe my GIFTED WARRIOR WEAPONS as MY 3 R's. They have helped me become "TRIUMPHANTLY RISEN."

REDEMPTION:

From what happened to me as a child, young adult and mature adult, starting from the hands of the man I called my father, who sexually abused me and joined my mother in physical and emotional abuse until I was placed into the Foster System at the tender age of 13.

Here I was physically assaulted, which I allowed, simply because that is what I was used to from past boyfriends to ex-husbands. I had six ex-husbands in all, yes Six, which I can now be proud to admit and not be ashamed to tell the whole world! And my name isn›t even Elizabeth!

RESILIENCE:

From not feeling wanted, loved, protected, worthy, good enough and appreciated to bouncing back to becoming PROUD of whom I have become and where I came from and for the strength and determination of SELF BELIEF that I, Anita Lucia La Pierre, deserved better! NEVER GIVING UP!

REDEMPTION:

From what happened to me from Birth to Present to survive it all "Victoriously" for myself and others because this has helped me so that I would not only care more about Anita, but also for my fellow mankind and all animals, for which we all deserve to be loved unconditionally.

To becoming a Strong Advocate for the sometimes forgotten, the Homeless or Houseless, Foster Children past and present, and Domestic Abuse Victims, for which I can say,

I survived from being all of the above.

I would invite you to consider some reflection questions:

- Do you fall into any of these categories?
- Which ones?
- Are you a Survivor, a Warrior?
- What was your significant event in your life for YOUR change?
- Which from above has played a role of you reaching out and helping others?

ABOUT ANITA LUCIA LA PIERRE

I am now a brave woman of faith, hope and new life.

I am merciful towards others, especially the less fortunate, broken and emotionally wounded.

I have become:

A certified, energizing, motivational speaker that provides hope and encouragement to others through my story and journey, titled: "You Are Not Alone."

Podcast Inspirational Guest where I share my truth about what it means to "Outreach to Others" and how to get involved to "Make a Difference."

Creator and Admin on Facebook

"Kindred Spirits, Warrior Women" Group Page—An encouragement and faith inspiration page.

Developer of "Be Happy, Be Kind" Homeless Hygiene Bags- An outreach mission that I created to offer care and compassion to others that have found themselves like myself in tough life conditions and circumstances with everyday hygiene products and Hope Ministry.

I have just completed a two month "Hygiene Bag" mission outreach car trip to ten different states along with many cities with my two precious fur babies (Dogs) Bentley and Riley as copilots, offering needed necessities and compassion to those who are in need and often ignored.

These major cities included: Albuquerque, Oklahoma City, Brownsville, Dallas, Fort Worth, Phoenix, Salt Lake City, Jackson, New Orleans, and Shreveport.

I am presently back in Albuquerque which is my home base.

Advocate for foster children of Albuquerque, New Mexico. I provide support to the city by donating clothing and hygiene products to help children who are placed into the system like I was, as they matter!

I am grateful and thankful today that my past has brought me to where I am today, A Warrior Woman!

"God created our toes pointed forward so we wouldn't walk backwards through our life."

Contact Anita for more information on her Speaker and Outreach Missions at Kindredspirits21@aol.com or on Facebook: www.facebook.com/BeautifulAnita

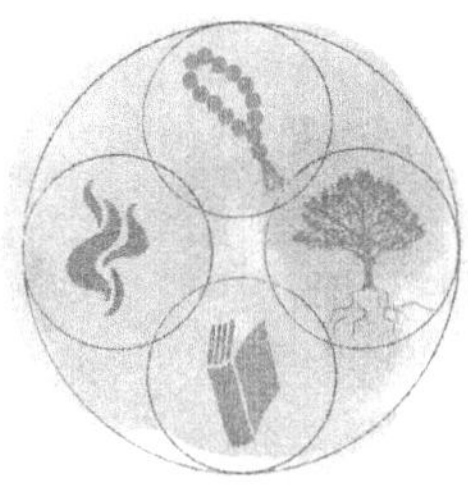

LOVE YOURSELF FIRST

Melissa A. Malland

I have always been the people-pleaser type, allowing others to determine my worth. What I didn't realize was how incredibly wrong it was to place my worth in the hands of others, especially a man. It took a traumatizing experience to ultimately open my eyes. My story speaks to women worldwide on how we can determine our own worth.

There I was with two little boys, ages six and three, with another baby boy on the way! It had been a very tumultuous pregnancy. At six weeks into the pregnancy the doctor told me that my hormone levels were extremely low and that I was going to lose the baby. I was devastated, but didn't give up hope. Perseverance is my strong suit and I prayed every day not to lose my baby. Then, shortly after that doctor's appointment, I began experiencing extreme nausea, vomiting, and fatigue. I was never so excited to be sick! By the time of my next doctor's appointment things were progressing in the right direction. However, life at home was beyond chaotic. I was raising two little boys, teaching middle school, and pursuing my Master's Degree in Education Administration. At times it felt like I was a single mother, as my husband, who is a police officer, recently became promoted to

Sergeant. It felt lonely and at times, I felt like we were two passing ships in the night. We made a pact to make sure date nights were a priority and scheduled them routinely.

My husband and I have a history together. We met while working on the Seaside Heights Boardwalk in 1991. I was 15 years old and he was 17 years old. I was attracted to his impatience and I the first day I met him I said to myself, "He's the one". We cliqued immediately and I thoroughly enjoyed his company. Besides being my love, he was my best friend. We did everything together and there was such a bond between us. So, when it was time for his prom and he asked me to go with him, I was over the moon excited. Thirty years later, and I still remember every detail about the dress. It was a navy blue, knee length, A-line dress, with short sleeves. It was such a classy dress and the color complimented my light skin tone. I couldn't wait to wear it and impress him. I was a Sophomore and he was a Senior, so I felt cool attending the Senior Prom! My mother and I went to the store to put the deposit down on my dress. The seamstress was going to begin alterations and then the dress was MINE!

It was less than a week later during my boyfriend's weekly phone call after his karate lesson. Our conversation was different that night and I could sense that there was something up with him. Then, he hit me with the worst gut punch, metaphorically speaking, by saying, "I've decided to take someone else to the prom." I immediately froze. I told him to hold on and ran into my mother's bedroom. My words couldn't come out fast enough. I belted out, "He's taking someone else to the prom" and the tears wouldn't stop. Then, we decided to break up and my heart was torn into pieces, beyond repair. I couldn't attend school the next day. When his prom day arrived, I stayed home on that day as well. There was, however, a silver lining in this dark cloud. Selfishly, I reveled in the stories I heard from my best friend who attended the same prom that my now, ex-boyfriend attended. So, his prom date left him immediately upon arrival to the venue, they only danced to one song, and even his friends said he made the worst decision by not taking me. I did smile when I heard this and found some comfort during this painful experience. I mean, here I am, 30 years later, still remembering this event. That is when I began to question everything about myself and my self-worth. What was wrong with me? Not skinny enough? Not pretty enough? Smart enough? It was from that point forward that I was NEVER the same.

Fast forward nine years later and at 25 years old, I finally said "I Do". Ironically enough, my first love and heart break came back to find me. He proposed one year after being back together and the rest is history, but it wasn't your happily ever after. So, there I was, a new wife, and those same insecurities were still there. Those feelings had never gone away, not while with him or with any other men during our time apart. My worries were amplified. Who would of thought that would be the case? He was finally mine and I should be secure, that wasn't the case. I was trying to be the perfect wife in all aspects. I tried to make him happy in every way possible, but I was competing with his profession and those individuals who became a part of his everyday life. He was a police officer and there were many functions to attend. I never wanted to attend those functions and the anxiety that would come with it was indescribable. There I was, comparing myself to all of these wives at those functions. Am I as pretty or as skinny? Is my face too round? I never enjoyed myself and all I wanted was my husband to be proud of me.

That wasn't my only competition. His job was very time consuming and demanding. We were only married for four months, living in a brand new house, when we got news that I was pregnant! It was such an exciting time, also a bit scary. My husband is a goal-oriented man whose ultimate goal was to rise through the ranks and one day become the chief. He was offered an undercover position that required him to work evenings. Again, I put my needs aside, wanting to be the perfect wife and knowing this would help his resume. I agreed for him to take this position. This fed my anxiety, as this occurred right before September 11, 2001. I was away from my family; alone and pregnant at night. My fear was that I would let him down if I didn't please him in any way, so I pushed through.

Fast forward to our second home and three little boys, now ages six, three, three months old. There we stood, my three month old in hand and my two older boys looking on, as their father was sworn in as Sergeant. It was a great moment for all, but it required some sacrifice for the family. My husband was assigned to work midnights and I took on the role of what felt like as a single mother. I still wanted to do anything and everything to please him, even though I sacrificed my own happiness in the process. Little did I realize that I was losing a piece of myself every day and the real me was fading away. I never held my husband back for securing his place at work by attending functions and showing his face. When he wanted to go out with the guys, despite the twist in my stomach, I smiled and said "Sure, honey." However, I repressed the hypocrisy in my life, which was a major issue because all my focus was on his happiness and my children.

I was always an outgoing and friendly person, one who stood out in the crowd. As a teacher, I became very close with a lot of my colleagues. There were events where we'd get together as a school and times where friends would get together for drinks by the beach. There were also friends that I grew up with and recently reconnected with. When it was my time to go out with friends, there was quite a bit of hesitation, which placed a lot of guilt on me. So much so that I began to decline the invites. I would repeatedly decline because of the guilt placed on me by my husband, as well as the need to please him. I became known as "Sell Out Melissa" within my school and people just stopped asking. I just continued to repress my feelings and move on, thinking of my husband and children. My self-worth always being an issue, reflected in simply wanting to please my husband.

The third best day of my entire life was the birth of my third son. This particular birth was a tumultuous one, which was fitting, because my pregnancy was filled with more downs, than ups. It was the most nerve wracking one out of the three. The pregnancy started with the fact that I was going to lose my baby. Historically I give birth to large babies so I was scheduled for a C-section. During the operation they had a great deal of difficulty getting my baby out. In fact, they had to push on my stomach to help retrieve my son. There was so much chaos when they finally pulled my baby out that I didn't have time to ask, "Is he okay?"

"Oh my goodness, he's so big," the nurses and doctors were shouting. "He's 10 pounds," someone said. "No way, he's bigger," someone else shouted. The doctor replied, "Hurry, put him on the scale." They placed my baby boy on the scale and he came into life weighing twelve pounds and three ounces. I was in shock and couldn't believe it. He had been the largest baby born, on March 10, 2008, in sixteen years! The doctors and nurses were stunned. My family and friends were in awe because I am a very petite person, which made it hard to believe that I delivered such a big baby.

My children have been my greatest pleasure since they were born with each birth as exciting as the previous one. There we sat, just my husband and I holding our newborn. What should've been such an intimate and special moment was clouded by my husband's job once again. There he sat in the chair diagonally across from the hospital bed, studying for his upcoming sergeant exam. I was torn and crying on the inside, but trying to still be the perfect wife, I continued to bury it. I continued to revel and admire my bouncing baby boy! My health was slightly declining with some blood pressure issues, but once I received clearance that I was healthy to go home, I couldn't wait to leave. The best years of my life were during the newborn stages of each child, that and having two younger boys at home waiting for me!

I didn't know what was happening. It came over me like dark

clouds before a storm. I wasn't myself. Where did I go? A new baby and two younger babies just wanting their mommy. I couldn't eat or sleep. The only thing I wanted near me was my new baby. I laid in bed every day while my family scratched their heads and tried force feeding me. The best way I could describe it was like someone else stepped into my body and I didn't have control of myself. It truly felt like an out of body experience. I hated it. I was screaming on the inside and wanted help. My OB-GYN saw me and diagnosed me with postpartum depression. She gave me some medications and sent me on my way. It wasn't working. My internist saw me and adjusted my medications, along with recommending me to a therapist. He had said if therapy didn't work, I would be put in an in-patient facility. No way! I couldn't be away from my kids. I wanted to do everything in my power to get back to "me" for my husband and kids.

This was the worst feeling of my life and I had no control over it. My best friend of over 20 years had abandoned me during my time of need. It crushed me to my core because I needed the support of those closest to me. My husband went back to work and my mother helped me as I started on the path to recovery. I was juggling three small boys, running a household, working on my Master's Degree, and trying hard to recover. Then, to add to what was already on my plate, my doctor had dropped more negative news on me. He was examining me and realized that I had a hernia that needed repair ASAP. After a cat scan, it was determined that I had two hernias and my diastasis recti was split in half and major surgery was eminent. I had never had surgery before in my life, but continued to push through. I still wanted to please everyone no matter what I was going through.

It wasn't until very recently that I found out the most devastating news of my life. I found out that during my time of need, despite my best friend checking out on me, my husband did as well. What I realized just a few months ago, was that I knew he was emotionally checked out during that time, but I didn't have time to recognize it. I knew, during that time, that I didn't feel comfort from him, which is why I attached myself to my kids. I had never felt a sense of security. Most of my marriage I acquiesced to make him happy and despite my efforts, my worst fear had happened. I gave him his freedom and stood by his side while I was on the sidelines.

This was the best thing that could've happened to me because it allowed me to return to myself and recognize my self-worth. Most importantly, I realized to never place my value or worth on a man. My message here is twofold, for you to recognize your worth and let it exude with confidence. Do not rely on what a man says or doesn't say, or what he does or doesn't do. It is simply up to you to feel it yourself and the right person will recognize and appreciate it. Also, postpartum is most definitely real and it can manifest in many different ways, so don't be afraid to seek help. Remember, women are strong and we can shine through the darkness and prevail. I have realized that the only acknowledgement I needed was from myself and placing my worth on a man was no longer a thought in my mind. It was time to pursue my dreams, follow my heart, reconnect with my true self and show the world my worth. This had proven to be the best thing to happen to me and my new mantra is "Love Yourself First".

ABOUT MELISSA A. MALLAND

Melissa Malland has been a teacher for 22 years. She is a mom of three boys, ages 19, 16, and 13 and she has been married for 22 years. Melissa possesses a Bachelor's Degree in education and a Master's Degree in Education Administration. She is licensed by the state of New Jersey to serve as a principal in any school within the state. Melissa currently lives in Toms River, at the Jersey Shore, and has done so since the age of eight. Melissa loves spending her free time with her family, taking walks, spending time at the beach, and reading.

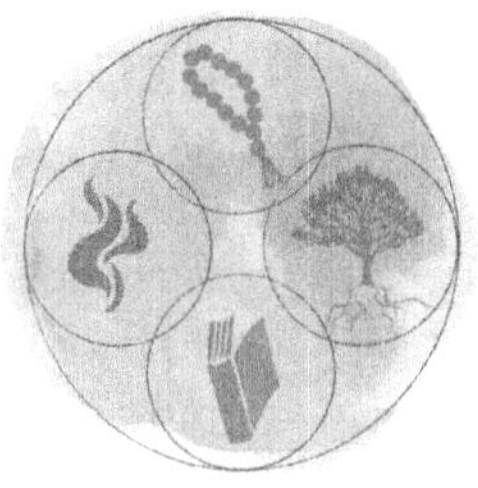

A HOARDER'S HEART

Melanie Renee

There was a loud knock at the door on a very frigid January afternoon. My heart dropped as I felt a wave of anxiety flood my heart. Who's there? No one mentioned that they were stopping over. I slowly, secretively peeled the curtain back to peek at whomever my unannounced visitor was. To my surprise, it was my neighbor from around the corner who I became friends with since moving into the neighborhood. I wanted to open the door, but I couldn't do it. I don't open the door for anyone who just stops by without my knowing. I was still too afraid, too vulnerable to expose what I was hiding inside my home. Normally, I would hide in the back bedroom and later create a lie that, "I must have been in the shower when you stopped by." I was ready to take my usual escape route when something inside of me told me to open the door. "No, I can't do that!" I thought, "I'll be so mortified, so embarrassed!" But the message tugging at my heart led me to walk towards the door as she continued knocking. I opened the door at a 30 degree angle, enough to fit my body through it and onto the porch without revealing what was behind me. She happily greeted me with a freshly baked container of warm muffins. I could see her breath dancing in the 20°F cold air as she told me how she missed me and wanted to say Hi. The guilt started banging at my heart like a screen door in a hurricane. I should be inviting her inside my home where it is warm and cozy. I should have her sit at my dining room table and offer her a hot cup of tea. But I can't do that. She will see my dirty little secret. The secret I've kept hidden my entire life because society has attached such an awful, hurtful stigma to it. No, we will have to freeze and keep this visit short. I explained how I couldn't invite her inside because we were remodeling the front room and the area was torn up. She smiled and said she understood, but I could tell she would've rather come inside. After 15 minutes we said our goodbyes and ended our visit to prevent any form of frostbite. I went back inside my warm home and started to cry until my cheeks were raw. I didn't want to live like this anymore. I didn't want to hide and I didn't want to fear judgment from others! I was tired of my home being so full of clutter that you couldn't use the backdoor anymore. I was tired of the goat trails I'd created so you could walk from room to room. I really didn't want my children to resent me when they grew up. Or worse, I didn't want them to develop hoarding disorder and live with this shame and pain too.

This is a burden that lays heavily on most people with hoarding disorder. Unfortunately, society labels us as dirty, lazy, selfish, materialistic, disgusting people. Naturally, we don't seek help in the fear of being rejected by someone, even a therapist. And to cope with those emotions we hoard even more to soothe our pain and isolation. We try to hide it at first, stowing items away in either a spare room, a basement, a storage locker or a space hidden from everyone else. But once you start entering Level 3 hoarding, your hiding places become more scarce as some rooms become filled to capacity. I was a strong Level 3 hoarder entering Level 4. To give you a visual, Hoarders Buried Alive shows extreme Level 5 hoarders with Squalor Disorder (also known as Diogenes Syndrome.) Generally, people don't understand why someone would do this to their house. They don't understand why a person would want to fill their homes with so much junk that it becomes unlivable. What is someone's thought process when they create a life of hoarding? And for that reason, I know that I am called to humanize hoarding disorder, to help people understand the true mentality behind the stuff. Once people start to understand and have compassion for people with hoarding disorder, then people who want to change will seek help. They won't be afraid to hide it anymore. They won't feel so ashamed and start on the path towards recovery. The first thing I want everyone to understand is that hoarding is a mental disorder. It stems from anxiety, depression, PTSD, ADHD, OCD, etc. It can be genetic and sometimes trauma can trigger it and bring it to life. I'm asking you to look past the stuff and into the person's mental state, their minds, their emotions, their feelings. I want you to look for the stories where they were deeply hurt because that's where hoarding became a coping mechanism for survival. Once you start healing those traumas, those negative emotions of fear, low self-esteem and isolation, they will begin to heal and items will start being decluttered from the home.

The birth of my hoarding disorder began between 5th and 6th grade. We had moved into a new home and I was starting at a new school in September. I was the new girl during my very awkward prepubescent stage of life. I was shy with huge glasses, frizzy hair and a little on the heavy side. No one in Seventeen magazine looked like me. In fact, they were showing me how to not look like myself, which made my self-esteem even lower. I was a prime target for bullies who tortured me. They called me names, teased me, pushed me, were disgusted by my presence. I was a sensitive kid so it tore me up inside. It was like they were putting my heart through a paper shredder. I didn't tell my parents because I was too sad to even explain it. Talking about it made it come alive and I wanted to run away from the pain. Instead, I came home and escaped into my room, it was my safe haven!

A place where all my plushies, artwork, crafts, barbies, and toys brought me comfort! They didn't hurt like the bullies in school did! Look at Joey McIntyre and Jordan Knight smiling at me from all my NKOTB posters! They didn't think I was weird and ugly. All of my collections, my stickers, crafts, drawings, Caboodles filled with make-up and Precious Moments figurines became my support group! In fact, they made me so happy that they became an expression of who I wanted to be! I was that happy, cheery, popular girl everyone loved in this fantasy world that I created in my bedroom. This was how I coped with being bullied during middlc school until 9th grade. In High School I developed into a new woman and we had another school merge with us. It was a fresh start to make new friends and the bullying lessened. I didn't need to depend on all my treasures to bring happiness throughout High School. It wasn't until after High School that I desperately sought for the comfort of those items again, but this time it was for survival.

Most people say they see their life flash before their eyes when facing certain death. I, however, didn't see that. What I saw was a perfectly round metal circle with such an eerie darkness inside of it. I knew in a moments time that dark cold circle could transition into a bright light with a propelling bullet racing towards my eyes. Was I going to die at 19? Was I only meant to be here for a short time? Was I never going to experience being a bride, a mother, a grandmother, a successful artist and writer? How would my parents handle this devastation? "I want to experience so many things before I gain my angel wings, please God, please let me live just a little while longer." Facing death felt more like time standing still, the seconds are minutes and the minutes feel like hours. It feels like your soul knows it is at the hourglass point of where life meets death, earth into heaven. The person who held my life's existence was my abusive boyfriend high on a concoction of crack, cocaine and heroin. He was out of his God damn mind. He yelled, "Do you love me? Say it, SAY IT!" My mouth moved as I desperately proclaimed my false love for him. I actually hated him, but this was no time to be honest. It was by God's grace that his best friend lifted his arm up into the air begging him to not do this. My ex-boyfriend listened to Billy, he always listened to him. Billy took the gun out of his hands, emptied the bullets and told him, "this isn't you man, this is not who you are!" They walked away together as Billy looked over his shoulder signaling me to get away. I don't think I ever ran that fast before, like a gazelle running away from the lion.

He wasn't like this in the beginning of the relationship. After a year though, he transformed into this monster once he became addicted to drugs. When he was high, he called me those awful names the bullies called me once before. The verbal abuse started to evolve into physical abuse. Once sober, he apologized for hurting me and he promised he would change and seek help. He claimed I was the only good thing in his life and he wanted me to help him heal. But the vicious cycle only continued and the change never occurred. I tried leaving him many times before, but he threatened to hurt my family and friends. Like a sacrificial lamb, I stayed to take the brunt of the abuse. To survive the trauma of an abusive relationship, I resorted back to my coping mechanism of finding comfort in things. I had a job now, so I would buy toys and collectibles to ease my pain. It was my way of holding onto the happy, joyful emotions of childhood so my heart didn't feel fear and depression. I loved 101 Dalmatians, Disney toys, Pokemon and anything Claire's sold to remind myself that I am that happy little girl inside. The toys, clothes, shoes, craft projects, make-up, drawings were all my escape from the torment. I created this world where I could be who I truly was, a free spirit who loved life and never lost her childlike wonderment. I never let go of anything, I couldn't let go of what protected me in my deepest anxious moments and cries for help. The items were my therapists, my support group, my lifeline, my hope for a better life. All of my precious collectibles kept me sane, strong and safe during the scariest time of my life. They became me. The abuse continued for about another year as I prayed for a way to escape without endangering my loved ones. Thankfully, that prayer got answered. It was when he got arrested for carjacking someone during a drug bender that he went to jail.

I finally got my chance to escape from him. I was set free. He couldn't hurt me anymore and I could become that girl I wanted to be. To deal with the PTSD of his abuse, I pretended like it never happened. I shoved all those memories and emotions into a mental box in the deepest abyss of my being. When he was released, his family sent him to California to get help. He did come back home, but he didn't try to find me. Years later though, he was killed in a horrific car accident at 26.

You can easily see how hoarding and physical items became my survival mechanism for trauma at a young age. I thought it was better than turning to drugs, alcohol, crime, more abusive relationships, etc. I made it out alive and my things reminded me of how strong I was inside. Life continued as I graduated college, fell in love, got married and had children. All the life events I longed for. I also had to hold onto every memento, favor, picture and piece of paper of those happy celebrations. Once I had children, the hoard just doubled as every bib, rattle, Onesies, toy and handprint drawing got packed away as my children grew older. The stuff was who they were as my babies. The attachment is so deep that I would have a full blown panic attack if I were to let go of it. There were other moments that triggered my hoarding as well. I always wanted to be a stay at home mom and left my job when my first son was born. It created a financial struggle causing stress to pay bills each month so the hoard rescued me again. I held onto everything because if I needed it, we had it on hand. Freecycle helped me get Christmas presents for my children, yard sales helped clothe my growing boys and I needed to keep everything for the next child too. After years of never decluttering, those open spaces in our home started to disappear.

The third bathroom was filled, the laundry room, the garage, the basement all started looking like storage lockers full of stuff. Now, I don't have rotting food, dirty diapers, empty soda cans, or fast food bags in my house. That is Squalor Disorder (Diogenes Syndrome) and separate from hoarding disorder. Though many people struggle with both disorders like the Hoarders show, I only hold onto a lifelong of functioning items. I can let go of trash and rubbish.

The intention of my story is to help you understand the thought process behind hoarding disorder. When you see a person's hoard, it is the physical manifestation of every thought, emotion, creativity and character trait of that person. The moment I decided to change was that frigid January day when I couldn't let my neighbor inside. I am a social butterfly who loves entertaining. But I need a 2 week notice so I can snowplow all my clutter into the basement. God laid on my heart that I would heal in my hoarding disorder and that I would make it a public journey. I knew it was my life's purpose to be a voice for those who were too scared and vulnerable. But it took me a few years before I gathered the strength to do so. In 2018, I started a YouTube channel called "A Hoarder's Heart." I use the channel to show my messes, explain my emotions, anxiety, ADHD and how I declutter the rooms as a hoarder. The channel took off and is continuing to grow with each view. It is a safe place for people with hoarding disorder to find love, acceptance and hope. And when you show people compassion and understanding, it helps them begin their journey of healing as well. It also helps people understand what is truly happening within a hoarder's mind. It lifts away the judgment because you realize it has nothing to do with laziness, filth and greed. It's actually their coping mechanism for their fear, anxiety and depression. They developed these deep rooted subconscious habits to cope with the stresses of life. But no matter how old you are, there is hope that you can redirect your life's path. I think the most rewarding part is that I receive messages every day from people thanking me for being so open, honest, and vulnerable as I put words to their emotions. I am happy to say that I have decluttered thousands of items from my hoarded house since starting the channel. I am currently writing steps that help people with hoarding disorder clean out their homes without overwhelming them. I also dream of creating support groups around the world. I am still in the beginning stages of this journey and I'm ready to shine my light brightly for the world to see! I will humanize hoarding disorder, not only for myself, but for all those who are ready to heal too. If you are ready for that change, I want you to know that the strength to heal is already within you. You do not need to solely seek for it in the physical world, you only need to connect within that inner strength inside your soul, the one that is intertwined with God and source energy. Once you let the light of your soul shine brightly, your life's legacy becomes alive on this earth. Your legacy is not how much money you leave behind, your legacy is how many people you serve.

ABOUT MELANIE RENEE

Melanie Renee is a #1 Best Selling Author and Content Creator whose work is focused on humanizing hoarding disorder. She explains the true mentality behind her hoarding on her YouTube Channel: A Hoarder's Heart. Her channel has helped thousands of women declutter their hoarded homes. She has a Bachelor's Degree in Communications from Rowan University and is currently seeking to advance her education.

Distinguished by her transparency, creative vision and passion to serve people, her YouTube channel gains thousands of new subscribers each month. Her intention is to create a global community where individuals feel accepted and understood while healing in their hoarding disorder. Her platforms also invites people into the world of hoarding so they can understand the emotions and thought processes beyond the stuff. It opens the door to find compassion and acceptance and helps repair damaged relationships caused by this disorder. She plans to grow her YouTube channel even more, start public speaking engagements and write more books. Her life's calling is to be a voice for those who are too fearful to speak for themselves. Her inspiration is fueled by her two loving sons and husband to provide a better quality of life for her family.

If you would like to connect with Melanie Renee and learn more about "A Hoarder's Heart" please visit:

YouTube Channel: A Hoarder's Heart
Instagram: @ahoardersheart
TikTok: @hoardersheart
www.hoardersheart.com
Email: hoardersheart@gmail.com

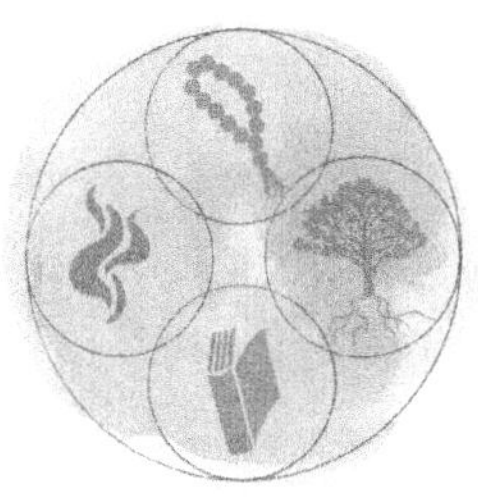

GIVE BACK AND IMPACT: BE A FORCE FOR GOOD

As we conclude *Women Who Shine*, we highlight a woman whose life's mission is to Give Back and Impact—a changemaker who shines her light into the world every day as a force for good. In this parting section highlighting women who Give Back and Impact, we feature
Ellie D. Shefi

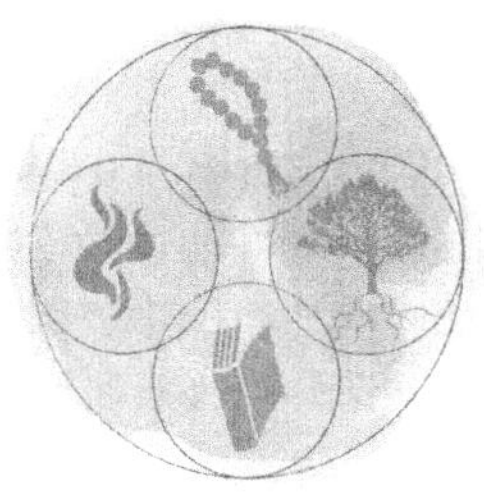

GIVE BACK AND IMPACT: BE A FORCE FOR GOOD

Ellie D. Shefi

At three years old, I wanted to be like Ruth Bader Ginsburg. At eight, I was nicknamed "Defender" because I spoke up for other kids who didn't have a voice.

At seventeen, I graduated from high school magna cum laude and went off to college with scholarships and grants galore.

But two years later, I was homeless, living out of the back of my 1980s Toyota Tercel hatchback, eating food thrown away by restaurants.

Nothing in my life's journey has been simple or easy. I've been beaten and assaulted. I've hidden behind a false identity in a remote location to escape an abusive relationship. I've spent years in and out of hospitals, flat on my back, because of a health condition that baffled doctors. Yet today I'm the staff attorney for a federal judge, the dean of a law school, a sought-after international speaker, best-selling author, entrepreneur, strategist, consultant, coach, mentor, and the founder of a nonprofit foundation that equips underserved youth with mindset, advocacy, and entrepreneurial tools to enable them to create the lives and the future they envision. I've dedicated my life to teaching others to find their voice and stand in their power so they can use their voice to amplify their impact in the world.

What made the difference? My belief that each of us can use our voice and our life to be a force for good: to help those who are in need; to speak up when we see injustice; to shine our light in the world. When we refuse to let obstacles keep us from our goals, we can turn even the worst circumstances into lessons that uplift, transform, and inspire others. In this chapter, I share seven lessons that helped me shine my light through even the darkest of circumstances. I hope that they help you get through your own tough times, whatever they may be, so you, too, can shine your light and be a force for good in the world.

#1: Speak up for what's right and find something worth fighting for.

Growing up, I went to school in a very diverse but under-resourced neighborhood in Long Beach, California. My friends' ethnicities, races, nationalities, and cultures ran the gamut—from Vietnamese, Cambodian, Indian, Thai, Tongan, Samoan, and Laotian, to Senegalese, Ugandan, Namibian, South African, Chinese, Japanese, Korean, Israeli, Iranian, Iraqi, Spanish, Columbian, Mexican, Venezuelan, and more. I noticed early on, however, that because of their economics, ethnic background, or the color of their skin, these friends were treated very differently than I was by shopkeepers, police, and passers-by. So, as early as elementary school, I started speaking up for my friends when they faced bigotry and unfair treatment in our community. As I grew up, I never stood by and stayed silent when I saw disparate treatment, racial injustice, or inequality. That's why, later in life, it was so painful when my voice was taken from me by abuse and domestic violence. I could no longer speak up for myself, much less advocate for others.

It took years, but eventually the drive to use my voice to fight for what was right helped me overcome the obstacles I faced.

Whenever you come up against forces that would dim your light and silence your voice, find something that you feel is worth fighting for. It will reignite your light.

#2: Choose, find, or make your own way.

Money was very tight as a child. If I wanted a new piece of clothing, toy, cassette tape, movie ticket, or other treat, I had to earn the money to buy it myself. Ever resourceful, I became an entrepreneur early in life so that I could pay for those extras. My first entrepreneurial endeavors included tutoring, proofreading and editing, choreographing dance numbers for groups, and teaching art and dance.

The skills I developed from these foundational entrepreneurial endeavors continued to serve me after I graduated from high school. I attended a small liberal arts college in the Los Angeles area that offered me enough in scholarships, grants, and work-study to cover its steep price tag. But after a couple of unfortunate incidents in my first year—and the administration's refusal to address them—I became disillusioned. When I didn't receive enough financial aid to cover the costs of my second year, I didn't bother to find the money to go back. Instead, I decided to make my own way, find my own place to live, and support myself. I knew that eventually I would go back to college to fulfill my dream of becoming an attorney—but I would do it on my terms.

All of us run into people or situations that try to hold us back. It takes great courage and commitment to turn away from those negative experiences and make your own way, especially when you have no idea what your next steps should be. But the very act of taking control over the direction of your life is the path to greater freedom and success.

#3: Practice a "How can I?" mentality.

As a teenager, I learned to practice a "How can I?" mentality. Rather than focusing on an obstacle, I asked, "How can I get around this to achieve my goals?" When I left college at eighteen, with no job and no money, I asked myself, "How can I make money?" This simple question led me to four other key questions for any entrepreneur: "What do I know? What do I do? What do I love? And how can I monetize it?" I knew that I could sell anything and I'd been teaching various subjects for almost a decade—and I enjoyed doing both. So, I looked in the classified ads section of the local newspaper and found a company that needed trainers to teach, manage, and motivate sales forces. I figured that if I could manage and motivate myself, I could do that for others, so I applied and got the job.

But there was always a bigger "How can I?" question in the back of my mind: "How can I make the money to go back to college, graduate, and go on to get my law degree?" When you believe that bigger opportunities lie on the other side of big obstacles, you'll smash through whatever is in the way. By asking "How can I?," you'll reveal more possibilities, and either find a solution or create one.

#4: Trust your instincts and live authentically, in alignment with your ethics.

I did well at the management training company. The teams I trained usually ranked number one in sales, and I was promoted very quickly to regional sales director. The company sent me to Colorado to run an office there, but I left after a few months. (It was way too cold for this California girl!) Then they asked me to go to Texas to launch a new office. It was going to be a great opportunity and I was very excited to put my "How can I?" mentality to work . . . until I arrived and met the person with whom I was supposed to open the new office. Something about her triggered alarm bells. Thankfully, because of my life experiences, I had already learned to trust my instincts. I called the company and informed them that I would not partner with her. Since she was already well established in that territory, my refusal to work with her left me out in the cold—alone, in a new state, with no job, and no money. But I was at peace, confident in my knowledge, skills, passions, drive, determination, and resourcefulness.

You see, I wasn't going to compromise my integrity for money or anything else. As Lisa Nichols says, "Conviction and convenience don't live on the same block." I always choose conviction over convenience. I live in alignment with my ethics and what I believe is right. And I'm going to make sure that I surround myself with people who are in alignment with my values and ethics, too.

But that decision to quit left me with a few problems! I was just nineteen years old. I was in a place where I didn't know anyone. I refused to go back home because I knew my family would never understand that living in integrity and being authentic and ethical were more important to me than the "convenience" of selling my soul for money or a job. Still, I had nowhere to live. I had no job. And I had no money. What was I to do?

#5: Necessity is the mother of invention.

I had quit my job before I got paid or reimbursed for my moving expenses, so I needed to figure out immediately how I was going to find a place to sleep, keep clean, and eat. All I had were a few belongings in the trunk of my hatchback, which became my home on wheels. Since I needed a safe place to park, I went to places like Motel 6, Super 8, and Red Roof Inn because they had well-lit parking areas, lots of cars coming and going, front desks that were attended 24/7, and enough security to ensure my car was safe, but they weren't so stringent that someone would ask me to leave, call the police, or have my car towed. If I slept in the back seat under a dark blanket, no one could see that I was living in my car.

For the restroom, I would walk into the hotel like I was a guest and then use the ladies' room off the lobby—but not so often that anyone at the front desk would ask me which room I was staying in. I'd also come in the hotel in the afternoons, after the housekeepers had finished cleaning the rooms. I'd take a bar of soap from the cleaning cart, then I'd drive to a fast-food restaurant that had a lot of foot traffic. I'd go into the single-stall restroom carrying my hotel bar of soap, my hairbrush, toothpaste, toothbrush, and deodorant in a small bag. I'd lock the restroom door and take a "bird bath" in the sink. Then I'd brush my teeth, brush my hair, put on deodorant, and go about my day.

Food in the mornings was easy. Some of the motels had a free continental breakfast and because they didn't keep track of who was a guest and who wasn't, I could walk in, grab a cup of coffee and a glazed doughnut stick wrapped in plastic (imagine a greasier version of a Twinkie), and perhaps an apple to have for lunch. I discovered that fast-food restaurants, like KFC and Taco Bell, always had food they would throw out at the end of the day, so, for dinner, I'd go in right before closing time and ask them to give it to me instead. "Well," they'd usually say, "we can't give it to you directly, but we'll bag it up and put it outside by the trash. You'll have to go and get it there." It wasn't glamorous, or even healthy, but I had food to eat while I was getting on my feet.

Comfortable? No. But comfort was not the goal: covering my basic needs of shelter, cleanliness, and food was. When you know who you are and what you stand for, and when you keep your eyes on your ultimate goal and refuse to give up regardless of your current circumstances, then you will do what is necessary even when it is *un*comfortable in the short term.

#6: Let ideas lead to inspired action.

I'd been one of the top managers/trainers at the company, and while the salespeople I trained created a lot of money for the business, I never reaped financial rewards from the results I produced. At first, it made me a little angry. Then I thought, "Wait: if I could do it for them, why can't I do it for me? I know how to teach and train. I know how to manage and motivate. I'm a great sales trainer, and every business needs salespeople. I'll start my own training business!"

That thought was a "yes" to three of the four questions I had asked when I got the job in the first place: "What do I know? What do I do? What do I love?" I just had to figure out how to monetize my idea when I had no office and no money to rent one. I had to turn inspiration into reality.

Back at the hotels, I sat in the lobbies and looked through the Help Wanted sections of the complimentary local newspapers. I saw dozens of ads from companies: "Salespeople wanted," "Management trainees wanted," "Receptionists wanted." I called these businesses and asked, "What skills would your managers (or salespeople or receptionists) need to have for you to hire them immediately?" Most companies had similar skills for each job category, and I had trained people in all of those skills. So, my plan was to find potential salespeople, managers, or receptionists, train them in the skills required, send them to the businesses, and collect referral fees. One obstacle remained, however: where would I do this training?

Even when you have a plan to reach your goal, you can run into roadblocks. But if you allow each obstacle to inspire you to come up with creative ways to get past that barrier, you'll keep moving forward. I started looking for an inexpensive space and found a building that offered a very small (120 square feet), very cheap office with a desk and a small closet. It had a low security deposit and two months' free rent; it included electricity, heat, air conditioning, and its own phone line.

Two months was enough time for me to start generating revenue, so I signed the lease for the location that would become my management training center. Bonus: I even moved out of my car and slept on a mat under the desk! As long as I was out of the building when the cleaning crew came by, no one knew I was living in the office. I used the communal bathroom down the hall and put food in the communal snack refrigerator. I was still eating food that KFC and Taco Bell tossed out, but, overall, it was a step up.

I was ready to put my business plan into action. I negotiated a deal on placing one- or two-line ads in the classified section of the local paper: "Receptionist/sales/management trainees wanted, no experience necessary, all training provided," and listed the office phone number. When candidates called, I interviewed them, and if they sounded promising, brought them in for group interviews, four people at a time. Even though the office was so small that we all had to stand, I role played with them to get a feel for how trainable they were, whether I could work with them, and how fast I could get them up to speed. Time was money, and I had to generate income as quickly as possible.

Luckily, one of my talents has always been to build the airplane while it's flying. I became super effective at interviewing, selecting the best candidates, training them as fast as possible, and sending them to companies. I then used the referral fees to place more classified ads. Within a few months, I generated enough money to move from my tiny one-room office into a bigger one. (And I negotiated another month's free rent.) The new office included a set of inexpensive folding chairs and a whiteboard, so I could hold trainings for 20 to 30 people at a time. I still slept under the desk and used the complex's communal bathroom, but I was able to buy inexpensive food from grocery stores instead of picking up bags next to fast-food dumpsters.

You might be wondering why I didn't use some of the initial business income to rent an apartment instead of getting a bigger office. It's because I never took my eye off the ultimate goal, which was to earn the money to return to college, go to law school, and become an attorney. That was my passion, my drive, and my inspiration. Everything I did was focused on making that goal real. And, at that point, spending money on an apartment instead of space to train more people, and thus earn more income, didn't further the goal.

#7: Look for ways to be a force for good.

Eventually I found a small, inexpensive one-bedroom apartment that I shared with two other people. Since they were a couple, they took the bedroom while I slept in the tiny living room. (Hey, it was a step up from the floor of my office.) Meanwhile, my management training company became a healthy, growing business. I paid the bills and watched my college fund increase month after month. And, after a few years, I established state residency, which meant I could pay in-state tuition rates. Within one more year I had saved enough to be able to go to college. I decided it was time to move on from my management training center and return to school full time.

I will always remember the day that I announced to my right-hand person, "Katie" (not her real name), that I was leaving the company. Katie was newly married, pregnant, and her military husband had just been deployed. Katie was my star pupil: I'd mentored her for over a year, and she knew my training program inside out. She was well equipped for success. I wanted her to take over the business, but I knew she couldn't afford to buy it. So, on the day I left for college, I told Katie that I was giving the business to her, no strings attached. I put everything—the lease, the classified ads, the phone account, and the client list—into her name. Then I handed her the keys, hugged her, and walked away.

Some people might say that giving away such a valuable asset was imprudent. But to me, the business was always a means to an end, not the end itself. I was happy to provide Katie with an opportunity that she needed but couldn't afford, and I left to pursue the goal that inspired me every day.

I believe anyone can decide to be a force for good in their life, their family, their community, and their world. Opportunities to shine our light appear constantly. The question is never, "Am I a force for good?" but "How can I be a force for good?"

It's Time to Shine Your Light!

Even after you achieve your goals and think you are doing all you can to be a force for good, you'll get a reminder that you need to up your game. I graduated from college and law school and became an attorney. One of my proudest moments was being sworn in as a member of the Bar of the United States Supreme Court by Justice Ruth Bader Ginsburg herself. For many years, I was happy being a force for good "behind the scenes" as a staff attorney for a federal judge. I wrote opinions on discrimination cases, prison condition cases, and civil rights cases—causes that I have long been passionate about. But a 2019 cancer diagnosis spurred an even stronger desire to be a visible force for good.

I can't be behind the scenes anymore. I want my light to be seen every day. Nothing will stand in my way of helping others find their voice, stand in their power, and change the world. It's why I help women, authors, and speakers use their voices to tell their stories and amplify their impact. It's why I founded my nonprofit, the Made 2 Change the World™ Foundation, a comprehensive youth program that provides underserved youth with the skills, resources, and mentorship they need to become tomorrow's leaders and use their voices and their lives to create the world they envision.

And it's why I share these lessons with you. No matter where you come from or what's happened in your life, you, too, can be a force for good. You have a unique voice, unique experiences, and unique gifts. You just need to declare how you want to use them in the world.

Claim your power. Determine your passion, purpose, and mission. Then shine your light and be the force for good you were born to be.

ABOUT ELLIE D. SHEFI

"Ellie is a transformational leader who is changing the world!" ~**Jack Canfield**

Having overcome a lifetime of adversity, including abuse, domestic violence, homelessness, cancer, and a myriad of other health issues that have seen her defy the doctors' death deadlines for over two decades, Ellie Shefi has mastered mindset, resiliency, and resourcefulness, and she has dedicated her life to being a force for good.

Ellie is an attorney, entrepreneur, speaker, strategist, consultant, and coach who provides her clients with practical, easy-to-implement tools and strategies that generate results. She is often interviewed in publications and on podcasts and television shows, including NBC, ABC, CBS, the New York Times, Forbes, Entrepreneur, Yahoo News, the LA Tribune, and TED Ed. Ellie helps entrepreneurs bring their business to life; authors get their book out of their head and into the world; and speakers amplify their message so they can scale their impact. She is the creator of You Are Not Your Scars™, a program that teaches women how to shed external labels and expectations, find their voice, stand in their power, and become the architects of their life and legacy.

Ellie is also the founder of the Made 2 Change the World™ Foundation (www.made2change.org), a nonprofit that equips and empowers the next generation with the tools, resources, and strategies they need to create the lives, communities, and world they envision.

A best-selling author, Ellie's books include *Unlocking Your Superpower: 8 Steps to Turn Your Existing Knowledge into Income*; *Sisters Rising: Stories of Remarkable Women Living Extraordinary Lives*; *The Authorities: Powerful Wisdom from Leaders in the Field* (co-authored with multiple New York Times #1 best-selling authors

Les Brown, Bob Proctor, and Marci Shimoff); and *SuccessOnomics* (co-authored with multiple New York Times #1 best-selling author Jack Canfield).

To connect with Ellie and learn more about her work, including how you can get involved with the Made 2 Change the World™ Foundation, please visit www.ellieshefi.com

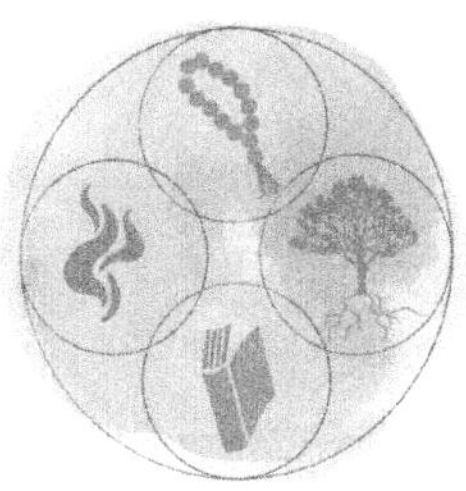

Have you ever dreamed of
becoming a published author?
Do you have a story to share?
Would the world benefit
from hearing your message?
Then we want to connect with you!

The *Inspired Impact Book Series* is looking to connect with women who desire to share their stories with the goal of inspiring others.

We want to hear your story!

Visit www.katebutlerbooks.com to learn more about becoming a Featured Author in the #1 International Best-selling *Inspired Impact Book Series.*

Everyone has a story to share!
Is it your time to create your legacy?

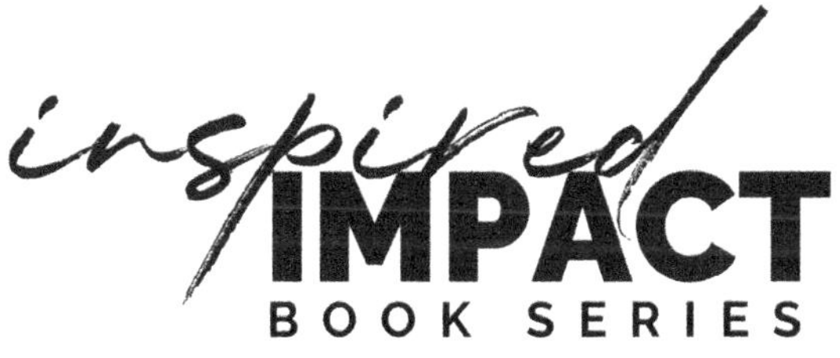

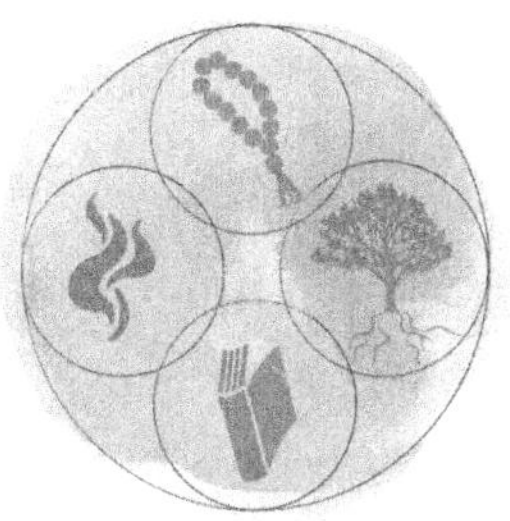

May Your Soul be uplifted, and the words of these pages inspire you to continue to SHINE your infinite light living the fullest expression of your divine life.

the women who shine

REPRINTED WITH PERMISSIONS

Taja V. Simpson
Maya Comerota
Diana Buckwalter
Denise McCormick
Kristi Ann Pawlowski
Candice Shepard
Tara Truax
Ivanna Mann Thrower Anderson
Heather Beebe
Tracey Watts Cirino
Brooke A. Conaway
Sarah Grafton
Susan E. Grubb, LPC
Gaby Juergens
Ann Klossing
Stacy Kuhen
Christine Lavulo
Shari Lillico
Christina Macro
Laurie Maddalena
Tatjana Obradovic
Dr. Lisa Patierne
Lori Parks
Maria Ramos
Ellie D. Shefi
Emma Alexandra Williams
Kristina Williams
Peggy Wright
Dianne A. Allen
Dr. Agatha Ampaire
Anita Lucia La Pierre
Melissa A. Malland
Melanie Renee

Made in the USA
Middletown, DE
13 September 2021

48190094R00186